One and All

The Logic of Chinese Sovereignty

Pang Laikwan

STANFORD UNIVERSITY PRESS
Stanford, California

Stanford University Press
Stanford, California

Printed and bound by CPI Group UK Ltd, Croydon, CR0 4YY

Library of Congress Cataloging-in-Publication Data

Names: Pang, Laikwan, author.
Title: One and all : the logic of Chinese sovereignty / Pang Laikwan.
Description: Stanford, California : Stanford University Press, [2024] | Includes bibliographical references and index.
Identifiers: LCCN 2023030951 (print) | LCCN 2023030952 (ebook) | ISBN 9781503638228 (hardback) | ISBN 9781503638815 (paperback) | ISBN 9781503638822 (ebook)
Subjects: LCSH: Sovereignty. | China—Politics and government—20th century.
Classification: LCC DS775.7 .P358 2023 (print) | LCC DS775.7 (ebook) | DDC 320.1/50951—dc23/eng/20230812
LC record available at https://lccn.loc.gov/2023030951
LC ebook record available at https://lccn.loc.gov/2023030952

Cover design: Laywan Kwan
Cover art: Xiao Chen, *Valley and Mountains, after Zhao Boju*, undated; late 17th–early 18th century, Qing dynasty, Hanging scroll; ink and color on silk, Painting: 221 x 94 cm. (87 x 37 in.) Mount: 328 x 11.5 cm. (129 1/8 x 4 1/2 in.) Princeton University Art Museum
Typeset by Newgen in Lora Regular 9.5/14

Contents

Part I
Concepts and Structures

Part II
Culture and Representation

Contents

List of Figures

Preface

After three years of crisis mode, the Chinese government has finally stopped calling COVID-19 a national enemy. In fact, the pandemic is seldom mentioned in the public media anymore. Despite the widespread protests against its zero-COVID policy and the immeasurable human toll the sudden rescinding of this policy has taken, the Chinese government seems to have survived what has widely been regarded as the biggest challenge to its sovereignty since 1989. Many predictions of political havoc are also proven wrong, and business is back as usual. At a time when many of us are standing on a threshold of history in awed silence, let us go back to the fateful and uncanny moment when only Chinese people were concerned about the spread of the coronavirus. It might give us some insights into how China's current sovereign logic is constructed and also lost in the interactions among the state, the people, and the enemy, which could be the virus or many other things.

Facing an unknown virus that was deadly and highly contagious, the People's Republic of China (PRC) central government imposed a lockdown in Wuhan and other cities in Hubei in late January 2020. Responding to the grievances, fear, and complaints heard everywhere in the country, the government worked to convince the populace of the omnipotence of state power under full control. Nevertheless, the PRC still struggled to pacify the grudging public, who suspected that a truth was being concealed.

Two weeks passed in which the PRC undertook major censorship and propaganda efforts regarding the spread of what would become COVID-19. On February 6, 2020, Doctor Li Wenliang died. His death unexpectedly triggered a new burst of national anger, one directed precisely against the government's suppressive opinion control. This was because Dr. Li was one of the earliest whistleblowers who had alerted the people to a new deadly virus denied by the government.

It had been Li who, in December 2019, had sent a message to fellow medics on his own social media account, warning of a virus similar to SARS. But he—along with the handful of other medical workers who also mentioned the mysterious virus in their own social media accounts—was identified and condemned by the government for spreading rumors. After signing a letter of repentance, Li was allowed to go back to work; this led to him contracting COVID. When news of his death went viral late on the evening of February 6, Chinese netizens roared, protesting that the whistleblower's death demonstrated the state's relentless crushing of freedom of speech.

But Dr. Li died twice.

The news of his death was first circulated on the internet around 9:30 p.m. on February 6, Beijing time, and was quickly confirmed by major Chinese newspapers such as the *People's Daily* and *Global Times*. Posts discussing his death on Weibo, China's biggest microblogging website, reached a billion hits, and there was an avalanche of demand for freedom of the press.[1] The World Health Organization (WHO) also announced Dr. Li's death on its Twitter account. A subsequent report in *The New York Times* interviewed a fellow doctor who had treated Dr. Li that evening and confirmed that he died at 9:10 p.m.[2] Later that night, though, news circulated that Dr. Li had not died. He was in critical condition, and he was undergoing emergency treatment at the hospital. But then the next morning, February 7, Dr. Li was finally pronounced dead in an official sense.

A rumor then widely circulated that Dr. Li had been attached to an ECMO machine for hours after his death was announced at 9:30 p.m. People suspected that this was to keep him alive until the government was ready to deal with the disaster. Some also speculated that keeping him alive was intended to shift the nation from anger to the wish for a miracle. Perhaps most importantly, the government wanted to buy time to control opinions on the internet. What is known is that, during the few hours between the two deaths, the government was able to wipe out most online discussion relating to demands for freedom of the press.

We do not know exactly what happened to Dr. Li. We may never know. But the fact is that the public did hear that Dr. Li died twice. And to many ordinary Chinese netizens, the period between the two deaths was one of the longest nights in recent memory.

China's most symbolic COVID victim died in a most surreal way: he could not simply be allowed to die. Instead, his death had to be completely controlled by the propaganda apparatus in order to demonstrate the united efforts of the sovereign power of the PRC state to protect the life of its subjects. Dr. Li's death crystallized the state's intense anxiety caused by an unknown external threat to its population. And so, within those few hours, the government struggled to repackage that death from a force of destruction to one showing the sovereign state's care of the people.

We might read this incident from two perspectives. First, Dr. Li's second death—accompanied by the full implementation of a propaganda machine promoting national mourning—can be seen as the sacrifice the state presented to the community in order to avoid the predicted social violence from erupting. Many cultural theorists, such as René Girard, have shown the tendency of societies to resort to the sacrificing of an individual (human or animal) as a scapegoat: this is so members can identify with one another through the sacrifice and form stronger social bonds, while the scapegoat will be viewed as the savior.[3] Dr. Li's second death could indeed be understood as the sacrifice orchestrated by the state, designed to coincide with the state's announcement of policies to fight the virus. Seen in hindsight, the second death of Dr. Li became the country's passage into a period of war, a state of exception that allowed the sovereign to exercise its power at full throttle. In the three long years that followed, the PRC continued and intensified such rhetoric of "the state versus the virus," simultaneously mediated by the people as objects of protection, management, and censorship.

There is another way to read Dr. Li's death: specifically, in how it reverberates with Giorgio Agamben's theorization of thanatopolitics—the politics of death—where the enormous power of the sovereign ruler is justified by his claimed ability to control/manage his own death as well as the death of his people. Agamben illustrates his theory by locating two different lives—one sacred and the other a bare life—embodied in the ancient Roman emperor and later the French and English sovereigns. When these sovereigns died, they were given two separate deaths, complete with two different sets of rituals. The king first died as an ordinary human, but an effigy was put together to extend his life so that he could be given a much more elaborate ritualistic death at an appropriate time. This reveals the throne's dual embodiment of both the sovereign, whose power lasts forever, and the bare life shared by every one of us.[4] To Agamben, the death rituals show the people how the sovereign is in full control of both lives.

Clearly, Dr. Li in 2020 was no king, but his "doctor identity" facilitated a metonymic slide between the sovereign and the care-provider in the age of COVID. The sovereign, like Dr. Li, dies with and for the people, but the sovereignty also lasts, to protect the people. Dr. Li's two deaths reveal a thanatopolitics: who can die, who must live, and how to die. . . . If the PRC's postsocialist sovereign legitimacy has been built on economic prosperity, COVID drastically changed the priority to the state's capacity to protect the lives of the people from death, given the ineffable fact of death's proximity. Similar to the king's physical death, Dr. Li first died as a bare life, but this first death was quickly appropriated by the state to put forth a second death, which could be seen as a symbol of sovereign unity and the population's perpetual life.[5] Dr. Li was also presented by the government as a national hero who had sacrificed himself for the health of the people.

In Europe, a king's death had to be ritualized to carry the symbolic values of the transcendence and eternity of the monarchic power. Correspondingly, the PRC also repackaged Dr. Li's death, transforming it from a symbol of sovereign failure to one of state power—specifically, the power to enable the population to last forever. Agamben's theory is most insightful in illustrating the innate connection between sovereign power and death.[6] It is his power to undergo and transcend death that makes the king the ruler. Each of us—as members of sovereignty—will die, but sovereignty itself does not. Indeed, this is a most basic logic of sovereignty: the people, as an abstract entity, will persevere against all odds, also denying any outside power to rule the people.

But Agamben's theorization of the omnipotence of the sovereign could be highly problematic, as it seems to display a silent affirmation of the state's power, however critical he is of the state's control over individuals and communities. Agamben's critical exposition of state power could easily become an endorsement of such reasoning, just as description could become prescription. Maybe Agamben only reinforces our existing state-phobia. As Michel Foucault argues, "state-phobia" is a pervasive sentiment in the modern world, and it assumes that the state has an intrinsic tendency to control and expand.[7] Indeed, maybe the state is never as powerful as we fear, and maybe the local community has its own ways to determine how lives continue.

This might explain why the second death of Dr. Li orchestrated by the state did not end the story. Dr. Li's life continues on his social media account, as netizens continue to leave comments on his Weibo social media page. On this very special page, we see strangers sending Dr. Li gratitude and affection, sharing their own daily anecdotes or expressing their personal frustrations, constructing an online "wailing wall."

However depoliticized they might be, the never-ending comments on this "wailing wall" demonstrate that he is not yet forgotten. Dr. Li's second death was meant to seal the coffin, but the people insisted on giving (a third) life to his persona in the public sphere. Remarkably, they do so not to resurrect him as an eternal hero but instead to let each other see and be seen. There were more than a million messages left on his Weibo account within the first year after his death. The contents of the messages range from expressions of gratitude to exhortations to remember, from everyday greetings to the sharing of daily happenings, attested in the four most frequently appeared terms in these messages: "Dr. Li," "today," "good night," and "hope."[8] After China dismantled its COVID controls in December of 2022, messages lamenting the death of their loved ones due to COVID also began to appear on this wailing wall.[9]

While these messages represent a tremendous diversity of sentiments and the mundane life of the people, the obscure thanatopolitics of trying to control Dr. Li's death is also ridiculed. It is clear that these online messages are flimsy and fleeting, quickly replaced by others. They tend to be depoliticized, representing the people's internalization of political discontent into their everyday life routine and petty struggles. It is also true that this Weibo account is monitored by the state, and it clearly does not represent an alternative Chinese sovereignty. Yet, taken together, the forgettable messages combine to build a resilient memory—at least the people do not just forget. Instead of seeing sovereignty as the manifestation of the singular will of a great number of people, this social account shows that sovereignty could be a community in which the diverse members are partially bound by hopes and suffering, through which they gain their limited autonomy from the dominant powers as well as the incalculability of the future.[10]

Dr. Li's active afterlife in social media is actually nothing special, but it is like many other social media pages of the deceased: although the person is already dead, friends and family members still leave messages on their account, affording opportunities for the bereaved to maintain bonds with the dead. A public and performative mourning is constructed through the memories, bereavement, and remembrance posted in the account.[11] These social media pages demonstrate that certain acts of reminiscence and publicness can rival state memories. It also shows that the individual is always situated in a community. However much state sovereignty is modeled on the self-mastery of an individual human agency, the state must learn how it is, first and foremost, a community made up of many individual citizens. The people are never One. It is through such recognition and actual experiences of plurality and change that *pouvoir constituant* could become resilient, supple, and constructive, engendering a polity that is the subject—instead of the object—of sovereign power.

Most recently, the Cyberspace Administration of China, PRC's internet regulator and censor, announced that even artificial intelligence must submit to the country's core socialist values.[12] While critics in the US and the EU also push their governments to impose tough regulations on AI, China is the first of the world's most technologically advanced countries to show the absolute will to keep AI under its jurisdiction. Facing an increasingly uncertain and fragile world, humankind has no option but to work with state sovereignty to find the fine balance between liberty and solidarity, to not lose their way in the jungle of self-interest and human emotions, while being faithful in building fair and accountable institutions to protect life and promote positive changes.

This is not another book trying to demonize the PRC. I am living in the reality of this sovereignty, and I do not have the luxury to abstract it into a totality. Instead, I want to address this sovereignty by reading its history critically. No one knows what the future holds, but with history in mind we should have the courage to walk further into the uncharted field, to develop a sovereignty that affirms life, cooperation, and an entangled humanity.

PANG LAIKWAN
Hong Kong
May 5, 2023

Acknowledgments

A major part of the book was written during my 2021–22 residency at the Center for Advanced Study in the Behavioral Sciences (CASBS) at Stanford University. I was blessed by the intellectual vigor generated at the center, constantly challenging and nourishing my thinking. In addition to the sincere friendship of many fellows, I would particularly like to thank Aisha Beliso-De Jesus, Megan Finn, Anna Grzymala-Busse, Amalia D. Kessler, Laurence Ralph, Helen V. Milner, and Neta Kligler-Vilenchik for their inspiring questions and comments as well as useful suggested readings, which have been reflected in the writing. During those months in the Bay Area, Elaine Tong cared for me in the most gentle and generous ways, and she will continue to be the ballast of my life. I also thank Nettie Wong, Fiona Ng, and La Francis Hui for their unyielding trust and sisterhood. Most importantly, I am so fortunate to have the love and understanding of KC and Hayden, who enabled me to take seven months off from my domestic duties to embark on a voyage of self-discovery.

I thank Dylan Kyung-lim White of Stanford University Press for his trust in this project from the beginning and his professional guidance and gracious facilitation throughout the process. Lai-Ping Hui and Rosanne Hui of Han Mo Xuan were very kind to grant me the copyrights to reproduce the four figures in chapter 5. Robert Hegel, Wai-Yee Li, Jie Li, and Joseph Li have read and shared their thoughts on some chapters and suggested further readings, and their goodwill means the world to me. As an overqualified research assistant, Ko Chun-kit provided me with not only precise answers but also stimulating questions—he is an anchor of this research. Han Zhuyuan, Wong Long-Hin, Hu Wenxi, Leung Po, and Lu Xin also assisted my research at different stages. Jie Li and David Wang at Harvard as well as Haiyan Lee and Ban Wang at Stanford invited me to share earlier versions of my book with their stimulating audiences. I was most honored by the invitation of Ming-Bao Yue and Peng Xu to give the Florence Liu Macauley Distinguished Lecture at the University of Hawai'i at Manoa. I would also like to express my sincere gratitude to the two anonymous reviewers of this book, who have shared their very constructive questions and comments with me. All mistakes contained in this book are mine.

An earlier version of chapter 6 appeared as "China's Post-Socialist Governmentality and the Garlic Chives Meme: Economic Sovereignty and Biopolitical Subjects" in *Theory, Culture, and Society* 39, no. 1 (2022). The research is generously supported by a GRF grant offered by the Hong Kong Research Grants Council as well as a publication grant from the Faculty of Arts of the Chinese University of Hong Kong. I am most grateful to the Chinese University of Hong Kong for granting me a sabbatical leave when I was most intellectually lost. Writing this book has been a miraculous, regenerative experience for me.

This book is dedicated to all those around the world defending the principle of plurality against the ubiquitous desire for uniformity.

Introduction

The current PRC state has persistently claimed its governance as uniquely Chinese: it neither follows others nor asks others to follow itself. But it is never clear exactly what this "Chinese path" is. Many Western critics use terms like "authoritarianism" or "totalitarianism" to fill in the gap, but these terms do not accurately describe the wide identification the current PRC sovereignty has enjoyed from many of its citizens. An uncritical use of such terms could also lend credence to a Eurocentric worldview, in which the non-West must forever be indebted to the tutelage of the West. Doubtlessly, the Chinese state is seeking greater centralization of power, and the room for public opinion has narrowed. But there are still multiple consultation processes in place to facilitate an effective government capable of responding (or not) to people's opinions, and there is also enough social and economic freedom that allows a certain degree of citizen self-realization.

What really characterizes the current "Chinese path," I believe, is the enormous weight given to the security of state sovereignty, which is the bottom line of all policies. State security in the PRC encompasses many fields, and the list keeps expanding, from cultural security to cyber security, which will be discussed in chapter 2, and more recently finance security and food security. Under this general security anxiety, society is monitored by intense censorship and self-censorship in the name of protecting the collective from all kinds of threats, real or imagined. I would use the term "sovereigntism" to describe how this state uses sovereignty as its supreme political doctrine. There is clearly an authoritarian dimension to this sovereigntism, but the people, theoretically, are not at the reception end of power; instead, they are considered the owner of the sovereignty. As the state, allegedly, is only the representative or embodiment of the people instead of the authority that instructs the people, sovereigntism does not need to feature an all-powerful leader. It is also not fascism, as the current PRC government emphasizes social harmony among class and ethnic groups, unlike other fascist regimes that tend to spread hatred within society. To the current Chinese government, any attempt to divide the people must be suppressed, as only with peace and unity can sovereignty last forever.

This sovereigntism pursued by the current PRC state is neither ontological nor epistemological, but it is primarily utilitarian, allowing the state to formulate changing policies and narratives to respond to different situations. This utilitarian sovereigntism employs contrasting logic, from autocracy to neoliberalism, selectively to support its internal and external policies, in ways that can potentially advance socialism, capitalism, nationalism, and globalization as long as they are deemed beneficial to the sovereignty. In the name of the well-being of the people in general, sovereigntism allows the state to adopt almost any measures, regardless of the underlying ideologies, to secure its sovereign interests. It is a state ideology composed of many ideologies, or we can also call it a state ideology without ideology.

Sovereignty has become a political fundamental, sacrosanct and incontestable, in China: because its integrity is not negotiable, the use of the term effectively ends all discussions. But we also discover that the policies and politics around this sovereigntism can quickly change, most evident in the sudden U-turn of the COVID policies at the end of 2022, the state's changing narratives about different global projects such as the Belt and Road Initiatives, not to say its crackdown on the leftist groups and LGBTQ+ movements in the nation in the last few years, all in the name of sovereign security. It is the arbitrary and empty quality of sovereigntism that makes individuals so afraid and obedient.

There are international and domestic dimensions of state sovereignty. Externally, state sovereignty is fundamental to the current world system composed of nation-state as basic units. For example, the PRC articulates the "community of shared future" as its internationalist vision, stressing a new global governance that values the interdependence and interconnectedness of all nations.[1] This "community of shared future" discourse is based on the state's absolute sovereignty, with the assumption that each state is an autonomous, self-determining subject represented by the state, with no role played by civil society. In other words, plurality describes international relations, but not domestic ones, as the state is itself an indivisible and autonomous unit.

This book is concerned primarily with the internal dimension of state sovereignty, with the full awareness that the state-people relation is always intertwined with the international environment. While state sovereignty supposedly engenders a fairer world with states respecting each other, the discourse of sovereigntism could be deeply antipolitical in domestic terms, as its unifying logic involves the attempt to conjure away the ineluctable contingency and plurality of political action. Instead of valuing debates and negotiations based on the principles of equality and plurality, sovereignty is often exercised through command and obedience. As Andrew Arato and Jean Cohen argue, whether sovereignty is asserted by the king, by a parliament, or in the name of the people, its hegemonic dimension cannot be jettisoned, because it implies the attempt to appropriate the collective by a single representative body at a specific instance.[2] All over the world, the more the state stresses sovereignty, the less the inherent plurality of the people could be expressed.

As such, the biggest puzzle the current Chinese government poses to its citizens and other people is the near impossibility of raising any criticism of the state, which can always resort to the right of the Chinese people to self-governing as the supreme political reason to fend off external and internal challenges. The people have occupied a mythical role here, which endorses and legitimizes the PRC's pronouncement of its strong commitment to non-negotiable territorial unity, common prosperity, and national autonomy. All state decisions can be legitimized as long as they are made in the name of the people. But there are never any systematized and continual procedures to prove the people's endorsement and choices.

Sovereigntism provides an illusion of unity and certainty for the people. This integrity of state sovereignty is understood as a trio: the coherence of and among people, territory, and history to the extent that each accounts for the others. For example, the Xi government points out that there is one Chinese dream that all Chinese share, which is the dream of restoring the national greatness lost in recent history. Indeed, the Chinese dream is presented more as a bygone fact than a future vision, that China is always already a unity of people and territory historically. This one people that shares the same country and history deserves the strength and pride that originally belonged to it. A central component of this Chinese dream is also the reunification with Taiwan, which, allegedly, has always been a part of China's territory.

To dialogue with this sovereigntism critically, we need to examine precisely the assumptions of the integrity of people, territory, and history in China. During the Long Twentieth Century, while the modern nation-state was adopted as China's political structure, the actual regimes hosting the nation-state changed rapidly: China was transformed from an empire to a republic, cutting a sharp turn into socialism and ending up in a postsocialist nation embracing state capitalism with utmost national pride. The successive governments introduced completely new socioeconomic political structures and reasoning, so the people were invited to identify with their states in very different ways. I believe the current sovereign logic of the PRC can be most productively interrogated by looking at the ways China's changing political economy have morphed along contrasting socio-political conditions as well as at the active participation, silent endorsement, and different degrees of resistance of different groups and individuals. As I will show in chapter 2, federalism and internationalism were widely accepted during the republican and socialist periods, respectively, and they both suggested a much looser sense of state unity than the current Chinese government does. The state sovereignty is both dynamic and active, seeking and being influenced by the people's endorsement, because the sovereign power must continuously be justified, sought, and explained. Careful historicization is the most effective way to expose the constructions that naturalize sovereignty as sacred and unchanging.

Instead of arguing that any one political system is by nature better than others, I would like in this book to understand China's changing sovereign logic within its own historical trajectory. There would never be a set of political principles the Chinese must follow, and I have no ambition and ability to prescribe a political ideology for China. But I think it is worthwhile an effort to understand China's current sovereign logic by examining what sovereignty has meant to different regimes in recent history. Not only would such a historical approach help us to understand China, but through it we can also identify and tackle some fundamental concerns related to state-building and democracy as universal predicaments in our increasingly divided world.

I will emphasize that this history of Chinese sovereignty is also a part of world history, which not only includes but is also largely shaped by the West. Therefore, this history would invalidate any political ideology of a fundamental difference between China and the West. Indeed, Machiavelli's famous book *The Prince*, written in the early sixteenth century, can be seen as one about sovereigntism: how to ensure the persistence and legitimacy of the sovereign power.[3] Today, while the current Western liberal democracy claims to have overcome this problem through the regular elections it structures to refresh the sovereign legitimacy, the sovereign anxiety does not just disappear. All over the world, states and the people reiterate their rights to sovereignty, identifying and condemning the intervention of internal and external forces that allegedly steal their autonomy. The nation-state has become—or is once again—the most powerful actor on the international stage. But a politics based on self-interest without common values would only bring the world to further fragmentations and conflict. While this book is an exploration of China's sovereign logic from a domestic perspective, this investigation is carried out with underlying global and contemporary concerns in mind.

Sovereignty and Legitimacy

To understand the development of modern sovereignty discourses in China, we need to begin in the nineteenth century, when the modern idea of state sovereignty first formed. While I will devote the next chapter to the exploration of traditional Chinese sovereign theory, let us begin here with the contestation of two competing Chinese concepts in the nineteenth century that relate to sovereignty: *fatong* 法統 and *zhuquan* 主權. Examining the historical context of these two new concepts during the early days of modern state sovereignty in China illuminates the hybrid nature of China's modern discourses on sovereignty, which draw on both Western and indigenous political ideas.

The term *fatong* was used primarily during the late Qing and early Republican period to refer to China's orthodox sovereign logic. It could be seen as the nineteenth-century form of the traditional terms *datong* 大統 or *zhengtong* 正統/政統, which describe the ruling power's propriety of possessing political legitimacy. *Datong* describes the legitimate sovereignty passed from one king to another, one regime to another. The new term *fatong* also had the same connotation, but it emphasized *fa*, the law. Adding the term *fa* into this traditional system, the original *datong* idea was modernized, replacing the spiritualist dimensions of monarchic sovereignty with the modern mandate of the legislature to sanction the legitimacy of the ruling power. As such, the sovereign with *fatong* is both the one approved by law and the one who makes law. But the transcendental dimension still lingered in the usage of the concept at that time. The term was used by different competing regimes, from the revolutionary party headed by Sun Yat-sen 孫逸仙 (or Sun Zhongshan 孫中山) (1866–1925) to the short-lived monarchy of Yuan Shikai 袁世凱 (1859–1916), as well as different warlords, to assert their sovereign legitimacy.[4] Even though the concept of *fatong* has now fallen out of fashion, recent debates between the leaders of the two parties still center on whether the Chinese Communist Party (CCP) or the Nationalist Party (Kuomintang, KMT) is the legitimate heir of the *fatong* of the Xinhai Revolution of 1911.[5]

Contesting *fatong* was the term *zhuquan*, which was an imported concept. The term itself could be found in ancient Chinese texts, loosely referring to the power of the emperor. But via the Japanese, the term was reintroduced by translators in the late nineteenth century to stand for the newly imported concept of Western modern state sovereignty.[6] After China's many confrontations with the West and the influx of Western concepts, *zhuquan* appeared with other new, fashionable words such as "nationalism," "revolution," and "constitution." These concepts all gradually settled in the collective Chinese mindset.

We should also note the wide appearance and usage of the term *zhuquan* right after the Hundred Days' Reform (戊戌變法).[7] In 1898, constitutionalists, including Kang Youwei 康有為 (1858–1927) and his student Liang Qichao 梁啟超 (1873–1929), convinced the young, aspiring Guangxu Emperor to initiate a constitution reform. But it lasted for only 100 days and was suppressed by the Empress Dowager Cixi to protect the power of the monarchy. It was around this period that the meanings of the term *zhuquan* subtly shifted: beginning as a technical term in international law, it changed into one embodying national survival and international justice. The sudden popularity of the term showed how, by the close of the nineteenth century, the people of China desired a new political system to keep up with and defend the nation against the West.

The two terms existed side by side. Modern *zhuquan* emphasizes the people's endorsement, while traditional *fatong* is sanctioned by a more abstract force originating from Heaven. *Zhuquan* is clearly an imported concept, while *fatong*, however much a product of the modern time, belongs to a Confucian-Legalist teaching that played an important role in facilitating the modern state to settle into the Chinese political consciousness.[8] I will devote chapter 1 to a discussion of the traditional political philosophy contributing to the idea of *fatong*. Entering the twentieth century, the term *fatong* was gradually phased out, but some of the meanings attached to *fatong* were integrated with *zhuquan* to form a new notion of political legitimacy that was supported by the people while remaining accountable to a higher abstract historical force.

To understand the sovereign logic of the current PRC state, it is important to remember that it inherits the discourses of both *zhuquan* and *fatong*, and it implies authority sanctioned by both the people and a larger historical logic. Both terms are highly paternalistic and masculine. The concepts of sovereignty associated with them are presented through metaphors for and a fondness of power and fraternity, while the people are depicted as willing to yield to the sovereign power in exchange for the protection it provides. This is even more the case in recent years, when the idea of the nation is increasingly muscularized, with the concepts related to *motherland* gradually replaced by those of *fatherland*.[9] In fact, sovereignty is so attractive due partly to the belief that the sovereign is both the master of himself and the controlling author of his own meaning, so that all the individuals identifying with such sovereignty also earn the same power. Sovereign discourses also often feature the rhetoric of competition, providing a problematic dichotomy of friends and foes, either triumph or demise. This desire for sovereign shelter as well as pride has constructed a relatively stable space of representation along with the dominant patriarchal society, which in turn justifies the power of the ruling sovereign.

The PRC's concern to prove its *fatong* is also demonstrated by the ruling regime's self-assumed task of writing the history of the previous sovereign power, which was also one of the most important tasks required of new sovereigns in traditional China. Without an institutionalized church as the transcendental source of power, the new sovereign had to demonstrate how much it had learned from the glories and failures of the previous incumbent to shape its wise and sensible rulership now and into the future. Following the dynastic practices, one of the first major scholarly assignments of the Republican government was to produce an official Qing history. The resultant *Qingshi gao* 清史稿 was rushed to publication in a non-finalized form in 1927 as the editorial team fretted over rapid regime change and political instability. The CCP, running one step ahead, diligently produced its internal party histories to justify the succession of leaders and their changing governing philosophy. Its three most powerful leaders—Mao, Deng, and Xi—all produced their own "Historical Resolution of the Party" documents (in 1945, 1981, and 2021, respectively) to articulate how their leadership had learned from the Party's history and how they were therefore justified to lead the nation.

This CCP tradition—that of seeking legitimacy by scrutinizing the Party's own mistakes and achievements as a form of important political ritual—is unique in the world. It can be seen as a combination of China's historical political economy with a strong pragmatism, which together compel the regime to establish its *fatong* through learning from historical lessons. Most importantly, without democracy, the modern Chinese ruling regimes have to find other ways to prove their sovereign legitimacy, and the abstract historical logic becomes handy: truth will always reveal itself in history retrospectively.

State Sovereignty from Europe to China

To understand the full meaning of modern state sovereignty in China, we have to go to Europe, where the concept was formed amidst the power contestation among empires, states, and the church. During the medieval period, the Holy Roman Empire, which considered itself the successor to the Roman Empire, claimed dominion over much of Western Europe, together with the Byzantine Empire and later the Ottoman Empire in the East. At the same time, the territorial state, semi-autonomous and with clear-enough borders, was also gradually formed in France, Italy, and Germany.[10] There was also the enormous power of the Catholic Church, which asserted its authority over princes and emperors. It was a time when states, smaller in size and characterized by a centralized government, coexisted and competed with the empires, which encompassed multiple nations with decentralized rule, while the church, representing divine power, intervened in the secular world as it wished. There were complex alignments and contestations among the three forces during the medieval period, whose end was characterized by, among other things, the singular Christendom coexisting with multiple imperial sovereignties being replaced by the system of modern European states, which themselves formed new empires within and beyond Europe.

The rise of the state was partly reflected in Jean Bodin's *Six Books of the Republic* (1576), which is frequently referred to as the first book in Europe theorizing state sovereignty. Asserting that both the pope and the emperor should be subject to the law,[11] the book put forward a theory of absolute and undivided sovereignty that can limit the power of both of them and reestablish social order. Bodin did not write to initiate a new sovereignty; he only wanted to justify the power of the existing monarchy and to subordinate the enormous power of the church to the state.[12] Significant social unrest in Europe during that time was the result of religious conflicts, and Bodin hoped that the elevation of the monarchy over such disputes would help promote religious tolerance.

Wars continued, most violently observed in the enormously destructive Thirty Years' War (1618–1648). After years of difficult negotiations among many European states and groups, the two Treaties of Westphalia in 1648 ended the conflict and brought peace to Europe, even as it effectively dissolved the Holy Roman Empire.[13] Borders were readjusted and recognized, and the Treaties confirmed the inviolability of state borders, so that each prince could rule his own territory respected by other princes.[14] The Peace of Westphalia is widely assumed as the foundation of modern state sovereignty.

This act of substantiating the power of monarchy also paved the way for the rise of a new concept of state sovereignty in Europe, with strong tensions and collaborations between the state and the people. This can be grasped by reading Thomas Hobbes's 1651 *Leviathan* together with Jean-Jacques Rousseau's 1762 *The Social Contract*. Hobbes's book was published right after the Peace of Westphalia was established, and it first articulated the parallel existence of monarchic sovereignty and popular sovereignty: alongside the sovereign power of the king, there were also the people who could make political decisions.[15] But since individuals tend to follow their divergent self-interest, they should submit to the absolute sovereign rule in exchange for peace and prosperity. Hobbes's book was the first to articulate that relations between the sovereign and the people were based on negotiation instead of natural submission.

Rousseau elaborated his social contract theory between the state and the people in *The Social Contract* by emphasizing the "general will" of the people, which he believed is essentially geared toward the common good of society. The task of the state is to follow and cultivate this "general will." Rousseau also articulated the differences between the sovereign from the government, differentiating the "Sovereign" as the lawmaking body from the "Prince" as the magistrate that enforces the laws. As such, he clearly separated the power of the people, in the form of the Sovereign, from work of the government, in the form of the Prince.[16] Through legislation, the people become their own masters, while the duty of the executive branch is to execute sovereign decisions.

Although written one century apart, the two books can be read together to understand the core implications of European modern state sovereignty. Hobbes focused on the importance of the state, while Rousseau was more concerned with the people. Hobbes argued that sovereign order cannot be established without a state collecting the power forfeited by the individuals, who otherwise would only act according to their desires and produce chaos.[17] Rousseau, on the other hand, emphasized that the government must heed the wishes of the people. We should see them as mutually defining each other, with modern sovereignty referring to both the state ruling the people and the people, through the state they establish, ruling themselves.

This state-people dynamic did not dissipate the unity of the state but actually reinforced its identity with the assumption of one-nation-one-state, and there was also the increasing personification of the state in Europe. Carl Schmitt traces it back to the allegorical tendency of Renaissance writers to present states as persons; later, the Enlightenment thinkers also described states as "moral persons" in international law.[18] In this new modern world, international relations became fashioned according to the social relations among individuals with mutual threats against each other. The liberalist values of individual autonomy and competition were applied to diplomatic relations, projecting the international community as a society composed of independent agents with defined rights and duties. Under such an ideology, the sovereign state—like the individual—also became atomized. The sovereign state has since been understood in terms of a sole person, implying that the state, like the person, is unified and coherent and has its own agency with respect to others.[19]

Therefore, the modern state sovereignty which is now adopted globally was a unique historical product of Europe's political economy, which witnessed the rise of the nation-state that appropriated political power from both the church and the empire to become a self-empowering political entity. In this way Kant was right to criticize the European international order for encouraging each state to see only its own majesty and to avoid submitting to any external constraint.[20] This European interstate system also announced a new political culture, proclaiming modern Europe's progressiveness, which is liberal democracy, against both its medieval past and other non-Western countries.[21] Without this theory of popular sovereignty, Europe's modernization and secularization projects could not be completed.

In addition to the competitions inside the continent, Europe's internal inter-state relations must also be read alongside its external expansion. The Westphalia Treaties mark not only the stability of state identity but also the transition from intense inter-state battles within Europe to an aggressive expansion directed outward through colonialism and imperialism. Wars did continue within Europe in the seventeenth and eighteenth centuries, but the common recognition of state sovereignty and borders allowed the European states to acquire enough peace with their neighboring countries so that they could focus on conquering the world. After Spain and Portugal, England, France, and the Dutch Republic also actively established their own overseas empires starting in the seventeenth century, displacing their direct internal rivalry to external competitions among each other in other parts of the world.

Arguably, this European order reached its height in the nineteenth century. Wars and other forces of change were welcomed as long as the overall European order was not jeopardized and preferably strengthened. Schmitt describes this system as delicate and civilized, and it was achieved by tacit understandings among the states. It regulated the European contest in a bracketed space—not to eliminate wars as such but to regulate them in a way that they did not challenge the stability of the entire European order.[22] But Schmitt remains silent on the brutality of this imperial system outside Europe.

While Schmitt praises this European coexistence as the manifestation of a higher civilization, Hannah Arendt is overcome with disdain. She protests that it was a most absurd phenomenon that modern European imperialism grew up in nation-states which more than any other political bodies were defined by boundaries and the limitations of possible conquest. For her, it was the countries' economic interests steeped in capitalism that drove modern European imperialism. In contrast to the political conquests in earlier empires, which were often followed by the integration of heterogenous peoples through a common law, the economic expansion central to modern imperialism did not alter the basic structure of the nation-state in Europe. The fall of the traditional land-based empires witnessed the rise of new sea-based imperial-colonial empires in which the conquering state ruled primarily by exercising tyranny in the conquered land with the consent of a presumably homogeneous population inside the state.[23] This modern European sovereignty was also undergirded by the community of European nations, respecting and competing with each other simultaneously. Or, despite the economic competitions, the interests of the individual state and those of the larger European order were mutually constitutive.[24] European economic imperialism based on internal peace and external invasion was probably the most important factor contributing to the idea of the modern sovereign state, whose respect for autonomy and equality among the European states became a means for European expansionism to thrive in the age of capitalism.

Not surprisingly, it was a different story when the modern sovereign state was adopted internationally. We must join Europe's internal diplomatic history and external colonial history to understand the options given to China as well as many other non-European countries. This modern European sovereignty theory was developed first to ease the intense intra- and inter-state wars in Europe and then to justify these European states' economic competition outside Europe. While property rights and sovereign rights are central to the European order, they do not apply to areas outside Europe. As such, the idea of modern state sovereignty that arrived in and was adopted by China in the late nineteenth century was riven with contradictions. China gave up its two-millennia-long imperial system after failing to resist the European

imperialist encroachment, in the hope that the principles of border inviolability and non-interference associated with modern sovereign states
could be employed to defend China from such imperialist intrusion. But
these principles had already been proved to be smoke and mirrors outside Europe. Sovereignty was only a means for the European countries
to engage in colonial and economic imperialism against a world to which
China belonged.

Some have argued that Japan was able to learn from the unfair treaties it signed with the European nations and the United States in the
mid-nineteenth century to maintain its territorial integrity and to assert
sovereignty over its territory. For example, while the Japanese government granted judicial jurisdiction to foreign consuls, all foreigners in
Japanese territory were bound to obey the laws of Japan.[25] The Japanese
success seemed to have convinced some Chinese scholars and officials
that a comprehensive command of international law was key to Qing's
sovereignty. But what really mattered, unfortunately, was not legal reasoning but power, in that Japan was powerful enough to defend and regenerate itself. While Qing failed to maintain its sovereignty under the
challenge of China's own revolutionaries, the Meiji Restoration led Japan
to its own imperialism, infringing on the sovereignty of weaker nations.
Neither the Chinese nor the Japanese development were exactly what
they had claimed to learn from modern European sovereign principles.

As it turns out, this Europe-based world system would be challenged
not by the victimized countries like China but by the rise of the United
States. A new international order began to coalesce after the First World
War, and the territorial-based state sovereignty would be compromised
by America's global domination.[26] There are two dimensions, economic
and political, of this new world order.

Economically, the modern state system was called into question by
late capitalism and the ascendance of the global finance system, undergirded by the US-centric global multilateral infrastructure that
facilitates transnational capital and information flows. Multilateral
economic institutions such as the World Trade Organization and the International Monetary Fund began to establish a pervasive and intrusive
presence in individual member states. This rise of transnational capitalist institutions also prompted critics to articulate the importance
of sovereign rights, specifically to regulate economic activities within
the state border against these different transnational forms.[27] China is

now meandering between the two positions, actively engaging in global investment and resolutely defending its economic sovereignty, as is required by the situation.

Politically, a wave of decolonization reinforced the value of independent sovereignty from the 1940s to the 1960s, when the British and French empires quickly disintegrated. This postcolonial politics found rapport with the Westphalian principle of sovereignty, and it is still the dominant political frame in China's diplomacy today. At the same time, a transnational governance of the global human rights regime also developed in the 1970s in order to keep an eye on authoritarian governance, and it succeeded in loosening individual state sovereignty to allow human rights concepts and global scrutiny to enter authoritarian countries.[28] Many critics and scholars, both in authoritarian and liberal democratic countries, criticized this transnational legal regime as undermining the state's autonomy. Some have argued that this is an attack on democracy too because democracy can only take place within a sovereign state.[29] Expectedly, the current Chinese government and some other non-Western countries have categorically rejected universal human rights as sovereignty-infringing.

The current PRC is enthusiastic about state sovereignty partly because it allows the government to guard, filter, and coordinate both the transnational capital flows and the use of certain universal political values in the country. While the Chinese state has suavely maneuvered the sovereignty discourses to facilitate its own agenda, it is important for critics to differentiate the two sets of traffic to provide a more acute analysis. Endorsing a strong state sovereignty would give the state the power to resist both, while a weak state could be exposed to both.

Sovereignty and Culture

Modern sovereignty is not only an economic-political ensemble, but most importantly it is also a culture. More precisely, sovereignty is a state-people-territory-history imagination. State sovereignty is both an institution and a political persuasion, involving many levels of operations and discursive practices. It is also a political theology, conveyed through apparatus of law, education, and propaganda. Before it is an institution, sovereignty is a culture, a general set of ideas, beliefs, and identification that permeates a community.

The performative dimension of modern state sovereignty is particularly prominent. Consider Boris Johnson's video address to the nation—broadcast an hour before the implementation of Brexit in February 2020—in which he heralded the country's "recaptured sovereignty" and hailed the rediscovery of the power of independent thought and action that the British had supposedly lost for decades. Meanwhile, across the English Channel, practically all the major candidates for the 2022 French presidential election emphasized French national sovereignty and called for a reduction of the power of the European Union. In the United States, when Donald Trump addressed the UN General Assembly in 2019, he asserted, "If you want democracy, hold on to your sovereignty. . . . And if you want peace, love your nation." We just do not quite know how he pieced together that logic. In the same year, Brazilian president Jair Bolsonaro responded to world criticism of his policies for deforestation of the Amazon by arguing that climate change was a conspiracy driven by hidden interests from abroad; he also insisted that "the Brazilian areas of the Amazon rainforest are sovereign territory." Sovereignty is so important to these leader performances partly because it is the national leader who embodies state sovereignty. At the same time, state sovereignty cannot be objectively proved and can only be performed.

Most scholars interested in modern sovereignty in China come from the fields of international relations or international law.[30] This scholarship helps us understand the struggles of China in a complicated world order. But this approach tends to pay less attention to the domestic dimension of sovereignty, specifically how the state communicates with the people to justify its power over them. In fact, diplomacy is often highly performative, meant for the local audience. In recent years, Chinese diplomats have often asserted China's sovereign rights in the "wolf warrior" style. Yet such assertions, while seemingly directed at the opponent government, are often in fact pitched more to the domestic audience, and they are often inconsistent.[31] Today, China's Foreign Ministry seems to have largely ignored its duties in maintaining good diplomatic relations with the world, and its spokespersons seem to take on the duties of the Central Propaganda Department and speak only to please domestic nationalist audiences hungry for national pride. The lionhearted performances of the diplomatic officers serve to show the people that they should be proud of their strong state, that the collective prosperity achieved so far is at risk, and therefore that they must submit to the sovereign order.

As the core constituent of state power, sovereignty is extremely abstract, which is always already generalized through all kinds of cultural means, not only via top-down state propaganda or education but also through the constructions by cultural mediators and the citizens themselves. Sovereignty is made up of thoughts, ideologies, and representations: they construct fictions, but they also contain the "truths" elicited by these constructions. Politics cannot be understood properly without considering affect and belief, however abstract and unreliable they may be. William Callahan, for example, has recently demonstrated how maps, as a form of cultural mediation, were diligently produced during the Republican period in China to indicate the territories "stolen" by European and Japanese imperialist regimes, and how the current Chinese government and prominent state intellectuals appeal to maps for evidence supporting Beijing's expansive claims in the South China Sea.[32] From a cultural perspective, we can conceptualize modern sovereignty as primarily a space where lineage and authority are established and challenged and where the mutual identification between the state and the people is operated in a field of open-ended language and representation.

In this book I pay particular attention to intellectual culture because sovereignty is primarily a claim, or an imagination, negotiated between the state and the people. Intellectuals are treated here not as philosophers who provide original and transcendental thoughts. Instead, I consider them as active players in the larger cultural-political field, who have led public opinion, have spoken for the masses, and have acted as vehicles of power. Their expressions provide us with glimpses of China's popular sovereignty: not only did these intellectuals shape political opinions; they also actively invented the expressions that articulate the general cultural milieu. But many of them also represented the state, conveying its sovereignty to the people. These intellectuals could be as biased, short-sighted, and imprudent as the general public and the state, but they were able to speak for the times.

But I also emphasize that sovereign power is not only a discursive effect. However much the state adopts different means to convince the people of its legitimacy, sovereignty is also a political reality, a construct that no political community can afford to avoid altogether. In general, state sovereignty is both a set of concrete state operations and a loose structure of discourses and credence that construct the political legitimacy of the state, and they face both outside and inside. Ultimately, modern sovereignty is a set of relation constructions: between the sovereign and the people; between one people and other people externally; and among the people internally. Here institutions matter as much as culture, so sovereignty cannot be reduced to nationalism. There are dynamic interactive relations—between culture and institutions, emotions and reasoning—inherent in all state sovereignty. The state cultivates the people's identification with its sovereign power, but the people also benefit from the sovereign power to develop their own ambitions. It also embodies the people's desire for stability and solidarity. Nationalism alone cannot encompass and explain such a complex dynamic, particularly considering that individuals act and position themselves for both strategical and emotional reasons.

This is the reason I separate the book into two parts: while the first part discusses primarily political reasonings and philosophical concepts, the second part focuses on cultural representations. I believe that a more sophisticated grasp of this history of sovereignty can be achieved only by reading the two parts side by side. Together, they show how state sovereignty is a power incarnated in concrete institutions and circulated among the people through representations and rhetoric. It is also an assemblage constantly collapsing and reconstructing, to the extent that it could never be permanently owned by any single party.

The Logic of the Self

Unity and permanence are central to the discourses of sovereignty that are often built around the logic of the self. Modern state sovereignty is established with the purpose of denying outside powers the possibility of ruling the people. It must seek legitimacy internally, and modern state sovereignty also becomes self-legitimizing. While this book focuses primarily on state sovereignty, we need to recognize that there are many forms of sovereignties, ones that pertain to individuals and groups, and they are often in conflict with each other: consider, for example, the antagonism between the indigenous people and the settler colonizers in many countries as well as those between an individual and his/her family. These many levels of sovereignty often become so entangled that they could not and should not be separated too quickly. Each case needs its own contextualization.

Self-control can be understood on two levels: externally, it rejects other people's attempts to command oneself; internally, it celebrates the self-management of impulses, emotions, and conduct for the sake of higher goals. This comprises a good part of our moral education. Scaling this behaviorism up to the state level, we find that discussions of state sovereignty often also hinge on a dual structure: externally against foreign interference and internally against domestic disorder. Indeed, our imagination of sovereignty tends to be based on a coherent and confident individual, capable of managing and controlling one's own self.[33] But because the state is composed of many individuals, the state as the representation of the people implies a power transaction, in the sense that the modern state operates through citizens' voluntary transference of their authority to the state. Collecting the power of the citizens, the state could become coercive due to, and despite, these originating forces. It is often difficult to differentiate "the sovereignty belongs to me" from "I belong to the sovereignty." This sovereign logic echoes the possessive propensity of private property ownership, giving rise to the idea that I own and am entitled to any value associated with my country.

No major political theorists in the West (with the possible exception of the anarchists) have denied the importance of the state in exercising sovereign power and protecting the body politic; indeed, even Karl Marx placed the withering of the state in the distant, utopian future. The state is still the most important form of political community in modern society, and the people express their political rights mostly via the state. This leads to the highly problematic circular logic of modern sovereignty: in order to maintain the people's sovereignty, we must protect state sovereignty at all costs; in order to end a hegemonic sovereignty, we need to develop another one.[34] Questions related to state sovereignty are mostly questions related to collective self-governance as well as its demise.

Indeed, sovereignty does not describe only the individual and the state but also many forms of political collective. Groups with different political ambitions and a different sense of belonging might also evince a will to sovereignty. Women are often considered objects instead of subjects of sovereignty,[35] while the sovereignty of indigenous groups is also often encroached by hostile political and economic forces.[36] To deter the state from collecting all the power, activists and artists have promoted different kinds of indigenous rights.[37] Critics—including myself—have also urged us to refocus back on the sovereign agency of individual political actor as well as the collectives they form.[38] But such approaches run the risks of overemphasizing the agency and liberty of the enlightened self. The more demanding political task is to understand the necessary entanglement of different levels of sovereignty, and to deal with the resulting disagreement and conflicts.

Needless to say, while we should critique the assumptions behind liberalism, we cannot jump to a wholesale denunciation of personal liberty and end up endorsing authoritarianism. China's current sovereign logic displays a strong animosity toward liberalism, where state economy and collective good matter more than personal liberty.[39] Its rapid economic development in the last three decades, as interpreted by many critics, proves the effectiveness of this sovereign logic. But the Chinese state has clearly exploited the people's willingness to negotiate personal liberty: the grave consequences of the state's enormous power in intruding into their private life has been painfully felt by citizens in the COVID-19 lockdowns. Our task is not to dichotomize authoritarianism and liberalism, knowing that each would be contaminated by the other in different ways, but to navigate and work through the entanglement to develop a more just and benevolent political space.

We must also differentiate sovereignty from government: each sovereignty is composed of a government, yet the sovereign and the government are clearly not the same thing. While the sovereign is the body that owns sovereignty—which is highly abstract—the government is an assemblage of concrete institutions with diversified bureaus, agendas, functions, and locations. In terms of the actual operation of the government, the state could be very fragile, and its bureaucracy is often far less efficient and powerful than the sovereign power would claim and hope. But the state's sovereignty does not necessarily suffer.

Both the state and its critics tend to overstate the unity and the power of the state, while the government often fails to achieve its ambitions.[40] Many states, whether democratic or autocratic, suffer from bureaucracy and incompetence. In fact, many patriotic Chinese citizens are highly critical of the inefficiency and sometimes corruption of their local governments. But they tend to separate the mundane bureaucracy from the Central Government, which embodies state sovereignty. The state is both a quotidian government and a symbolic site of sovereign power, and the latter is conjured by countless citizens who identify with it and submit to its authority. The government's day-to-day operation might be inefficient, but this does not cancel out the originating power of the sovereignty that existed prior to the institution.

Consider the acts of Hu Xijin 胡錫進, the former editor-in-chief of the CCP-sponsored tabloid newspaper *Global Times* and one of the most popular opinion leaders in China today. In early May 2022, Hu challenged the "dynamic zero-COVID" policy on his Weibo account at a moment when Beijing, where he lived, was about to enter a lockdown after Shanghai's almost catastrophic lockdown. But one day later, Chairman Xi offered a strong statement to reiterate the importance of a zero-COVID policy and reemphasized that this national policy could not be challenged. Hu's message was immediately deleted, replaced by a new message urging the Chinese people to believe in and follow the commands of the CCP. Hu quite sincerely stressed that this obedience was a result of both "reason and belief."[41] Reason and belief do not go together in our common sense, yet sovereignty is a combination of the two. Hu's self-correction points out how sovereignty is composed of both institution and symbols, such that reasons and affects are both essential parts of the state-people relationship. The Chinese people could be critical of government policies, but they obey sovereign demands for reason and belief.[42]

In Europe, such a distinction was first identified by Bodin in the sixteenth century. He separated the state agent that exercised authority from the authorizing sovereignty that empowered this state agent for such power.[43] Following up on this idea were French Revolution thinkers such as Abbé Sieyes, who described this dual structure of modern sovereignty with two terms: *pouvoir constituant* (constituent power), the power that legitimizes the state, and *pouvoir constitué* (constituted power), the power legitimized by the former to become the constitutional order and government structure.[44] In the context of the French Revolution, the two terms combined to describe the logic of popular sovereignty: the new Republic was empowered by the people to make laws and develop the government apparatus so as to manage the people. The slipshod operation of state apparatus might dissipate the originating constituent power, but they are not the same thing.

With the many entanglements operating, sovereignty cuts both ways: it can be hegemonic, and it can be the force to fight hegemony.

In the words of anthropologist Audra Simpson, who works on indigenous rights, "Only critique can help us distinguish between sovereignty as Western exceptionalism and dominance, and sovereignty as Indigenous belonging, dignity, and justice."[45] Accepting and modifying Simpson's recommendation to describe my project, I would say that only critique can help us distinguish sovereignty as state exceptionalism and dominance, and sovereignty as sensible collective governance based on justice, plurality, and adaptation to external change. To me, scholarly critique not only betrays the innate complexity of all sovereignty claims but also encourages us not to shy away from offering informed and difficult moral-political judgment.

———

There are two main types of movement and segmentation, according to Gilles Deleuze, that make up our assemblages of desire.[46] On the one hand, there are the constant efforts of territorialization and reterritorialization exercised by power, producing segmentary lines as boundaries to classify people and things. On the other hand, there are also acts and effects of deterritorialization resulting from, first, individuals constantly crossing thresholds and initiating transformations (for instance, migrants and dissidents) and, second, the flight lines appearing around marginalized characters, mostly unconsciously, making a loop or dashing toward an unknown destination.[47] In spite of his differentiation, Deleuze acknowledges that in the real world, it is impossible to separate these divergent movements and segmentations. Deleuze also makes it clear that acts of territorialization are immanent and general and that they include not only those acts belonging specifically to the state but also many of our daily operations: consider, for example, how much time we spend every day busily constructing and guarding our own space. His model is very helpful for us to understand sovereign power, which is tasked precisely to territorialize, create lines in order to sort people out, offer them a form, and give them a sense of agency and unity. At the same time, the meanderings and flight lines of individuals and groups would also cut across or bend the sovereign power in subtle and violent ways.

The book is composed of two parts, which loosely correspond to Deleuze's ideas of territorialization and deterritorialization. This structure also demonstrates my approach to studying China's modern state sovereignty from a wider frame of reference. The first part studies the key political ideologies in a continuous and dynamic history, while the second part discusses the cultural representations of specific media in specific historical periods by individuals. It is important that we do not read the sovereign story simply from the state's perspective, which is a problem of Agamben's sovereignty theory. Instead, state sovereignty is constantly deterritorized and reterritorized by people of all kinds. I find it important to juxtapose the two approaches to illustrate how sovereignty is both a top-down political theology and a vast set of popular cultural expressions. This approach also shows that any appropriation of state sovereignty as transcendental and unchanging is bound to be problematic. To facilitate its control, the state often presents (and conceptualizes) sovereignty in terms of border-making: demarcating inside and outside, defining propriety and debauchery. But this stabilization would necessarily be challenged by the people (or, to use the Deleuzian term, desire), whose actions would turn sovereignty into a messy and unstable entanglement. Even those supporting it could create static and embarrassment, and the intellectuals best embody the ambiguities.

Part I treats the concept and ideology of state sovereignty in China as a continual presence, tracing its historical roots and demonstrating how it has transformed in the Long Twentieth Century along with the rapidly changing political systems. The three chapters in this part also theorize and historicize the internal contradictions inherent in this term. Following this introduction, chapter 1 focuses on China's traditional sovereign philosophy, at the core of which is the idea of *Tian*. Two thousand years ago thinkers of different schools reinterpreted existing political ideas and created new ones to form a Confucian-Legalist sovereign theory. This sovereign worldview combined religious, moral, and political ideas to legitimize imperial sovereign power. This conceptual framework has been enormously effective and significant in the subsequent development of the Chinese imperial system, the end of which by no means terminated its influence in modern times. This chapter also discusses the essential role intellectuals played in sustaining this sovereign theory.

While sovereignty is generally understood as a self-contained concept, chapters 2 and 3 explore sovereignty in relative terms—that is, against external threats and internal challenges—to show that it is never unified. Chapter 2 offers a concise reading of the fiction of unity constructed in different periods of modern and contemporary China, demonstrating how the ideology of unity is central to sovereignty. The ruling regimes might be changing rapidly, but they all have to manipulate the myth of unity and to appropriate China's internal plurality and changes in international relations to empower the state's sovereignty. This chapter also discusses the close connection between the state's ethnic policies and its international relations. Providing a chronicle of major political events in modern and contemporary China, this chapter also serves as the historical background for the rest of the book.

Picking up some of the discussions of Heaven's mandate in chapter 1 and the tensions between threats and unity in chapter 2, chapter 3 focuses on the ideas of revolution in this history, examining how the ruling regimes both revere and fear revolution. Both the Republic of China (ROC) and the PRC obtained their sovereignty through revolutions, and the ruling regimes have incessantly returned to their revolutionary victory as their source of legitimacy. But the sovereign powers also fear revolutions the most, trying to repress seeds of dissent at all costs. Demonstrating how revolution was central to both the KMT and the CCP sovereign power, this chapter challenges our assumption that sovereignty is an entity of stability and permanence. It also shows how violence is central to state sovereignty.

Part II focuses on the unique manifestations of major sovereign concepts in the different political systems. Each of the chapters in this part also examines a particular form of cultural representation, with the purpose of revealing the fictive and imaginative dimensions of sovereignty. Together they show how culture and representations sustain and challenge sovereignty. Chapter 4 focuses on the idea of popular sovereignty first forged by Sun Yat-sen's revolutionary party around the first decade of the twentieth century, and the response on the part of a new generation of intellectuals. The abstract idea of the "people" is foundational to basically all contemporary political discourses, which assume that it is the people who precede and give form to the political institution. This chapter examines how the sovereign power constructed the Chinese people as modern citizens in the 1920s, how some scholars substantiated it, and how others doubted the capacity of the Chinese people to be their own rulers.

If chapter 4 analyzes how some republican intellectuals refused to endorse the state's sovereign discourse, chapter 5 shows that many socialist intellectuals volunteered to be a part of the state propaganda. This chapter discusses the national landscape represented in the new state-sponsored genre of modern ink brush paintings. These works were invested with heavy political, aesthetic, and economic values, and they revealed the mutual appropriation between the socialist nation-building and traditional Confucian and Daoist aesthetics. Artists were subjected to intense political scrutiny, although some also gained political capital by producing works to support the state ideology. This chapter also analyzes the assumptions behind territorial sovereignty and examines how traditional Chinese paintings were tasked to aestheticize land as an abstract possession of sovereign power.

Chapter 6 focuses on biopower in contemporary China. Globally speaking, state sovereignty might have been challenged and diffused by neoliberalism and globalization. But postsocialist China has demonstrated the opposite trend, with increasing centralization of state power. Focusing on a few internet-based memes and videos for political mockery and self-mockery, this chapter explores how the ordinary people live in a powerful state whose political legitimacy is built on its economic promises to the people. This "social contract" can be a result of the state benefiting from a people tired of the political instability they have experienced. But such heavy reliance on economic interests also produces economic "involution" and promotes class consciousness in China, which could become the biggest challenge to the current sovereign power.

A brief conclusion is provided to remind us how this book on modern and contemporary China is also relevant to today's world, when a new wave of international antagonism is on the rise and when natural and human-made disasters loom large. It is urgent for us to develop a better global governance for humanity beyond national borders and to reflect on a sovereignty that commits more on comradeship of differences than coercion into one.

Concepts and Structures

One

The Mandate of Heaven

Few would deny that the COVID pandemic has been one of the most serious challenges to the PRC's sovereignty in recent years. In early 2020, at a time when many Chinese were still immersed in the fear of the unknown virus and the agony of the fierce lockdown, dissent was directed in subtle ways at Xi Jinping's autocratic leadership. In March of that year, a senior China observer in the United States commented that "Xi has been stripped of his air of invincibility and that is calling into question his 'mandate of Heaven.'"[1] The term "Heaven's mandate" (*Tianming* 天命) is used here to describe Xi's falling out of favor with both Heaven and the people, in other words losing his legitimacy as China's ruler. At that time, similar uses of the expression could also be found in Chinese commentaries outside China. Not a few believe that the deadly virus could well derail Xi's sovereignty. As it turned out, the successful containment of the virus by the draconian lockdown policies actually strengthened the sovereign legitimacy in the first two years. The discussions of Xi losing the mandate of Heaven appeared again at the end of 2022, when the virus spread ferociously in the country.[2] But with the confirmation of Xi's third term as China's president in 2023, such queries quickly faded into obscurity.

Tianming belongs to those who rule. But when Heaven is disappointed with the performance of the sovereign, Heaven will send a natural calamity to Earth or give rebels the chance to rise up in order to show that Heaven's mandate has shifted. For example, the Tangshan earthquake, which according to China's official announcement killed more than 240,000 people, took place on July 28, 1976, and it was seen by many people as a sign of Heaven denouncing Mao, who as it happened would die a month later. The term also suggests a centralized political power, which demands the loyalty of all people to the ruling power.[3]

Tianming is an ancient Chinese concept. For example, in the famous 770 BCE poem "Zhao min" 召旻 ("Zhao is foreboding"), collected in *Shijing* 詩經 (*Book of Songs*), the anonymous poet described the natural disasters accompanying the vicious and indolent performances of King You of the Zhou dynasty 周幽王 (c. 795–771 BCE).

Far distant Heaven hates and terrorizes us,	旻天疾威
Heaven liberally sends down death,	天篤降喪
And wears us out with famine, our grain not ripening and our vegetables not ripening.	瘨我饑饉
People are all adrift and fleeing,	民卒流亡
Our settlements and borderlands are utterly deserted.	我居圉卒荒
Heaven sends down its crime net,	天降罪罟
And the "*mao*-crickets at its roots and the bandit-locusts at its nodules" cause government's collapse by their squabbling in your royal palace;	蟊賊內訌
Your royal-palace['s] disorderly castrati-officials have no deference,	昏椓靡共
They've crumbled into such chaos, being devious and evasive;	潰潰回遹
And those going to calm and pacify our country!	實靖夷我邦
. . .	
Of old, when the Former Kings, the founders of our [Z]hou dynasty, received the Mandate from Heaven	昔先王受命
They had such as the Duke of Shao	有如召公
And daily expanded our state by one hundred li-miles,	日辟國百里。

Whereas nowadays our state is daily contracted by one hundred li-miles	今也日蹙國百里。
Alas, so sad!	於乎哀哉
Rulers nowadays	維今之人
Don't esteem men of venerable experience.[4]	不尚有舊。

The poet described how the world was beset by natural and human disasters, which were both acts of God. The poem also suggested that the disasters were sent by Heaven due to the impotence of the king. The former kings had received the Mandate from Heaven to form the dynasty,[5] but the current one lost it. With the poor performance of the king, both he *and* the innocent people had to suffer. The justice wielded by *Tian* can be ferocious.

Tian can be loosely translated as "Heaven." As in English, the Chinese concept suggests many related ideas: the sky, the place where gods, angels, and deities live, and the embodiment of the highest divine force. Its mandate, or command, is good, just, and inevitable, because *Tian* accords with the best interests of humankind and is beyond the control of any single individual or interest group. It is considered the archetypal origin of all Chinese religions. Different schools of thought also offered their own interpretations of *Tian*. Confucius told his pupil that "*Tian* does not speak, yet the four seasons unfold, and all things come into being," while Mozi asserted that *Tian* inclines to propriety and dislikes discord. The Daoist master Laozi described that *Tian* is not benevolent, and it treats everything as a straw dog, while in the book *Guanzi* it is claimed that *Tian* is fair and has no biases, therefore things both beautiful and ugly exist side by side.[6] While the emphasis of these passages differ, together they portray a *Tian* that does not conform to the wants and desires of any human individuals, yet it ultimately accords with the collective interests of humankind. *Tian* also became a political theology, standing for a divine approval of the legitimacy of the ruling regime—or of its competitor, who will become the next ruler.

But the Chinese concept is also decidedly secular, implying a *propriety* of social and cosmic order: whoever receives the mandate must be the one who can maintain the world order and satisfy the needs of the people. *Tian* provides the foundation of the Chinese moral universe, in which humans and things are properly placed and harmoniously related. But it is also the ultimate judge. As shown in this ancient poem, *Tian* could become ruthless when it was not satisfied with the performances of the sovereign power, whereupon it inflicted natural disasters and enabled revolutions. From these, the people could decipher its mandate.

Before we enter the modern and contemporary periods, in this chapter I want to delineate the traditional Confucian-Legalist sovereign theory with *Tian* at the center. *Tian* is simultaneously a spiritual concept, a moral construct, and a mode of assessing political power, and it was used in Imperial China to support the stability of the ruling power. The term can be found in the earliest Chinese texts, such as the *Book of Songs* mentioned above, as well as *Shangshu* 尚書 (*Book of Documents*) and *Daodejing* 道德經 (*Tao Te Ching*), which, it is believed, collected writings from the 1000s BCE to the 200s BCE.[7] According to these texts, the term *Tian* was already used widely in Western Zhou dynasty (1045–771 BCE), which witnessed the first political regime in China to administer a unified empire of enormous size for a long duration. Robert Eno argues that part of Zhou's success can be attributed to the belief in *Tian*, which was virtually the personal deity of the Zhou throne, as the king was the only one permitted to communicate with *Tian* through sacrifice. With the endorsement of *Tian*, Zhou rule was nothing more than an agency for the will of *Tian*, and the government was an organ for the discharge of religious and political responsibility.[8]

Thinkers after the Zhou dynasty began to present *Tian* as the source of not only political power but also all human virtues, which could be acquired by gifted individuals; this was most obvious in the case of Confucius, who could communicate with *Tian* directly and who therefore qualified as the Sage—as the morally superior person who could communicate between *Tian* and humans.[9] The term gradually becomes, among ordinary people, the ultimate source of transcendental moral force arbitrating justice, and it also confers political legitimacy and prescribes duties to the king. The term *Tian* is also used in Japanese and Korean societies with similar implications, and it is a fundamental concept in Confucian sovereign ideology across geographical locations until today.

The unique power of *Tian* in China must be understood in terms of the absence of institutionalized religion there. This contrasts with, for example, Islamic countries, where the sovereign power cannot be legitimate if it does not operate on Divine Law (shari'a) and serve the cause of Islam.[10] Likewise, in sixteenth-century France, Jean Bodin emphasized that sovereignty must be bound by the laws of nature prescribed by God.[11] Even today, the separation of church and state is central to political life in the Western democratic countries, but the church, with its supreme moral authority, still wields different degrees of influence in state policy in many Western states.[12] Carl Schmitt argues that, deep down, the modern secularized state is consecrated by some divine residue: "all significant concepts of the modern theory of the state are secularized theological concepts."[13] But we must keep in mind that while Schmitt suggests a universal phenomenon, his observation is based entirely on the European situation. Monotheism does not exist in China, and there was also not a religious institution similar to the Christian Church in the West, which both legitimized and competed with the secular state. Instead, Confucianism explicitly asks the people to disregard the supernatural. Our attention should be directed to the people's wellbeing, upon which the legitimacy of the sovereign power is measured. Only when the government failed to exercise the heaven's mandate would the supernatural force of *Tian* intervene and bestow disasters.

But this does not mean religion is absent in Chinese political culture. Daoist practices and ancestral worship permeate people's everyday lives. Religious activities were also extremely important in the daily operation of the imperial court, which earned its political authority by connecting with *Tian*.[14] *Tian*, as the invisible, ineffable, and unfathomable authority, could be seen as the abstract agency embodying this coexistence of secularization and spiritualism in China. This Confucian political order overlaps with a rigid social and moral economy, which together designate the emperor as a part (instead of the soul) of the world, submitting the Chinese sovereign to a cosmic order of propriety and harmony.

Without a set of codified laws, the normative Confucian sovereign theory is highly adaptive, practical, and subject to interpretations. Sovereign legitimacy is not measured against a set of moral-religious principles; instead, legitimacy depends on the general economic and moral performance of the government.[15] Inevitably, the actual power and responsibilities of the Chinese Emperor were shared by an extensive bureaucracy and local magistrates, upon which his sovereign legitimacy depended. The Confucian scholar-officials also had the fundamental responsibility of advising the Emperor to abide by the people's best interests. But the absolute authority the Emperor possessed in the human world was not up to the ordinary people or the officials to challenge. Only *Tian* could do that. But this supreme force—unlike Yahweh and other ancient gods who have distinct identity and consciousness above humans—is also primarily the expression of the people. It might sound contradictory, that the emperor could not be challenged by the human world but must also be accountable to the people. But this ambiguous power relation sustained the Chinese dynastic system for two millennia. In fact, *Tian* could be seen as a built-in mechanism—though only a self-supervising one—within a monarchic structure to encourage the absolutist sovereign to be more accountable to the people.

In the following, I decipher three interrelated concepts—*Tianming* (Heaven's mandate), *Tianzi* (emperor), and *Tianxia* (all under heaven)—to explain the fundamental structure of this Confucian-Legalist sovereign theory. I focus on the time spanning the "Spring and Autumn" period to the Han dynasty to explore how a sovereign theory was formulated, coalesced, and carried over. For brevity's sake, I must sacrifice some of the nuance and complexity of the concepts in order to create a more readable narrative. The chapter ends by briefly examining the roles played by intellectuals in sustaining and propagating this sovereign system.

Heaven's Mandate—*Tianming*

China's earliest civilization with written records can be dated back to the Yinshang period or the Yin period in the Shang dynasty (c. 1300–1045 BCE). At this time, many were worshiped at the court, including *Shangdi* the high god, imperial ancestors, and nature deities, showing how the god and ancestors were summoned together to support sovereign power.[16] The term *Tian* appeared in the subsequent Western Zhou period partly to designate this general moral-religious entity comprising the divine force. Western Zhou was considered by later Confucian scholars as their utopian past, embodying the highest point of Chinese civilization. It was purportedly a period when feudalism was practiced in a world of moral propriety, where individuals happily played their assigned social roles, resulting in a prosperous and harmonious society. But this dynasty was gradually corrupted, and during the reign of King You, whom we just met in the aforementioned poem, its capital was ransacked by "barbarians." The new King Ping escaped to the East and established a new capital along with other rising powers, which commenced the Eastern Zhou period. This Eastern Zhou period has been further divided by historians into two periods: "Spring and Autumn" (770–476 BCE) and "Warring States" (475–221 BCE), when Zhou had to compete with the many newly emerging states. After five hundred years of interstate wars, the final victory of Ying Zheng of the Qin state unified the vast territory and established the short-lived Qin dynasty (221–207 BCE), to be succeeded by the Han dynasty (206 BCE–220 CE).

China during the "Spring and Autumn" and "Warring States" periods was not unlike medieval Europe, where many states existed together uneasily, characterized by incessant battles on the one hand and their mutual influences on the other. Although there was not a church in China to mediate and balance the conflicts, the competing states shared similar written official languages. This was also the period when most of the classical schools of thought were formed. Writings and artifacts of the period suggest that the idea of *Tian* was used among the states.

Like *Tian*, the term *Tianming*, Heaven's mandate, also first appeared in the Western Zhou dynasty, and it described the act of *Tian* conferring on the king the power to rule on earth after accepting the sacrifices the king offered. It was also during this period that *Tian* gradually transformed from a personalized god to the originator of the universal pan-moral-political order. According to historian Yu Ying-shih, a myth of the pre-Zhou period shows that the first king, in order to legitimize his enormous power, took up the role originally belonging to the shaman and monopolized the communication between the supernatural and the ordinary people.[17] This is the origin of *Tianming*, also the earliest version of Chinese sovereign theory.

A moral dimension was added to the term around Confucius's time (551–479 BCE), when Confucius claimed that he could communicate with *Tian* directly and understand *Tianming*.[18] The thinker's self-proclaimed ability in communicating with *Tian* expanded the meanings of the term *Tianming*, which now described not only sovereign legitimacy but also the cosmic-secular order accessible to the Sage. From then on, there are two major features of this Chinese sovereign theory: sovereignty belongs to the sovereign, but sovereignty is also based on the approval of the people.

Let us focus on how the term functions in the *Book of Documents*, which collected official documents and other prose writings produced during approximately the 2000–1000 BCE period. The date of the texts and the compilation as well as the accuracy of the historical materials found there have been subject to endless academic debate. Even so, certain chapters are generally understood to be true records of the Western Zhou period. We can also safely infer that the book was a product of scholarly efforts during the consecutive "Spring and Autumn" and "Warring States" periods. During that time, existing historical writings were systematically compiled into discrete volumes, including not only the *Book of Documents* but also the *Analects* (*Lunyu* 論語) and the *Mencius* (*Mengzi* 孟子).

The "Announcement to the Prince of Kang" (*Kanggao* 康誥) chapter in the *Book of Documents* records a conversation between the Emperor Wu of Zhou and his brother, the Duke of Zhou. The Emperor instructed his younger brother to remember the great enterprise of their father, Emperor Wen, and that "the mandate [of Heaven] does not rest on one person forever."[19] Emperor Wu asserted that despite the great achievement of their father, the blessing of *Tian* was not automatic; instead, the brothers had to go to some trouble to establish that they were, respectively, a great king and a great prince.

This idea of the mandate not resting in any one person appeared in many later Confucian texts, showing how the idea was influential in Confucian political thinking. For example, it is criticized in *Zuozhuan* 左傳 (Zuo tradition) that the Lu rulers have indulged their negligence for generations, and therefore it is natural that the people do not take pity on Lord Zhao of Lu being expelled and dying outside the kingdom: "There is no constant relation between rulers and subjects."[20] In *Liji* 禮記 (*Book of Rites*), on the other hand, Confucius is cited as saying that only those who can practice good governance can retain the mandate, while those who cannot maintain goodness will lose it.[21] Central to the concept of *Tianming* is that it changes hands, so that those who want to maintain it must work for it.

But how? Another central dimension of *Tianming* is its consent to the people. A line from the chapter "Great Declaration" (*Taishi* 泰誓) in the *Book of Documents* explains: "Heaven sees what the people see; Heaven listens to what the people listen to."[22] This line suggests an inherent sensory and psychological connection between Heaven and the people. With such strong interconnection, Heaven's will (*Tianyi* 天意) necessarily reflects the popular will (*minyi* 民意).[23]

Taken together, we can see the dialectical dimension of *Tian*. Being the source of all power, *Tian* is simultaneously unfathomable and easily observed. While human beings must submit to its omnipotence, *Tian* also listens to the people and sees their suffering, and it will protect the people by exercising its mandate. Accordingly, *Tianming* changes, but its alliance with the people does not change. Although it is impossible to understand the reasoning of *Tian*, we could locate its mandate in the historical unfolding in human society, knowing that it only endorses those rulers who practice goodness. Its mandate does not stay with one ruler forever, but it is consistent in aligning with the people.[24]

It is also important to note that coercive force is central to this sovereign theory. Without a clear road map to indicate how a corrupt ruler can be removed, the theory of Heaven's mandate indirectly supports the exercise of brute force. On the one hand, should one see a sovereign dynasty that is no longer able to rule, those who believe they have the mandate could and should employ forces to seize power. On the other hand, the current ruler, who believes that he still possesses the mandate, is entitled to suppress dissident voices; this is where Legalism (*Fajia* 法家), which emphasizes penal codes and imperial authority, becomes useful.

Confucian classics therefore provide legitimacy and guidelines both for political authority and for dissenters against that authority to fight each other.[25] Dynasty change is an inevitable and necessary part of the Confucian historical structure, which acknowledges that rulers can become so corrupted that Heaven must block them. The revolutionaries who successfully overturned the regime were not autonomous individuals as such, but they exercised *Tianming*. More accurately, the chosen rebels are both active players in their own ambitions and passive vehicles for Heaven to exercise its mandate. This approval of revolution also gives the people the hope that political change is possible, that the future can be better than the present, if the ambitious ones are courageous enough to try. The many revolutions and rebellions punctuating the two-millennia-long political history of Imperial China witnessed how this opaque Heaven's mandate operated: political power is equated with force, but political power without the approval of the people is also illegitimate.

This sovereign philosophy actually brought relative social stability and prosperity to China for two millennia. While the sovereign powers changed, the underlying sovereign logic did not. Compared with medieval Europe—where the rulers and state bureaucracies were weaker and needed to seek the collaboration of the people for taxation and conscription[26]—the Chinese imperial courts tended to have few incentives to share their political power with the ordinary people. But it has also been argued that the Chinese people supported this imperial social order because it provided a secure and predictable political environment for people to lead their lives. For a good part of their reign, the Chinese dynasties were more stable, richer, and more commanding than their European counterparts. The Chinese people, correspondingly, were also less motivated to demand power from their emperors. There were rebels daring or desperate enough to challenge the throne, but many ordinary people were persuaded that *Tian* would overthrow those incapable or illegitimate rulers. China continued to engage in countless wars in the following periods, but almost all dynasties, with different degrees of modification, adopted the administration structure, political ideology, and legal codes inherited from the previous ones.

The Kingship—*Tianzi*

Embodying *Tianming* is *Tianzi*—that is, the king embodies Heaven as the Son of Heaven. And the king's most important job is to maintain *Tianming* and pass it to his heir. Similar to the term *Tianming*, the uses of *Tianzi* can be dated back to the Western Zhou dynasty, when it referred to the King of Zhou. Found in texts compiled during the "Spring and Autumn" and "Warring States" periods, the term was associated not only with rituals and divine power but also with effective government and military strength. The two were also related: the king who treated the people well would necessarily be able to win wars.[27] *Tianzi* was indeed an important concept in early Chinese philosophy, not only because he is the king, but also because he is the boss of the philosophers. Most of the thinkers at that time were advisors to the kings, and most of the schools of thought were developed around kingships: advice for the kings on how to be a better sovereign. Let us look at some examples.

Daoism emphasizes a governance of doing nothing, and it tends not to comment on governance. But in the Daoist classic *Zhuangzi* we find the interesting chapter "Delight in the Sword Fight." Here, King Wen of the Zhao state sought advice from Zhuangzi, who told him that there were three kinds of swords: those belonging to the Son of Heaven, to the feudal prince, and to the common individual. Zhuangzi elaborates how the *Tianzi* sword was made by elements from different regions, embraced by tribes of all kinds, bound by nature, and approved by the universe. It is therefore in harmony with nature and cosmic energy; consequently, once that sword is used, "All under Heaven" (*Tianxia*) would submit to it.[28] But Zhuangzi laments that while King Wen was himself the *Tianzi*, he chose the sword of the ordinary people, which is employed to "slash through the neck and scoop out the liver and lungs." Since the sword is a symbol of aggression, Zhuangzi reminds the king to give up militancy and follow the natural law of nature and abandon swordsmanship as his means to exercise his ambition. The story ends with the suicide of all the swordsmen in the state, indirectly suggesting the success of the Zhuangzi in persuading the King to give up violence.

Mohism, on the other hand, believes that the duty of *Tianzi* is to maintain order proactively and realistically. Mozi believes that each person has their own view, and a society composed of myriad people would be overwhelmed by the multiple conflictual views. In order to avoid society from running amok, instead of pleasing everyone *Tianzi* must assert one view authoritatively and unify the nation.[29] Like Hobbes, Mozi believes that people tend to be selfish and cannot cooperate on their own. They must rely on *Tianzi* to manage disputes and establish structural relations to form stable communities.

There were also many discussions about whether it is justifiable to exile or kill a ruler who is incompetent. For example, in *Zuozhuan* we find descriptions and comments devoted to those rulers who fell victim to assassination, and their fates were deemed justified if these kings were improper toward their ministers; committed debauchery, adultery, inconstancy; or were tyrannical. It was believed that good government is the only way to validate the ruler, and the exercise of power on all levels must be tempered by advice, remonstrance, and correction.[30]

The "Spring and Autumn" period was a time when "a hundred schools of thought were contending with each other," and this relatively liberal environment was a direct result of the political environment witnessing the vigorous contestation of many *Tianzi*. There was only one *Tianzi* in Zhou at any one time, and his supreme power was rooted from his unique presence. But as China entered the "Spring and Autumn" period, there were now multiple kings competing for power. *Tianzi* reappeared as the singular supreme emperor for the unified Qin empire after 221 BCE after Qin defeated other states.[31] The "Spring and Autumn" and "Warring States" periods differed from the preceding Western Zhou dynasty and the following Qin dynasty in the proliferation of many competing rulers, which directly affected the intellectual culture.

Many Chinese political historians agree that the Qin dynasty was a turning point in Chinese history, not only in terms of the unification of the vast land but also as a radical restructuring of the intellectual culture, wiping out the previous pluralistic environment. The world of the Warring States resembled a huge market of talent, as statesmen and thinkers could travel around in search of better patrons. The rulers, in turn, competed with each other for talented thinkers and helpful advisers, although the advisers could also be ruthlessly punished and killed by their bosses. After unification Qin adopted Legalism as its ruling ideology, emphasizing draconian laws and severe punishment to maintain social order.[32] Qin's imperial unification marked a major shift in the balance of power: now there was only one emperor—and thus one employer—to whom all the thinkers had to submit. Perhaps this is why Legalist theorists, as Qin's official advisors, emphasized centralization of power, unification of measurement, and the unified system of laws. With the ideological support of Legalism, the supreme power of the *Tianzi* must not be challenged, while a weak people was considered essential to a strong sovereign.

As the first Chinese empire, the Qin lasted a mere fifteen years, followed by the Han dynasty, considered one of the most glorious ones in Chinese history. Han inherited and further improved the Qin's state administrative capacity. A new centralized bureaucracy was also developed, supported by the newly developed national imperial examination (this would be further strengthened in the Song dynasty), which provided channels for talented individuals to enter the ruling elite. That said, those chosen by the exams were still mostly the sons of the elite class.[33] Regional kingdoms gradually submitted to the Han Empire as dependent states, and Emperor Wu of Han was elevated as the supreme overlord, who governed a territory much larger than Qin. To contrast themselves from the Qin's coercive control, the Han Emperors began to grant some cultural and political autonomy to the regional power, which, however, was gradually taken back.[34] Overall, Han *Tianzi*, supported by a professional bureaucracy, was able to unify much of the known world and embody the total secular power of *Tian*.

To the state-supported intellectuals, when one sovereign finally defeated others and developed an empire, the more pressing ideological project was to legitimize this enormous imperial power, glorifying the *Tianzi* and the stability he commanded. After the Qin's quick deterioration, scholars of the Han dynasty worked to achieve two distinct goals: first, to depict Qin's emperors as tyrannical and corrupted; and second, to develop a new sovereign theory that would legitimize the supreme power of the Han *Tianzi*. The Han was clearly successful in demonizing the First Emperor of Qin, with an impact felt to this day.[35] Let us focus on the second.

The Han period was a time when different schools of thought were integrated into an official philosophy, most obviously observed in the integration of Confucianism and Legalism. The two were among the competing doctrines during "Spring and Autumn" and "Warring States" periods. But during the Han period, Confucianism, which would be the official ideology and teaching of most dynasties thereafter, incorporated much of Legalist doctrine to strengthen its effectiveness as a set of governance instruction. We can say that the relationship between Confucianism and Legalism in traditional Chinese sovereignty was one of reciprocal causation. On the discursive level, Confucianism considered law an inferior means of control, especially when compared with morality (*de* 德) and rituals (*li* 禮). Law should be used primarily as a subsidiary tool, in situations with certain determined evildoers who cannot be affected by moral instruction.[36] But in practice, the law in Confucian China was overwhelmingly penal in emphasis, clearly influenced by Legalism.[37] The political philosophy that dominated Imperial China would be better described as Confucian-Legalist,[38] which combined the advantages of rituals (*li*) and law (*fa* 法), building a logic of governance emphasizing both strong moral codes and extensive instructions for punishment.[39]

But the punishments applied only to ordinary people; there was a lack of legal codes and reasoning and legal operations to constrict the conduct of the Emperor. There might be certain institutional arrangements built into the system to maintain some balance of power and procedural rationality, but there were no written decrees specifying how to prevent the Emperor from abusing his power. This contrasts with medieval Europe, where public laws, such as the Magna Carta, existed to subject, however ineffectively, the sovereign to the consent of the social elites and the representatives of the people.[40] Instead, the Confucian system relies on an extensive bureaucratic system and rigid moral teaching to confine the conduct of the sovereign, while Legalism legitimizes the sovereign to subject the people to its total power.

Han scholars studiously integrated not only Confucianism and Legalism but other schools of thought found in the Warring Periods to create a new sovereign ideology. This was most clearly observed in the works of Dong Zhongshu (董仲舒, c. 179 BCE to 104 BCE), who systematically pulled together, if not invented, a political theology of imperial sovereignty combining the secular and the spiritual. He theoretically combined the Confucianism of his time with early Daoist thinking, constructing a divine force that substantiates imperial Chinese sovereignty. His most important text was *Chunqiu fanlu* (春秋繁露,Luxuriant Dew of the Spring and Autumn Annals), a commentary on the canonical Confucian text *Spring and Autumn Annals*. Dong referred elaborately to the ancient cosmic theory of Five Phases (*wu xing* 五行), the Daoist dualistic thinking of *yinyang* 陰陽, and the archaic Huang Lao religious thought and practices popular at that time, all to theorize how proper imperial sovereignty aligns with the divine structure.[41] At the same time, Chinese religions, now also beginning to be influenced by state bureaucracy, structured their institutions accordingly.

With his new theory, Dong Zhongshu also explained the role of the Emperor in the Confucian cosmology: "The King is authorized by Heaven, and it is the intention of Heaven to confer the King [this role]. The King, therefore, is called *Tianzi*. The King sees Heaven as his father, respecting Heaven with filial piety."[42] Reiterating the term *Tianzi* used in Western Zhou, Dong emphasized the Han emperor as the iconic symbol of an enormous empire. As such, many responsibilities were assigned to the Emperor, of which the most important was that he must practice and embody moral propriety (*zhengxin* 正心)[43] so that he could possess both morality (*de*) and the force (*li* 力) to lead the people.

As Dong explained, the Chinese character representing "king," *wang* 王, portrays the notion as a central column connecting the three horizontal lines: these represent Heaven, the people, and the earth, the three layers of the universal political cosmology.[44] The king must be responsible to Heaven above, the Earth below, and the people on the horizon. Following the principles of Heaven, the king rules the people with benevolence and acts without self-interest.[45] But under Dong's theory, the people were only passive recipients of Heaven's jurisdiction, and they did not have any direct methods to determine who their ruler should be. This conceptualization of the people as passive subjects yearning for a good ruler would curtail the practices and imaginations of democracy in China, and this culture can arguably be observed even today.

With Confucianism and Legalism operating at the same time, the king was understood as an embodiment of both kindness and coercion, benevolence and tyranny. This could be demonstrated in the way the two terms *wangdao* 王道 (the way of the king) and *badao* 霸道 (the way of the hegemon) define each other. *Wangdao* is a Confucian term used to praise the moral and political capacity of kings.[46] The term is often contrasted with *badao*, which referenced a king's coercion, arrogance, and despotism in counterpoint to his benevolent governance of *wangdao*.[47] The Confucian tradition associated with Mencius emphasized the importance of the king to practice *wangdao* and discard *baodao*. However, King Xuan of the Han dynasty made it clear that a sophisticated governance combining both *wangdao* and *badao* characterized the core political practices of his Han dynasty.[48]

This pair of traditional sovereign concepts has been continually used even in modern China. In a 1924 speech given in Japan that advocated the solidarity of East Asian countries to fight western imperialism, Sun Yat-sen declared, "The oriental culture practices the kingly way of *wangdao*, the occidental culture practices the hegemon's *badao*." He reminded his Chinese and Japanese audience to stick with the *wangdao* culture of Chinese humanism against the *badao* culture of Western imperialism.[49] Sun's successor, Chiang Kai-shek (1887–1975), also used the *wangdao* concepts to describe and substantiate the KMT governance, indirectly proposing himself as the modern embodiment of the Confucian sage-king.[50]

Around the same time, the two terms were also picked up by Mao Zedong, who reverted to the Han practices of using them both. Amid the war against Japan, Mao announced that the CCP embraced *both* the king's way and the hegemon's way: "Our king's way is political principle, and our hegemon's way is discipline; both are essential."[51] Mao re-adopted the ancient dialectical ways of government, showing his appropriation of both the Confucian and the Legalist thoughts (that is, honoring both morality and discipline).

Today, the Xi government reverts to a more conservative usage of the terms. Widely seen in today's mainstream political discourses, *badao* is assigned once again to describe Western imperial power, while *wangdao* describes China's own power. Qiang Shigong, a professor of legal studies at Peking University and a main adviser of Hong Kong affairs to the Central Party, has argued that the PRC sovereignty embodies not only Bodin's theorization that sovereignty is the state's absolute and permanent power but also the traditional Confucian concept of righteous governance, *wangdao*. It is this duality, according to Qiang, that makes the PRC such a great state.[52] Such intellectual distinctions have real-world implications. To Qiang, it is the responsibility of the Hong Kong people to respect and appreciate this *wangdao* governance. But to a key figure of Taiwan's Democratic Progressive Party, the PRC's recent Hong Kong policies are manifestations of extreme *badao*.[53] The sovereign ideology and terminologies developed two millennia ago continued to define political conflicts today.

Unity Under Heaven—*Tianxia*

Receiving the *Tianming* mandate, the assignment tasked to *Tianzi*, the king, is to rule *Tianxia* 天下, which literally means "everything under Heaven." The concept has attracted a lot of scholarly attention in recent years, due primarily to the much-discussed "rise of China." Through the elucidation of *Tianxia*, recent scholars have demonstrated China's unique worldview rooted in its long history to be differentiated from the political theories developed around the rights-bearing individual, an ideology central to Western liberal democracy.

It is argued that the prominent presence of *Tianxia* in traditional Chinese thoughts implies that China has always been a multinational country, with a civilization composed of many cultures.[54] *Tianxia* has also been celebrated by some scholars as cosmopolitan, non-coercive, and interest-sharing; such a reading, as some claim, informs the PRC's postsocialist foreign policy as promoting consensus and cooperation against the antagonist confrontations found in liberalism or Marxism.[55] It is also argued that the *Tianxia* philosophy aspires toward a universal idealism of peace that belongs to humanity in general and should not be treated as an ideology of a sealed civilization to feed the current feeling of civilization clash.[56]

Other scholars, however, point out how this conception of Tianxia has primarily been an imperialist ideology and a contemporary reimagination of cultural-political coercion. Under this reading, the narrative of Tianxia is constructed to convince the people of the legitimacy of China's past imperial acts and structure as well as its modern nationalist discourses. Critics argue that the state and statist scholars use deep historical and civilization content to justify the current Chinese state's domestic authority and global position.[57]

Overall, Tianxia is not a consistent concept, let alone a coherent philosophy. Loosely speaking, the term is first and foremost a geographical region. The space then signifies a set of traditional Chinese visions of world order as well as a body of cultural practices and mechanisms of domination that involve both coercive and consensual strategies. Historically, Tianxia was sometimes used to refer to the territory within China proper and sometimes the world outside. Thus, it is both the territorial object to be conquered and the original world order that is always already here and will remain here forever. The way Tianxia was articulated in China could be compared with the political practices of many premodern political regimes: they might be nonterritorial—such as those political centers dominating the hinterlands with their non-permanent, ill-defined borders—or they were empires that directly or indirectly controlled a large territory. These premodern geopolitical imaginations are often based not on actual territory but on the imagined conception of cosmology: blending the physical territory of different regions with narratives in official texts, as well as mythological stories of religious figures, corresponding to different terrains of knowledge.[58]

As the concept continued to be used in China, Tianxia increasingly became a geopolitical imagination related to sovereign power, referring to a territorial boundary and a political unity waiting to be, or that already was, unified. Tianxia also implies a world of propriety, in which peace is attained through everyone playing their proper roles. Thus, Tianxia embodies the traditional Chinese sovereign power in the sense that it links political power and moral propriety; moreover, it exists *ex nihilo*, and is permanent. While it is clear that Tianxia is a sovereign concept representing Chinese imperialistic logic being both its object and its moral principle, there are debates about whether it is hegemonic or liberating. Either way, the term is heavily ideological. Contemporary critics must be aware that their interpretations, as well as my own, also continue to contribute to the ideological construction.

In order to better understand this usage of the term *Tianxia*—as a spatial concept referring to both sovereign territory and cosmic order as well as an imperial order constructed based on both soft and hard power—we again may want to go back to history to investigate how the concept was formed. Like *Tianming*, the term *Tianxia* was purportedly first used in the Western Zhou dynasty, and it could also be found in the classics compiled during the "Spring and Autumn" and "Warring States" period, such as *Yijing* 易經 (*The Book of Change*), *Zuo Tradition*, *Book of Rites*, and the *Mencius*.[59] One prominent use of the term is related to feudalism. During the Western Zhou period, the emperor conferred rank, land, and slaves on his trusted relatives and meritorious officers in exchange for their allegiance, forming China's first established feudal system.[60] Under this form of feudalism, *Tianxia* was the Western Zhou kingdom deliberately divided in order to maintain unity. But *Tianxia* was also used to refer to the world outside the feudal order.[61] Soon, the feudal lords became powerful and challenged Zhou itself. This was how China entered the "Spring and Autumn" and "Warring States" period.

The *Tianxia* discussions of this period were characterized by political and philosophical openness. We can find some versions of freedom of expression, juridical rights, and economic rights enjoyed by the people allowed in *Tianxia*.[62] But the people were also exhausted by the constant warfare, and they desired political stability. Some scholars argue that the *Tianxia* that appeared in the texts of the time was associated with a longing for peace and order, as well as a yearning for the Kingly Way of *wangdao*.[63] But other scholars also point out that the term did not show a clear set of structured meanings at that time; instead, in most cases it loosely denoted a vast territory in which people lived harmoniously in archaic times.[64]

Entering the subsequent Qin dynasty, the term *Tianxia* was often used with a more concrete meaning: that of the sovereign territory. For example, in an important official document that announced the unification of the empire, it was written: "In the twenty-sixth year, the emperor conquered all the princes under Heaven [*Tianxia*], and the people had great peace. He established the title of 'Emperor' [*Huangdi*] for himself."[65] Here, *Tianxia* was used to refer to the combination of the original Qin territory and the other kingdoms that had recently been conquered. The following line in this edict demands that standardization must follow: "Measurements [of different places] are standardized. If they are not unified, or if there are doubts, they should be unified."[66] In this new political environment, *Tianxia* is meant to be unified, and this unification is represented by the standardization of the many practices found across the new imperial territory. Only through such standardization and consolidation can a proper order of the world be restored.[67] The term *Tianxia* was then widely used to describe and celebrate the Emperor's military prowess, turning the world from division to unification, restoring the ideal way of *Tianxia*.[68]

Entering the Han dynasty, state scholars such as Dong Zhongshu tried to standardize the meaning of *Tianxia*. Dong described *Tianxia* as the world order structured with a concentric circle of three layers of different types of people. He wrote: "The nation [*guo* 國] is on the inside and the various feudal kingdoms are on the outside; the feudal kingdoms are on the inside while the barbarians are on the outside."[69] He also argued that the people of *Tianxia* loved the Emperor out of their own devotion and passions in the same way that they loved their parents, so that their submission was a manifestation of the natural order.[70] This hierarchical structure described the totality of the imperial sovereignty. Such unity and order were thereafter to become foundational to Chinese sovereignty.

The meanings of the term became more stable after Han. As a world system, *Tianxia* positions China, or *hua* 華, at the center; meanwhile, other nations, or *yi* 夷, paid their respects, culturally and economically, to the Chinese court and in return were blessed with political autonomy. The term also implies natural order or propriety, endorsing the legitimacy of the current imperial structure. In other words, while *Tianxia* was the object over which the sovereign ruled, *Tianxia* also informed *how* the Emperor should rule. Those who submit themselves to *Tianxia* are good emperors, while those who consider themselves to be masters of *Tianxia* are bad emperors. To realize *Tianxia*, in its best shape, is the ultimate task of all sovereigns.

Overall, the coercive dimensions of imperialistic control and the idealistic wishes of peaceful, but hierarchical, coexistence of different people are both parts of this concept. Geopolitically, *Tianxia* clearly differs from the structure of the modern nation-state, which defines clear state borders and citizenry. But it would be too much of a stretch to praise it as a form of cosmopolitanism. In fact, it is not appropriate to translate *Tianixa* into cosmopolitanism, as some did, because the Greek concept is based on the local cohabitation of different people living in the polis, while *Tianxia* comprises a much larger geographical area without the implication of cohabitation experiences. *Tianxia* is an imagination of a relaxed cultural-political-territorial construct composed of trans-ethnic and trans-regional alliances. But there is also the Han Confucian culture as an attending force at the center, pulling—sometimes through force, sometimes through culture—the loosely connected peripheral people together within a clear hierarchical structure.

Ideologically, *Tianxia* portrays, or imagines, harmony between the internal (the Han civilization) and the external (the adjacent nations), between humanity (the cultured) and nature (the uncivilized). It also embodies a cosmology of complex interconnections within a hierarchical order, founded on harmony. In reality, though, this *Tianxia* order had been fiercely maintained by military actions. In times of peace, the tributary system was relatively effective to maintain a certain amicable relation of the Chinese imperial court and adjacent kingdoms. But *Tianxia* is also the product of bloody warfare. Overall, while there were many cultural and economic exchanges within the Chinese empires, such order was heavily maintained by military muscle and coercive controls.

The political structures of the ruling power varied substantially from the Han dynasty to the Qing dynasty, which ended in 1911. Imperial China was not a stagnant entity, but its ideological and territorial landscape was always changing. Yet, overall, the loose *Tian* sovereign structure—connecting *Tianming*, *Tianzi*, and *Tianxia*—stayed resilient. Confucianism dictates that only those Emperors who exhibited humility to Heaven and a moral integrity to the people could bring *Tianxia* together. This was supplemented by Legalism, which argued that the people must be heavily controlled and that they must submit to the total power of the Emperor.

In fact, not only China but Japan and Korea also developed their own nation-based Confucian *Tianxia* systems—which, not surprisingly, feature each respective country as the center.[71] Sharing the same lexicon, it is also not surprising that certain commentators of the three East Asian nations support their own *Tianxia* systems as congenial while being critical of the *Tianxia* ideology of others as imperialism, founded on military strength and expansionism instead of respect for modern state sovereignty. For example, there are Japanese scholars today arguing that the "nine-dash-line" in the South China Sea is part of China's advancement based on its *Tianxia* worldview.[72] Critics in East Asia, who might defend their own diplomatic policies as cosmopolitan, are likely to be much more critical of their neighboring countries as aggressive, however much they share the same deep-rooted political imagination.

The Confucian Scholar-Officials

China's traditional political economy could be seen as composed of two systems: there was *zhengtong*, which, as mentioned in the introduction, refers to the political legitimacy of sovereign power approved by *Tian*. But parallel to actual political sovereignty, there was also sovereign philosophy (道統 *daotong*), which the scholar-officials, or the so-called literati class, possessed.[73] It is widely agreed that the term *daotong* was first coined by the Tang scholar Han Yu 韓愈 (768–824), who collected existing ideas and asserted that the authentic *dao* belongs to Confucianism, instead of Buddhism or Daoism, and it had been passed down through generations of Confucian masters.[74] Entering the Song dynasty, *daotong* began to be contrasted with *zhengtong*, and their separation and collaboration characterized the uniqueness of China's sovereign system. In fact, if it is the relationship between popular sovereignty and state sovereignty that sits at the core of modern political power, we can argue that it was the mutual support and empowerment between *daotong* and *zhengtong* that made up China's traditional sovereignty.

The Confucian literati were convinced that they possessed *daotong*, the sovereign philosophy, and they struggled to maintain some moral independence from the imperial court, particularly if it was untrustworthy. This, arguably, was the result of their intellectual forebears in the "Spring and Autumn" and "Warring States" periods, who traveled among nations to seek an audience with different kings. Confucius is the most typical representative of those who claimed to possess *daotong* philosophy but not the *zhengtong* ruling power: he was not a permanent part of the ruling power, but he advised different rulers—those willing to listen—how to rule. This also explains why he claimed that he could directly connect with *Tian* and understand *Tianming*. While the literati did not exercise sovereign power, it was nonetheless believed that they possessed its "truth." Therefore, the literati were able to advise the rulers how to rule, which also made them extremely powerful.

While the literati were convinced that they could shape good government, the sovereign power also relied heavily on scholars to sustain its sovereignty. The imperial examination system was generally effective, generating a relatively successful meritocratic system. The rulers were also convinced that the pious recital of the Confucian classics demanded by the examination on the students represented an act of faith in moral values and submission to imperial sovereignty. As the government was theoretically open to talented men through the imperial examination system, the people—particularly the powerful clans—were also convinced that they could gain political power by submitting their most intelligent young men for vigorous education. The sovereign and the public officials gradually developed a political symbiosis.

While the Confucian literati were crucial in holding up the imperial system, the relation between the monarchy and the scholar-officials fluctuated from dynasty to dynasty and from emperor to emperor. There was not a static way of governance supported by a fixed sovereign-literati coalition. The collaboration between the imperial court and the Confucian officials seemed to be most complementary and productive in the Song dynasty. But it was not the case for either Tang or Ming. Many Ming emperors, for example, were despotic; they valued Legalism and deplored the Confucian teachings that privileged the people.[75] In turn, a significant number of Confucian scholars were critical of their monarchy's autocracy and disapproved of the court's centralization of power. The Ming Confucian master Gu Yanwu 顧炎武 (1613–1682) contrasted the idea of Tianxia with guojia 國家 (nation).[76] Gu believed that too many people cared only about the state, which was much less important than Tianxia. If every Chinese person participated in the revival of Tianxia idealism, the nation would automatically become strong.[77] Huang Zongxi 黃宗羲 (1610–1695), a contemporary of Gu's, also offered a critique: in antiquity, the sage-kings had considered Tianxia as the host and the king to be simply the guest; today, the relation was reversed, which led to disasters everywhere.[78] Huang criticized the emperor as selfish, sacrificing the interests of the people for his own benefit.[79]

The literati also relied on cultural means, particularly literature, to criticize the sovereigns. Some of the greatest writers in premodern

China, from Tao Yuanming 陶淵明 (365–427) to Liu Zongyuan 柳宗元 (773–819) and Su Shi 蘇軾 (1037–1101), were trained as Confucian scholars but at some point failed in their official careers. They then utilized non-Confucian thinking, such as Daoism and Buddhism, to articulate a non-Confucian cultural-political order. Their works are characterized by humanistic insights, criticism of social inequality, and delight in nature, but deep down they could still be highly concerned about politics and tended to use non-Confucian means to express their Confucian sensibility. The literati's criticism of the political establishment in fact reinforced the belief of their possession of the *daotong* sovereign philosophy, which was considered by many of them to be higher than the *zhengtong* sovereign power. While the people did not speak, the Confucian scholar-officials spoke for them.

But we must acknowledge that other than the few exceptions mentioned above, generations of Confucian scholars tended to refrain from critical reflection on the legitimacy of the sovereign power because the literati class and the monarchy depended on each other for survival. It has been argued that since China was primarily an agricultural nation, the sovereign tended to let things take their own course instead of being ambitious in driving events such as conquering other nations.[80] This conservative sovereign power was supported by an equally conservative literati class, which encouraged the people to submit to the existing social hierarchy and not to question the sovereign power. This Confucian-Legalist system was hierarchical and authoritarian. Even so, it was supported by pervasive moral teaching and an elaborate bureaucracy so as to guarantee some kind of self-constraints and balance of power.

Overall, the Confucian political culture was devoted to bringing happiness to the people. To achieve this, the officials—so deeply immersed in Confucian philosophy—took responsibility in demanding, albeit often tepidly, the ruling regime to prioritize the same philosophy, while asking the people to submit to the power of the sovereign. They taught the people to respect the rigid social and political hierarchies; and they also reminded the Emperor, repeatedly, to love the people.[81] The Confucian-Legalist sovereign philosophy—which is built around respecting *Tian* on the part of the sovereign and around submission and moral liability on the part of the people—discourages the people from questioning the sovereign power, but it also teaches the rulers to exercise their power according to the people's needs. As mentioned, other than sending down natural disasters as a last resort to disown the sovereign, *Tian* does not speak. As such, the literati class became enormously important as Heaven's spokesperson: mediating the sovereign and the people, as well as sustaining the integrity and vigor of this political system.[82]

Such an operation, with intellectuals functioning as a crucial pivot, continued all the way into the late Qing reform. The Constitutional Reform Movement, for example, was pushed primarily by intellectuals such as Kang Youwei, who successfully convinced young Emperor Guangxu to incorporate the Western political structure into the Chinese order. The reform ultimately failed. Yet Kang wrote to his potential overseas donors that Guangxu's good fortune (escaping assassination and regaining his power after being imprisoned) proved that he was still blessed by *Tianming*.[83] What Kang did not mention was the pressure placed upon the Qing court, deriving from the wide civil appeal inside the country as well as overseas Chinese, not to dethrone Guangxu.[84] To carry on his political project, Kang also wanted to show that he still possessed the *daotong* sovereign philosophy, while his westernized political project was indeed endorsed by *Tianming*.

In response to Kang's letter, his major intellectual rival, Zhang Taiyan, criticized the Constitutionalist Reform Movement as a project motivated by Kang's own desire for wealth and glory. Zhang was most critical of Kang using regressive concepts such as *Tianming* to support Qing's sovereign power.

> To get rid of the chaos and to return to propriety, what matters is not the absence or presence of *Tianming*, but how difficult it is for humans to achieve the goal by their own efforts. Between revolution and constitutionalism, I think it is easier to conduct a successful revolution than trying a constitutional reform.[85]

In chapter 3 we will return to the idea of how revolution took over *Tianming* as the source of sovereign legitimacy in modern China. Here, let us be reminded of the urgency with which the revolutionaries regarded the task of debunking the power of *Tian*. Zhang wrote a series of essays to explain how *Tian* should be understood not as a divine being but as a physical existence with atoms, forces, and planets. Zhang is such an important intellectual figure in modern China partly because he called for a fundamental change to China's political thinking: dissociate sovereign power from *Tianming* and reassociate it to human's capacity and political realism. He also encouraged a new generation of intellectuals to free itself from the narrowminded *daotong* philosophy and to learn from different schools of thought to develop a more emancipatory politics suitable to the Chinese. Despite his deep respect for Chinese culture, Zhang argues that *Tian* should be completely abandoned for a modern concept of sovereignty to take root in China. Zhang's project remains sound even in the twenty-first century.

China's traditional sovereign theory provides a dynamic interpretation of the co-dependence between the ruling monarchy and the ruled subjects, justifying the enormous power of the former while at the same time demanding the sovereign to be responsible for the latter's happiness. It also exhorts the people to rise up against those rulers who were incapable of the tasks, although this history still abounds with tyrannical kings and submissive people. Without a religious institution to explain and distribute power, *Tian* is so commanding and yet could be interpreted so freely by the people. *Tian* becomes the dual embodiment of divinity and humanity, the transcendental and the mundane, such that *Tianzi* the ruler and *Tianxia* the ruled are, at least in theory, equal parts of the same system.

For thousands of years the ruling regimes in China adopted *Tian* as a divine force to legitimize their sovereignty, but it is important to note that it is blatantly a historical construction, put together particularly by the literati-officials for their own benefits. Confucius' deliberate announcement of his ability to understand *Tianming* was crucial to the success of this sovereign theory, allowing him and his class to monopolize the mediating role between the ruler and the ruled. Protecting the interests of different parties, this sovereign theory created one of the most lasting political structures in human history.

But this Chinese sovereign philosophy, in which the people are passive subjects content with the status quo or waiting for changes, would be defeated by the more aggressive European modern state sovereignty at the turn of the twentieth century. The dynastic political structure that emphasizes regular rejuvenation would give way to the Western nation-state system, which implies more stability with its fixture of territory and population, while is balanced by the supervision of the people through various electoral mechanisms. The current PRC sovereign logic can be seen as one incorporating parts of both the traditional Confucian system and the modern system first developed in Europe: the ruling regime is not democratically elected, but it provides the security stemmed from the nation-state system. It remains to be seen how this modern Chinese sovereignty might realize the eternal peace and prosperity it promises without the built-in processes of regeneration observed in both the traditional Chinese system—in terms of dynastic rotation—and the Western democratic system—in terms of regular elections.

Two

Fables of Unity

"Safeguarding national unity and territorial integrity is the sacred right of every sovereign country"—this might be the most frequently heard line in the PRC's diplomacy of recent years. The statement carries two implicit messages. Externally, some foreign parties are hostile to China's rise, and China must be strong to guard its sovereign rights and integrity. Internally, there are schemes within the country (often promoted by foreign hostile forces), such as the independence movements of Tibet, Xinjiang, Taiwan, and Hong Kong, which aspire to separate a certain region from China. The two types of of threat, which often collaborate, challenge the unity of the state and China's sovereignty. To safeguard national unity and territorial integrity, the state must persistently identify and suppress external and internal enemies. In such sovereign discourses, it is often confusing, but it is also of little importance which of the many seemingly colluding forces is the originating one. The primary thing is that the sovereign actively seeks out enemies in order to demonstrate the urgency of unity.

The traditional and modern sovereign logics in China share an obsession with unity, and this theme forms the focus of this chapter.[1] The sovereign desire for unity is clearly not unique to China but is inherent in the history of modern nation-state, established through struggles against imperial control and interstate wars. There is a core contradiction that defines sovereignty: to maintain the group's autonomy, we must sacrifice the members' autonomy. Unity is the linchpin of this structure, with the assumption, supported by some historical experiences, that only a unified people is strong enough to defend itself from others.

It is true that each modern nation-state is basically represented by one government, but this does not mean that sovereignty, in practice, is singular, indivisible, and unified. In the real world, there are always international and intranational bodies involved in making decisions along with the states, and the states are also constantly influencing each other to make decisions. In most polities, there are different levels of control and compromise operating simultaneously, and the ideas of absolute autonomy and indivisibility, although long regarded as necessary attributes of sovereignty, do not match empirical observation. Scholars have demonstrated that governments tend to construct the unity of the state as a myth to hide the stratification of its process and practices.[2] Our social and political reality is always more unruly and inchoate than any singular power is capable of containing, not to mention the intrinsically pluralizing nature of culture.

Indivisibility is a pivotal concept in modern sovereignty, articulated repeatedly by some of the most important European political thinkers in modern times, from Bodin to Hobbes, to construct the identity of the state and to justify its authority?[3] As I delineated in the introduction, there is a specific history to this construction of state indivisibility in modern Europe, which witnessed the transference of sovereignty from the church to the monarchy and ultimately the people. The emphasis on the unification of the state also enabled the European states to direct their aggressive energies, which would otherwise have been spent on the incessant internal civic and religious wars, to external colonialism and imperialism.

While it was Carl Schmitt who most insightfully explored this history—I find his analysis convincing—his underlying politics deserve our scrutiny. Schmitt implies that it was the newly acquired autonomy and indivisibility of the modern sovereign state that qualified this European civilization as the most advanced historically and culturally, so that it has some license to conquer the world.[4] This praise is clearly problematic in terms of its justification for European external expansion.

But more problematically, Schmitt implicitly encourages modern societies to renounce internal political negotiations and demand absolute unity within the state.[5] Accentuating external threats and suppressing the natural existence of internal diversity become the inextricable core components of modern European sovereignty. Schmitt famously argues that "the political" consists in the construction of friends and foes as well as the struggles between them; the sovereign state arises as a means of organizing and channeling such political struggles.[6] This dichotomization of friends and foes is further developed in his analysis of the European *nomos*, in which he differentiates internal and external antagonisms, highlighting how the indivisible sovereignty of modern European states plays down the internal plurality immanent in society to justify their external aggressions.

Overall, modern sovereign unity refers to both the singularity of the will of the state and the unification of the state and society. Enemies never disappear; they are identified and constructed to justify the constant efforts of state unity. The sovereign power is always manipulating the dynamic between unity and difference, suppressing and highlighting those threats against the coherence of sovereignty at the same time. Such discourses could not be held together without many coercive mechanisms and the creation of a climate of fear busily operating in tandem. Needless to say, they often fail.

In China, the consistent thread that ties the various ruling powers from the late nineteenth century to the early twenty-first century might be the common ardor for unity. There were many occasions where a more pluralized sovereignty could be introduced, but time and again such doors were closed. While unity is a myth for all sovereign orders, the situations in modern China were particularly troublesome, because China was seldom really unified and autonomous. Space constraints dictate that I explore this complex history in a selective and non-exhaustive way. I focus on some major phenomena that showed disunity in this history, and I also explore how the sovereign power responded. The elements here include racial tension, regionalism, international hegemony, and simply the external world, which the various ruling regimes struggled to tame. I will also bring in relatively underdiscussed concepts in China's contexts, such as federalism and cultural sovereignty, to help us understand this history. However diversely these threats against unity were constructed within their historical contexts, they all demonstrate how sovereignty is not only challenged by but also constructs enemies to legitimize its demand for unity.

Qing's Racial Dynamics

One of the most important factors that construct the unity of modern nation-state is race. While most modern nations are multiracial, the racial groups must be properly incorporated into the singular sovereignty. In China, like in many other places, the avoidance of racial discord is a perennial governance problem for ruling regimes. To understand the dynamics between racial tensions and sovereign unity in modern China, we need to go back to the Qing dynasty.

After being practiced for two millennia, the Confucian-Legalist sovereign order discussed in the previous chapter gradually crumbled during the Qing dynasty (1636–1912). Its end was a prolonged process rather than an abrupt collapse. There are many ways to understand this process. Here I choose to focus on race, a concept signifying not only the Western concept imported during the nineteenth century but also the cultural and ancestral structure that differentiated the ruling class from the subordinate groups central to Qing's governance. Qing's imperial sovereignty was based largely on a careful divide-and-rule governance along racial lines. If in the nineteenth century the Chinese gradually came to believe that in order to survive as one people they needed to acquire modern state sovereignty, it is not a surprise that racial difference quickly became a site of contestation. Race played a major role in Qing's disintegration.

Let us first focus on the traditional conceptualization of racial differences in Qing China. The Manchu ruling class, via the Han officials, enthusiastically adopted the Confucian sovereign philosophy to rule over many cultural-ethnic groups. The ideas of *Tian* proved particularly useful to the vast Qing empire. Responding to a failed anti-Qing rebellion in 1730, Emperor Yongzheng asserted that while the Manchu had once been the barbarians, they had successfully acquired the Han culture and were now the civilized ones. Relying on the Confucian orthodoxy of *Tianming*, he argued that since the Manchu defeated the Ming dynasty, it was clear that *Tian* designated them to rule *Tianxia*, legitimizing its rule over diverse groups of people.[7] *Tianxia* now signified the

Qing territory, doubling the size of Ming's, where many ethnic groups were united under a proper political and cultural order, with the Qing monarch at the center supported by a largely Han bureaucracy.

The "Gongyang School" was central to this project. This comprised scholars devoted to the *Gongyang Commentary on the Spring and Autumn Annals* 春秋公羊傳 compiled during the "Spring and Autumn" and "Warring States" periods, in which the idea of "grand unity/origin" (*dayitong* 大一統) was emphasized.[8] In the Han dynasty, the *Gongyang Commentary* was considered one of the canonical Confucian texts, and Confucian statesmen such as Dong Zhongshu were particularly attracted to the idea of "grand unity" to support the legitimacy of the Han empire. But the text was gradually consigned to oblivion. Then, more than one and a half millennia later, in the Qing era, the *Gongyang Commentary* experienced a vigorous revival, testifying to a new shift in statecraft from cultivating the people's personal morals, which had been central to the dominant Confucian teaching developed since the Song dynasty, to an emphasis on imperial unification. These Gongyang scholars tried to follow the government of the Han dynasty that played down racial differences and emphasized the smooth operation of a grand unified empire while also strictly following the teaching of the Confucian classics. Moreover, the Gongyang tradition established a respect for the law by paying special attention to the presence of terminologies and rhetoric for making judgment in the Confucian classics. As such, the Gongyang scholars helped the Qing dynasty to establish a legal consciousness that would form the basis for modern state sovereignty.[9]

It is clear that the modern concept of race defined biologically was absence in imperial China, but the differentiation of ethnic groups was central to Chinese history, particularly in the Qing dynasty, which was ruled by a non-Han ethnic minority group. The Manchu claimed their superiority as the ruling class through their ethnic integrity, legitimized around ritual practices as well as premised on identity based on bloodline.[10] If the race invented in the West focuses on bodily features as well as affective and intelligence excellence/deficiency, the Manchu emphasizes rituals and family. After establishing the vast Qing empire, the Manchu strategically reinterpreted their past ideologically to justify their current conquest and rulership, so that political legitimacy no longer relied on the approval of political peers, as it had before entering China, but on biological connections.[11] The heredity-based eight-banner system in which all Manchu households had been placed for administrative and military purposes was also instrumental in maintaining the authenticity of the Manchu bloodline. It also shaped an exclusive identity based on myth, lineage, geography, and culture, which were presented as belonging only to the ruling Manchu people.[12] Borrowing the Confucian concept of *Tianming*, the Manchu origin myth justifies the political supremacy for the Manchu empire as the chosen one. Together the Manchu was careful to shape an exclusive identity that belonged only to them, whose ascendency over the ruled was legitimized by a loose sense of cultural-biological superiority.[13]

The complex imperial order of the Qing was hierarchical on two different fronts. Politically, the Manchus were clearly at the center, with the Han and other minorities occupying different positions subservient to the Manchus. Culturally, Confucianism was dominant, with other non-Han, non-Manchu cultures placed on the margins. The Manchurian monarchy practiced Confucianism in public, while its own culture, which was considered private, belonged only to the ruling elite. Being a multinational empire, the unity of the Qing imperial structure was established through some recognition of the diversity of the people with their own cultures and histories, facilitated by complex discursive operations and negotiations around systems of differences.[14] This political unity was achieved through a decree of hierarchy, mandated loyalty, constant negotiations, and the centrality of the Emperor as the Son of Heaven. While diversity was recognized and celebrated in this structure, the central and undivided power of the Emperor was not negotiable, which signified the unity of the empire.

The Confucian Han literati was central in holding this complex system together. They were used by the Qing court to govern the vast empire, and they were also well aware of the racial inequality existing between the rulers and the subjects. But instead of criticizing the disparity, they utilized the Confucian concepts in ways that did not challenge the Qing's legitimacy, while promoting more equality between the Manchus and the Han. In fact, the rise of the Gongyang School could be seen as the deliberate strategy of the Han literati to privilege cultural authority over racial difference for its own survival.[15]

While the multiracial empire found ways to hold the groups together for three centuries, racial differences came to haunt and challenge the Qing through a completely different historical force, that being Western imperialism. Beginning in the mid nineteenth century, Qing experienced repeated military setbacks in the two Opium Wars (1841–1842, 1857–1860), the Sino-French War (1884–1885), the first Sino-Japanese War (1894–1895), and the War with Eight Nation Alliance (1900). These military losses, at the hands of the various European countries, the United States, Japan, and Russia, forced the Qing court to grant favorable tariffs, trade concessions, and territory to the victorious imperial powers.[16]

With India as the precedent, what now loomed large on the horizon in China was the complete colonization of the Chinese people by the West. The task of protecting the culture from extinction instilled a strong sense of urgency in the Chinese scholar-officials for fundamental social reform. But to these elites with vested interests, the reform could not go too far in challenging the Qing rule. To achieve the proper balance, the literati separated racial/cultural essence from technological and administrative knowledge such that the former would not be corrupted by the latter. This dichotomization between inferior but coercive Western knowledge and the superior Chinese, including both the Han and the Manchu, cultural and political essence was most vividly captured in the line of Wei Yuan 魏源 (1794–1857): "learning from the strength of the barbarians in order to subdue the barbarians" (shi yi zhi chang ji yi zhi yi 師夷之長技以制夷).[17] The Chinese were willing to change their country only on a "superficial" level related to technical knowledge; however, the foundational political structure and cultural values that represented the racial superiority of the Chinese must remain untouched. Most importantly, Qing sovereignty must be protected.

It was also around this time that Western notions of race were imported. While ethnic taxonomies had been important to the governance of the great Qing empire since the seventeenth century, the Western idea of race was a different category, one allegedly supported by science emphasizing essential bodily and mental differences. The idea of the people of East Asia as belonging to a single "yellow race" was invented by European scientists in the eighteenth century and imported to China later.[18] The color yellow was associated with many racist stereotypes in the original Western formulation, but the Chinese accepted it as a positive self-identity, partly because yellow was an honorable color in China. The Chinese intellectuals were happy to call the Chinese race yellow also because of their general admiration of Western scholarship as scientific.[19]

With the concept of racial difference increasingly circulating in China as a new episteme, a new kind of racism was also cultivated, one that was no longer based on levels of civilization but rather the essential superiority or inferiority innate to a racial group. Not surprisingly, many Chinese intellectuals also comfortably adopted the discriminatory attitudes toward people of darker color. Yan Fu, for example, described the African descendants as born slaves.[20] The idea of racial war—that is, that the yellow, the white, the brown, and the black were bound to compete with each other for survival under the theory of social Darwinism—also gained traction.[21]

The Japanese, despite its war with the Qing, were generally not considered a race different from the Chinese. Instead, major thinkers of the time, such as Kang Youwei and Sun Yat-sen, saw East Asian countries as branches of the same race. They were convinced that Japan's success story of self-strengthening provided a model for China, and it also showed that the yellow race could stand on par with the white race. In fact, the pan-Asianism popular among many Asian scholars at that time was explicitly based on the notion of a common race and a shared cultural heritage of East Asian countries.[22]

This new conceptualization of race initiated and fueled different racial discourses, which were in turn used to support different political positions and to interpret different phenomena. Racial discourses were ideologically attractive partly because race was considered nonideological; it was "scientific," and it was also very visible. Race was particularly important in the formation of a new sovereign consciousness. Some intellectuals directly associated the idea of sovereignty with racial strength, arguing that those countries with strong sovereignty had a strong people.[23] But this Han-based Chinese race did not come into existence on its own; it was defined against the enemy races: the European and the Manchu.

First, the imported idea of race was appropriated by the Chinese as a means to respond to Western imperialism and their love-hate attitude to the white people. Social Darwinism was originally developed in Europe as an ideology for nationalism and imperialism to account for European colonialism as the natural course of history.[24] In contrast, the late Qing Han intellectuals adopted the idea to justify their defense against Western imperialism. The admiration of Western culture and technology was clearly developing, but a fundamental condescension was also resulted.

Racist discourses were employed to support the Boxer Rebellion of 1900, when many Westerners living in China—including missionaries—were attacked. There were popular views considering the Western body as hideous and weird, representing an inferior or barbarian race that justified the disdain that the Chinese showed it.[25] Some Chinese critics attributed the Boxer Rebellion as righteous from the opposite direction, describing it a result of the justified anger of the Chinese toward the racial contempt the Westerners shown toward the Chinese residents.[26] In major cities, there was increasing racial stigmatization found among the people, whereas more and more foreigners were seen on the streets who looked and acted strikingly different. The apparent distinctions of these people posed a fundamental challenge to the Chinese people, whose long civilization and worldview had not included these foreign cultures.

Race was also utilized in the rhetoric of international trade at that time. The modern nation-states of Western Europe emerged primarily as the outcome of war and in preparation for war. These were dominated by the process of territory consolidation and the state's subsequent monopolization of violence. But later generations of states, such as those in Latin America, came into being as a result of international trade promoted by imperialism. Local elites urged constructing a suitable market and proper business environment for local and foreign investors in the new capitalist order.[27] With the international power hierarchy already in place, in which Great Britain and other European states dominated international trade, local business and political elites in latecomer states could only play by their rules, hoping to benefit the most from international trade.

Similar to many other non-European countries, China in the late nineteenth century also underwent a similar need to create a modern market and entrepreneurial environment suitable for local businesspeople to engage in international trade.[28] Many Latin American and African countries were more open to—or less able to resist—transforming both their economic and their political systems to adapt to the new world system. But we do not see a comparable effort in China to open up its national market to integrate into the international economy. Consider how late Qing businessmen repackaged their international trade as efforts of national "self-strengthening," transforming economic strategies into a form of racial competition with the West. Avoiding any fundamental transformation of the political system, social and political elites articulated a racial dichotomization between the barbarian West, which possessed utilitarian knowledge, and civilized China, which symbolized the highest cultural achievement. At a time when many Chinese believed that their country had to be thoroughly westernized, racial discourse was adopted to facilitate China's embrace of the world while preventing itself from transforming so fundamentally as to lose its cultural integrity.

Second, race was deployed in many anti-Manchu discourses. The gradual decline of the Qing's imperial power in the late nineteenth century and the emphasis on racial conflicts between China and the West encouraged repressed Han-Manchu conflicts to surface.[29] While the Japanese and the Chinese were considered to be members of the same race, the Manchu were not. Many revolutionaries, at least before Qing was toppled, were faithful to the one-nation-one-state project, and the idea of race helped them to conceptualize a Han nation-state to expel the Manchu people. Those in the Chinese Revolutionary Alliance (*Tongmenghui* 同盟會) established in Japan in 1905 were particularly eager to advance a racial-ethnic nationalism to expel the Manchus, driven by an exclusive identity politics against both the Manchu and Western races.[30] Many considered the Han nation and the Han people to be the defining unit of integrity and solidarity for a genuine modern Chinese sovereignty. This racialization discourse of Han-Manchu antagonism has improbably persisted to the present day. As Kevin Carrico demonstrates, today's Han Clothing Movement was inherently driven by a conspiracy theory against the Manchu as a barbarian and genocidal force against Han.[31]

The imported concept of race, which is always used ideologically, helped some intellectuals to resist the Qing empire and others to do the exact opposite. Constitutionalists like Liang Qichao advanced a Greater Nationalism that incorporated the different racial/ethnic groups of the Qing empire to unite and fight the Western imperialist invaders as racial enemies. Liang was eager to reform the ancient empire to a young constitutional state, but he did not use the nation-state model and instead conceptualized modern China to be a multi-racial country while facing the aggressions of other races. We know that Sun Yat-sen would soon take the same position, shifting from biological nationalism to civil nationalism as the ideology to drive the revolution, as he acknowledged the need to galvanize the identification of all ethnic groups for the new state. Sun then advanced the cosmopolitan idea of "The Five Races Under One Union" and asserted that the five main ethnic groups—the Han, the Manchus, the Mongols, the Hui/Uyghur, and the Tibetans—were brothers and shared the same Chinese blood.[32] Because of its implication of collective identity, race became a flexible and convenient discursive category to present China's unity, enabling them to include some and to exclude others as the situations require.

But race is also fundamentally different from culture, another indicator of collective identity. The Western discourses of race are biological in nature, promoting racism by describing and discriminating bodies as innately abled or disabled.[33] While these ideas have had an impact on modern China, culture as a nonbiological concept is arguably more important in China in describing collective identity. During the late Qing period, race and culture were both used. While racism was a strong force in the new revolutionary discourses, there were also many revolutionaries insisting on culture over race to define Chinese identity so that they could defend their traditional culture as more inclusive than Western culture.[34]

But some thinkers did highlight race. An interesting example can be found in an essay written in 1907 by Zhang Taiyan, who tried to defend and explicate the name "Zhonghua minguo" (中華民國) Sun Yat-sen had suggested two years earlier for the new Republic he had promised to establish.[35] Zhang consulted elaborate historical evidence and affirmed that the term Zhonghua (中華) originally referred, very loosely, to a racial group and a geographical location, not a culture, therefore refuting the Constitutionalists who accepted the Manchurian rule from a culturalist perspective. Zhang argued that the Han and the Manchus had always been two distinct racial groups. Wary of racism, Zhang emphasized that the new Chinese Republic must not treat ethnic groups the same way that the United States treated those of African descent; the right to vote and the right to hold political office must be granted to the minorities—on condition that they learned the Chinese language. But he also used the phrase "zhuquan zaiwo" 主權在我 (sovereignty resides in me) to argue for the importance of sovereignty during the cultural assimilation process. However successfully the Manchu or other ethnic minorities have acquired the Chinese culture and language, he argued, the Han people must maintain their own sovereignty, unlike the situation of the Qing dynasty in which the Han lost their sovereignty.

We know that Zhang, as well as many of his revolutionary fellows, would change his attitude after the 1911 Revolution from Han essentialism to cultural assimilation, seemingly refuting his own racialist politics. But Zhang's idea of "sovereignty resides in me" might be the most crucial factor for us to understand this change. The concern was to make sure the Han owned their sovereignty, not the other ethnic groups. Zhang acutely reminds us that between race and sovereignty, it was the latter that dominated the political consciousness of the time, although the former was much more widely utilized.

The Demise of Political Pluralism in the Republican Era

In two royal memoranda written to Emperor Tongzhi, top Qing minister Li Hongzhang 李鴻章 (1823–1901) repeatedly asserted that the Qing dynasty was "caught in a historical period of extreme change, one unprecedented in the three millennia of Chinese history." Li argued that foreign nations had never previously intruded into China's territory so easily and on such a scale. But he also added that this unprecedented era could also be a monumental juncture of positive change, if the Emperor was willing to initiate radical reform and develop China into a powerful, unified modern nation.[36] Although the two memoranda were likely intended as a demand from a minister to his boss for a higher military budget, Li's observation in the 1870s has been widely quoted as a penetrating insight into this era. But probably most unexpected to Li is his description of "changes unprecedented in the three millennia of Chinese history" becomes a repeated claim throughout the Long Twentieth Century. The challenges China faced only intensified.

The first enormous historical change witnessed in modern China was introduced not by foreign forces but by internal rebels: the 1911 Xinhai Revolution ended the imperial structure that had endured in various forms for two millennia. This, in turn, brought about China's first modern nation-state, but no power was able to pull the vast territory together. Qing's political unity was dismantled by the revolutionaries, whose new sovereignty, however, did not bring about a new unity. At first, the people were overwhelmed with wonder; it seemed that what had been revealed was the hollowness of not only the Qing dynasty but the entire dynastic system, which had been supposed to last forever. Quickly, though, the initial joy and curiosity were replaced by frustration and disillusionment, as political instability intensified and the control of the country was divided by miliary cliques. China was caught up in a series of power struggles and internal wars, while foreign powers continued to interfere in China's politics.

While racial tensions had been the key factor challenging China's sovereign unity, as the Republican period began the entire political institution fell apart, and the Nationalist Party struggled to maintain some facade of sovereign unity. When the vast empire finally crumbled, the latent ethnic and regional tensions inherent in the vast territory and population that found their origins in the imperial structure emerged and intensified. China had never been culturally homogeneous; instead, it was made up of regions with distinct histories and identities. Without the imperial framework organizing the linguistic and cultural differences, regionalism resurfaced. Yet the Republican state was too weak to channel and suppress discontent. Entering the early Republican period, the disparities between north and south, east and west sharpened. Decentralization within China could be productive for a new democracy to experiment itself, as China was indeed a huge multiethnic, multicultural country demanding ongoing dialogue and mutual respect among different groups. But political pluralism was not permitted to grow. A unified state was chosen over federalism, and local democracy was abandoned for the establishment of a strong sovereign state.

The story went back to the Wuchang Uprising on October 10, 1911, when many cities and provinces claimed independence. Amidst the chaos, the ROC was established in Nanjing, and it received the support of many of such temporary governments which joined this first modern republic in Asia. After his election as the first Provisional President, Sun Yat-sen quickly agreed to yield the presidency to Yuan Shikai, who was more capable of negotiating with the powers located in Northern China. Yuan maintained the country's capital in Beijing; this regime was known as the Beiyang or Beiping government. The Beiyang period was extremely unstable, characterized by rapidly changing leadership, constitution, and political structures. Sun led another revolution in 1913 in an attempt to unseat Yuan but failed. Instead, Yuan proclaimed himself as the Emperor of the new Empire of China in 1915, but he died before his coronation. Thus, the imperial system was derailed before it was officially restored.

With Yuan's death, the warlords strengthened power in their regional bases, with the Beiyang government continuing to operate vigorously to pull the fragmented country, in vain, together. These regional powers had been expanding since the late Qing, when the imperial court was too weak to manage the vast country. Now, with the fall of the Qing empire, regional warlords—collaborating with and receiving support from Western imperial administrators, Japanese armies, Christian organizations, and the Comintern—initiated some of China's first modern nation-state-building projects within these regions.[37] Different parts of China developed unequally, further upending the myth of nation-state unity.

In spite of the fragmented nation, the Beiyang government proactively sought entrance into the international order as a sovereign country. For example, China joined the Allies in World War I, in part to qualify China as an independent sovereign nation. But even with such efforts, the Beiyang government still failed to assert its sovereign rights internationally. Consider that the 1919 Treaty of Versailles—which vowed to honor the Westphalian system and reestablish the international order by reinstating the independence of the sovereign states—ended up sacrificing China's sovereignty by giving Germany's former possessions in Shandong to Japan. Many Chinese people felt betrayed, and it also initiated the May Fourth Movement, which is discussed further in chapter 4.

Yet, however disunited the early Republican state was, the Beiyang period could be described as one of the most open societies in Chinese history due to the high degree of political experimentation of the moment. Different versions of partial democracy were introduced, while different levels of provincial and city councils were established, composed of representatives elected through different mechanisms. And it was at this time that the separation of powers was first introduced in China. Following the late Qing legal reform, the Beiyang and different warlord governments struggled to establish a modern juridical system with many political and financial challenges.[38] Five different constitutions were written from 1912 to 1925, each differed from its predecessor quite substantially, endorsing different political systems ranging from the congressional/cabinet system, which emphasized negotiation, to the presidential system, which showcased the leadership of a singular leader. Intensely debated were also the different ways to achieve checks and balances.[39] Overall, there were many good attempts to improve the constitution for the new republic along with politicians' selfish schemes, and the country also plunged into political confusion alongside the sincere desire to develop China into a truly democratic country.

Contemporary critics have characterized China in the 1910s and early 1920s as being thrown back to the "Five Dynasties" period (907–979), when China experienced terrible internal divisions and new regimes succeeded each other rapidly. It was a time when sovereign unity was absent, and it was also a rare moment of political plurality in modern China. Intellectuals and political activists conceptualized and welcomed different models for China's political system, and a strong central government was clearly not the only option.

Such political pluralism was most pertinently manifested in the federation movement. Called "Self-Ruled Provinces Alliance" (聯省自治, *liansheng zizhi*), the movement was promoted and accepted by so many leading intellectuals of different camps, including Liang Qichao, Zhang Taiyan, Zhang Dongsun 張東蓀 (1886–1973), Zhang Shizhao 章士釗 (1881–1973), and Hu Shi 胡適 (1891–1962) in the late 1910s and early 1920s.[40] Rarely had a political agenda received so much support from such a wide spectrum.[41] These thinkers believed that sovereign unity could be forged from of the collaboration of discrete self-ruling political communities.

While the opinions of the various intellectuals differed, they generally agreed that provinces should develop their self-governance capacity and then voluntarily form a united federation, in part to protect the administrative independence of local authorities from the arbitrariness of the central government. Local self-rule (地方自治 *difang zizhi*) had been widely celebrated in the late Qing era. This was due largely to the local governing practices on which the Qing had relied to rule over the vast empire for centuries, but also—crucially—to the increasing incompetence of the central government from late Qing to the Republican times. Furthermore, observing the political stability of the United States alongside the bankruptcy of China's imperial authoritarianism, many Chinese intellectuals began to advance the idea that the federation system would give the people more room to exercise democracy. Some intellectuals also tried to justify political decentralization with support from canonical texts. Revolutionary and poet Gao Xu 高旭 (1877–1925), for example, located evidence in *Zhouli* 周禮 (Rites of Zhou) to assert that China had a long history of decentralization and that it was the duty of the modern Chinese to respect this Chinese political spirit.[42]

The idea of federalism also received support from warlords of Hunan, Guangdong, Sichuan, and Zhejiang, among others; they had their own different political agendas in mind. Some local governments, for example, used "self-rule" as the excuse to demand new taxation, and the warlords also used the opportunity to centralize financial, administrative, and military power.[43] But there were also sincere wishes to advance democracy. Chen Jiongming 陳炯明 (1878–1933), for example, was committed to introducing a political infrastructure germane to democracy in Guangdong province he ruled by separating the civil and military administrations, and he was also very keen on developing Guangzhou into a modern city.[44] Hunan province went so far to establish its own constitution, universal suffrage, and levels of council supported by popular vote.[45] These arrangements were obviously short-lived. But it was a time when many warlords ran their territories like a state, devoting efforts to improving transportation infrastructure, promoting education, engaging in economic planning, and organizing social surveys.[46] These efforts reinforced the capacity of governance on a regional basis while also discrediting the notion that modernization must be carried by a unified nation.

But Sun Yat-sen never supported the "Self-Ruled Provinces Alliance," and as the 1920s began he shifted from keen advocacy of local democracy to a categorical rejection of federalism. He denounced his comrades' suggestion of staying in Guangdong and cultivating democracy there; instead, he insisted on fighting the Beiyang government with the aim of taking the entire country back.[47] A nation-state that was both unified and strong has been KMT's prime political agenda ever since. The CCP, on the other hand, also changed its attitude toward federalism from approval to disapproval, noticing how the power of certain warlords was expanding, which jeopardized the survival of the communist party.[48] Indeed, the wide support of a Chinese federation—instead of a single state—disappeared in China almost entirely after the KMT finally consolidated its nationwide control in 1927. The sovereign concept of China could have been very different if the competing political forces during the first years in the Republican period had been able to find ways to coexist and if the hotly debated federal system had been able to bear fruit.

Complicating the federation movement was minority governance. Right before the Xinhai Revolution, Sun changed his Han nationalism—the concept that all ethnic minorities in the region would soon be assimilated into the Han-centric civilization—to multinationalism, which was communicated in the slogan of "Harmony of the Five Ethnic Groups." The new government considered the Qing map as its own, inheriting the vast imperial territory (including the Xinjiang, Tibet, and Mongolia areas) as that of the new nation-state. But it was unclear what governance structure should be adopted to replace Qing's original imperialist multiethnic governance. Some ethnic groups actually regained some autonomy, while outside imperialist forces, particularly the Soviet Union, Great Britain, and Japan, eyed encroachment possibilities. The ROC was too weak to keep the vast Qing territory intact.

In the border area, the northern part of Mongolia gained independence immediately after the fall of the Qing, establishing the Mongolian People's Republic in 1921 with the support of the Soviet Union, while Inner Mongolia joined China—albeit with hesitation. In the West, the Simla Conference (1913–1914), conducted by representatives of Britain, Tibet, and China, failed to establish a national borderline for Tibet. The Dalai Lama's government may have remained in power throughout the first half of the twentieth century, but Tibet lacked clear international recognition of its territorial boundary and political status.[49] Since then, various Chinese governments have claimed Tibet under their sovereignty, while Tibet has constantly demanded and exercised different degrees of self-rule. Analogously, the Xinjiang area was also considered a part of China's sovereignty and has been internationally recognized as such since 1912. Yet twice parts of the region claimed short-lived independence under the names of First East Turkestan Republic (1933–1934) and Second East Turkestan Republic (1944–1949), a legacy that lasts to this day.[50] During the Republican period, despite the claims of Chinese sovereignty, Xinjiang remained under the sway of Soviet power and the rule of different Han warlords as well as the region's many ethnic groups. Hong Kong and Macau continued to be colonies of the United Kingdom and Portugal, although the treaties had been signed by the already disintegrated Qing dynasty.

Until his death, Sun emphasized unity over diversity, fought the warlords, and promoted the "evolution" of ethnic groups to become an assimilated Chinese civilization.[51] The KMT finally unified the nation in 1927, with the capital set in Nanjing, and this sovereign regime is generally known as the Nanjing regime, differentiated from the earlier Beiyang

regime. Internationally, the newly unified Republic's diplomats negotiated with Western powers to end extraterritoriality by attempting—
mostly in vain—to terminate all of the so-called unequal treaties.[52]
Domestically, the KMT also struggled to claim authority over the areas
complicated by extraterritorial arrangements.[53] At the same time, the
KMT launched a series of actions, including the so-called April 12 massacre in Shanghai, to purge its communist members, ending the United
Front between the two parties. While the 1927 Nationalist Revolution
united the country under the rule of the KMT, it also initiated a civil war
with the CCP that would last for almost two decades.[54]

Perhaps the most symbolic failure of KMT's unified sovereignty was
Japan establishing Manchukuo, a de facto Japanese colony, within Chinese territory in 1931, comprising three provinces in the northeast.
Manchuria has been a strategic location in East Asia, a region of interest
to China, Japan, and Korea, each of which busily churned out scholarship to prove their historical sovereignty of the region.[55] When Japan
finally succeeded in usurping the land from China, the KMT government
refused to engage in military action to expel this occupation; instead, it
sought the adjudication of international regimes to reject the formation
of the puppet state. Responding to China's outcry, the League of Nations
requested that Japan retreat to resolve the regional tensions. Japan responded by withdrawing from the League of Nations, going on to form
the new Asiatic League of Nations, which it spearheaded. Manchukuo,
under the sway of Japan, established its own government and legal
structure, claiming independent sovereignty in 1932.[56] The international
community did not show strong opposition, and this sent an implicit
message to Japan that its tactics had been effective, granting the newly
acquired territory structures of modern government with the effective
apparatus of law and planning. Moreover, Manchukuo also absorbed the
traditional Confucian order as well as mystical "Asianist" conceptions of
the human spirit and solidarity into its governance.[57]

Of course, the sovereign claims of Manchukuo were highly decep-
tive, and this so-called sovereign state was only a puppet government of
imperialist Japan. But many local residents and intellectuals supported
the independence of the region under its own distinguished cultural
heritage and identity. China claimed the three provinces as its own,
while Manchukuo requested that the world respect its sovereignty—
even though Japan was the real sovereign power controlling the entire

scheme. Overall, this incident has been interpreted in terms of national shame by the current CCP, but it also showed how China was never a unified one during the Republican period. History has shut down certain doors that could have led to new configurations of a modern Chinese state.

It should also be noted that neither the Beiyang government nor the Nanjing government was successful in penetrating rural China. Instead, the rural communal leaders were able to maintain their power and authority over their communities, and they did so by combining the symbolic resources of lineages with other economic, administrative, and interpersonal relations in the cultural nexus.[58] This social reality of enduring local power also proved how relevant the federation proposal was. While the new centralized government established in 1927 attempted to infiltrate their control into the vast rural area, many of its actions complicated the original power structure and exacerbated rivalry among the local leaders, creating new tensions in the villages. The KMT regime struggled to practice administrative and fiscal centralization, and it also exercised the rationalization and standardization required by modern government in addition to providing modern education and promoting industrial development. But these policies, which tended to be city-focused, failed to integrate well with the existing rural structure, which in turn hampered the central state capacity in institution building.[59]

All in all, the KMT's political will to build strong modern state sovereignty did not translate into an effective administrative capacity. The protracted war with Japan further dwindled the party's state-building ambition. After 1949, the CCP would inherit this political assignment, and it outperformed the KMT in centralizing power. Finally, a unified modern China came into being.

Sino-Soviet Relations and Ethnic Policies in Socialist China

Although it inherited a dilapidated government from the ROC, the PRC successfully pulled the nation together. In this, the brand-new socialist state realized the long-standing aspiration (since at least the nineteenth century) for a strong and unified modern sovereign state. But now the new regime had to face a completely different international environment in which an external superpower, the Soviet Union, influenced its internal governance on many levels. The ROC struggled to hold the internal parts together, and then the unified PRC shifted its attention to come to terms with this external Big Brother, which would soon be denounced to maintain the PRC sovereign integrity. In the previous section I discussed sovereign unity from a domestic perspective by focusing on the antagonistic or obstinate factors within the country; here I investigate how Chinese sovereignty dealt with those external forces that threatened its unity.

Following the instruction of the Soviet Union, the young PRC gave much attention to state planning and the role of formal laws and regulations in nation-building, trying to develop a regularized system with professional cadres.[60] The new regime also relied on local party members to reorganize the state structure in the entire country. The student arguably outperformed the teacher, particularly in the rural areas, in galvanizing the people through many forms of mass mobilization campaigns as well as policies blending coercive actions and normative appeals.[61] The Soviet method of five-year plans proved to be useful for the young socialist state to consolidate different strengths of the bureaucracy and society for economic development. Successfully building a new state following Soviet methods, the PRC also secured a prominent seat in the Soviet world order. But this, in turn, offered a new challenge to the young state: how could the PRC consolidate its hard-fought sovereign unity within the new socialist international order in which the Soviet Union was the commander?

Such questions of state unity and international collaboration, implying autonomy and dependence, in the emerging Soviet world order were poignant. In fact, even in the first years after the 1917 revolution, sovereignty was already a central political problem in the newly formed Soviet Union. Similar to Republican China, the Soviet Union inherited the vast territory from the Russian empire, which was itself composed of many ethnic groups. To differentiate itself from the coercive tsarist empire, the new socialist government classified non-Russians into "nationals" entitled to their own territory and culture. Lenin also supported the right of nations to self-determination, meant to show the superiority of the Soviet ideology to both Western colonialism and the previous Russian imperialism.[62]

In addition to its internal order, the Soviet Union also needed to legitimize its leadership position in the international Socialist order it spearheaded, an order that was supposedly formed by the voluntary participation of socialist parties all over the world. For its own survival, the new Soviet state considered the promotion of socialist revolutions around the world one of its prime duties, but it also stressed the importance of cooperation and mutual respect with international revolutionaries. The international revolutionary coalition was meant to be egalitarian instead of coercive.

However, the hypocrisy of equity became particularly obvious after World War II, when the Soviet Union assisted the establishment of communist regimes in Eastern Europe. Despite increasing criticism—particularly from the people of the subsidiary countries—Moscow did not alleviate its heavy-handed intervention in its "brotherly" countries. Instead, the Soviet Union advocated the idea of "limited sovereignty" to describe the fraternal diplomatic relations with other socialist countries in the Soviet Bloc, allowing the Soviet Union to intervene in countries where socialist rule was supposedly under threat.[63] The Soviet Union challenged the modern state sovereignty principles by allowing itself to infringe on the domestic policies of other communist countries. Correspondingly, the American interventions in Europe and East Asia after World War II also went well beyond what modern sovereignty principles would have tolerated. In contrast to the general belief that the autonomous and indivisible state became universal after the war, the two major international alliances substantially undermined the sovereign principles.

To provide balance to the hegemonic dimension of state sovereignty, international law and supranational institutions were produced by the consent of states, assuming that the identity, autonomy, and equality of each polity would still be maintained.[64] However, the international alliances developed during the Cold War period clearly privileged the American and Soviet leadership, which corroded the autonomy of individual states. Caught between these two major international networks, the PRC began as a stern member of the Moscow-based socialist order. But after the death of Stalin, along with Mao's increasing distrust of Khrushchev, efforts were made in China to distance itself from the Soviet Union. In his 1956 "On the Ten Major Relationships" speech, Mao critiqued the notion of the PRC modeling its state building completely on—and for—the Soviet Union.[65] By 1960, all the Soviet experts were ordered to leave the country. Since then, the PRC state has focused on developing China's own methods of nation-building. It also increasingly projected an image of hypocrisy of the Soviet Union, persuading those inside and outside China how the Soviet Union acted for its own benefit.[66]

Now, war efforts were directed as much against the Soviet Union as against the United States. In the Ninth People's Congress of the PRC in 1969, the Soviet Union was finally denounced as conducting "socialist imperialism," parallel to the "capitalist imperialism" of the United States. On the verge of war with the Soviet Union, the PRC advanced most fiercely its sovereignty against the Soviet Union's hegemony. As an official diplomatic statement announced, "What exactly does the theory of 'limited sovereignty' mean? It means that the sovereignty exercised by the Soviet revisionist social-imperialists is 'unlimited.'"[67]

On the face of it, China's sovereignty claim was meant to challenge the two great powers on the world stage. But concurrently, its claim was also part of an effort to construct an international alliance of developing countries. It was not until 1974 that the "Three Worlds" framework—which placed China as the leader of the developing world—was first officially announced in the United Nations. Yet two decades earlier, at the 1955 Bandung Conference, similar diplomacy and ideologies were already being developed. It was at this conference that China first tried to shift its diplomatic emphasis to the other developing countries, so as to counter both the United States and the Soviet Union. It was here that the PRC raised the official discourse of "South-South Cooperation," which promoted and promised solidarity among the global oppressed, initiating its own Third World alliance.

With the new Third World alliance forged, the PRC offered a critique befitting its vision of itself as the champion of the developing world: all people in the entire Asia, Africa, and Latin American regions were against US imperialism; meanwhile, it also accused the Soviet Union, following its imperialist ambitions, of trying to turn other socialist countries into suppliers of raw material and markets for goods.[68] Against the imperialism of both the United States and the Soviet Union, China's Third World project was allegedly supported by the doctrine of state sovereignty, in which each country and people could make their own decisions and decide their future. In a meeting with the Prime Minister of the newly independent Laos in 1958, Mao made it clear that while the PRC would do everything it could to support the political struggles of different peoples, it would not intervene in their internal politics, nor would it promote Socialism and Maoism in these countries. It was up to the individual countries to decide their own policies.[69] Until now, this has still been a key diplomatic policy—indeed, we could say that the PRC has refrained from developing too intimate a strategic partnership with any country.

But domestically, governance of the PRC minorities was more intrusive and controversial, precisely because the ethnic groups were considered to fall within China's sovereignty. In an effort to emulate the Soviet Union as well as to differentiate itself from KMT's Han-centered assimilation ideology, the besieged CCP in the early 1930s formulated its ethnic policy and advanced the right of nations to self-determination to secure support from the ethnic groups.[70] But the idea of self-determination (zijue 自決) was gradually replaced by that of self-government (zizhi 自治),[71] suggesting that the groups were no longer given the right to claim independence. While the Soviet Union organized different ethnic groups into nations with their own cultures and languages, the PRC classified them as minority groups and offered them limited self-autonomy within the five Autonomous Regions.

The major question guiding the CCP's ethnic policies was a deeply ideological one: should the new government use class to classify all people, or should culture be used as the key identity marker? Classical Marxism proclaims that it is economic class, not nationality or cultural identity, that is the main structural force dividing people in capitalist society. The CCP emphasized class struggles throughout the Mao era, but from time to time the state also realized the enormous importance of cultural identity to the ethnic groups. The CCP seemed to oscillate between the two options, creating inconsistency and sometimes abuses of power. Particularly during the time when radical assimilation policies were upheld which damaged the integrity of the groups, insurrectionist movements came into being. Religious autonomy also created perennial disputes. The 1959 Tibetan uprising, for example, was initiated by the Tibetan people's support of Dalai Lama. Ethnic tensions could be worsened in cases where the concerned minority groups lived in places with territorial disputes and conflicts of interest with other countries. Xinjiang, for example, has been the site of contestations between the Chinese and the Soviet forces, as well as other regional groups. The ethnic issues were often caught between international tensions and national solidarity, exemplifying the internal contradictions of many sovereignty discourses.

Overall, Socialist China was a much more powerful sovereign state than its immediate predecessor, and it was also able to pull together a huge territory more or less according to the Qing map. But its sovereign unity was achieved at a high price. It was caught up in the polarizing Cold War structure in which state sovereignty was compromised, and the central government also time and again suppressed the cultural identities of ethnic groups instead of helping them flourish, causing deep wounds. China's sovereign structure could have been a radically different one if the Maoist ideology had been able to develop into some fruition, where international collaboration was not based on sovereign interests but common political values, where respect for racial differences reconciled with the socialist ideal of equality. Although the actual term "sovereignty" was seldom mentioned in the socialist period, its logic permeated and muddled China's politics in profound ways.

Cultural and Cyber Sovereignty in Postsocialist China

There are many social and political indicators that distinguish China's socialist period from the postsocialist period that followed. But I want to point out the dominance of the concept of sovereignty as a subtle mark differentiating the two eras. Compared to the socialist period, sovereignty has been much more emphasized in the last two decades, and it has also replaced key Maoist principles such as class struggle or proletarian dictatorship to become China's new governance doctrine. Along this rise of sovereigntism, the concept of "security" dominates all policy making, weaving together the dense sovereign discourses in China and reflecting how sovereign power is not secure on many fronts. Furthermore, the idea of state security, a term hardly heard during the socialist period, is now raised widely in policy circles not only in China but around the world, witnessing the global propensity for state competition and confrontation. But unique to the PRC's current political rhetoric is the way that security and unity are often used together, and the National Security Law implemented in 2015 clearly defines that the protection of national security means the protection of national *unity* (Article 2). A revision of the sovereign security discourse would also help us understand how national unity is conceptualized by this government.

While the term *sovereignty* was seldom used in the socialist period, since the 1990s a flurry of related concepts—such as economic sovereignty, cultural sovereignty, and cyber sovereignty—have entered official PRC discourses. In turn, these have initiated the development of new policies and laws. These resulted primarily from Deng's open-door policies, introducing, allegedly, many economic and political risks to which the PRC has responded by calling for comprehensive sovereign control. The dominant structure of antagonism shifted from the Cold War standoff during the socialist period to a love-hate relationship with the West in the postsocialist period. I will explore in detail the meanings of economic sovereignty in postsocialist China in chapter 6. Here let us explore how the discourses around cultural sovereignty and cyber sovereignty evolved in the last two decades.

Cultural sovereignty is a concept that first appeared in the 1990s. It signified a new approach to culture from the perspective of state sovereignty: culture is no longer treated as a propaganda tool to convey the state's ideology, as in the socialist period, but it is a demonstration of national strength, particularly in the form of national pride showing its superiority over other cultures. Obviously, it also resembled the culturalism found in traditional Chinese traditions, in which the Confucian culture was considered the most important factor pulling *Tianxia* together. But there is also a decidedly modern dimension to this new discourse, which denounced those foreign powers trying to use culture to impede China's state sovereignty. Culture is conceptualized in the international stage in the form of competition.

The notion of cultural sovereignty has often been used together with an opposite concept, cultural hegemony, which tends to refer to the popular culture and cultural influences of the United States, Japan, and more recently South Korea. As China gradually opened up its cultural market after the 1980s, many Chinese were uneasy about the number of young people consuming foreign cultural products, as well as the values associated with such imports. In response, the discourse of cultural sovereignty promotes the development of Chinese cultural industries and also protects the Chinese people from the contamination of foreign culture. At the same time, the concept also legitimizes the state to have the absolute rights and autonomy to develop its own cultural policies based on national situations and needs. In many cases ethnic policies are also considered a part of China's cultural sovereignty. While China's cultural sovereignty praises traditional values and cultural propriety, related discourses identify Hollywood films, Korean TV dramas, and Japanese tourism as external threats corrupting the Chinese people. This cultural narcissism and anxiety can also be interpreted as a running thread comprising the sovereign logic since the late Qing—culture is the deepest source of pride and anxiety in this modern sovereign journey.

China's cultural sovereignty can also be understood as the Chinese response to the discourse of soft power. This is a concept made popular by Joseph Nye, who used the term to explain the enormous global influence of American culture.[72] To develop its own soft power, China should also produce knowledge and culture to be consumed and appreciated by the Chinese people as well as people all over the world.[73] The Confucius Institutes project can be seen as a key component of the international side of this campaign, meant to show the world China has a superior civilization that should be respected, studied, and admired. The government also actively supports its own cultural industry, with the intention of making China a cultural superpower comparable to the United States.[74]

We have yet to see any successful popular Chinese cultural products being widely accepted abroad. Instead, we see Chinese capital invested in major cultural enterprises of Hollywood and South Korea, aiming particularly to support, and to introduce pro-China ideas to, foreign-made products targeting PRC markets.[75] Such activities have come to a halt recently largely due to COVID and the increasing tensions between China and some parts of the world. Overall, soft power is no longer emphasized as a key policy factor in China. While Chinese citizens are increasingly attracted to consume China-made cultural products, the state has also intensified the ideological control of this home-grown fare. As the PRC state has become increasingly confident about its cultural control, the term *cultural sovereignty* is not in fashion.

Entering the 2010s, the prominence of the term *cultural sovereignty* has been gradually replaced by the new emphasis on cyber sovereignty, which has become, arguably, the top task of the state in protecting its sovereignty. As most of the cultural activities and communication now take place online, digital content censorship becomes a very effective means to shape and police people's thinking and expressions. If the concept of cultural sovereignty is primarily productive, meant to encourage the Chinese people to be proud of their own culture, cyber sovereignty is largely repressive, as a project to extend the PRC's censorship apparatus to the cyber world. Cyber sovereignty, first termed information sovereignty, was originally presented as a response to external threats, emphasizing the development of defensive mechanisms to prevent China's knowledge and information from being stolen by outside enterprises. But cyber sovereignty soon morphed to become an all-comprehensive state project to steer public opinion and cultivate identification.

In 2010, the Chinese government published its first comprehensive justification of its approach to cyberspace governance in a white paper, stating that the internet is under the jurisdiction of Chinese sovereignty, and all activities there must obey Chinese laws and regulations.[76] This new policy awareness coincided with the rise of sovereigntism in China, with the establishment of a National Security Commission 中央國家安全委員會 in 2013. Headed by Xi Jinping himself, this body was formed to consolidate the different security apparatuses under the party and the state as well as to step up the government's internal policing capacity. The committee also represents the state's concerted efforts in strengthening the ideology of sovereignty. It announces that the most important task of the state is to provide security to the people, but this ambition cannot be achieved without the proper protection of political security, economic security, military security, cultural security, and so on. This committee would become increasingly important under Xi's leadership, and it would spearhead the implementation of Hong Kong's National Security Law as well as the national pandemic policies in 2020.[77]

Xi advanced the idea of cyber sovereignty in 2014, asserting the importance of the state's capability in providing a safe online culture free from infiltration by Western anti-Chinese forces.[78] The Cyberspace Administration of China (CAC), which was established at this time, has become one of the most important apparatuses in today's PRC state security system. Its duties include censoring the domestic internet, but it also actively chases down and penalizes those users and websites that spread "rumors." The "Great Firewall," composed not only of high-power algorithms but also an army of individual internet inspectors, seems to be capable of blocking any keywords, memes, unwelcome messages, and even newly invented codewords deemed "dangerous" in social media. Sensitive words that are censored range from Winnie the Pooh, which first appeared as memes likened to Xi in the 2010s, to "Beijing" and "bravery" right after the Sitong Bridge protest in October 2022[79] as well as any major national topics the government considered threatening to social stability. Some scholars also estimate that that the state hired more than 2 million individuals as internet mobilizers, also called the Internet water army, and trolls to shape national opinions.[80] This tight censorship both bars Chinese netizens from reaching the outside world and restricts international rivals in the domestic market.

The concerns about cyber sovereignty have been raised in many other countries, as it is widely argued that state sovereignty has been weakened by the internet. Many governments envy the effectiveness of PRC's control, which is almost impossible to replicate because the PRC government began it in the early days of internet development. It has also successfully nurtured national tech giants such as Baidu, Tencent, Alibaba, Bytedance, and Meituan for a closed-circuit internet ecology completely under state jurisdiction and policing. While the internet was first developed with free rein in the West, China has tried to police this most intractable domain to a homogeneous one.

Netizens might have their own strategies of bypassing censorship, such as using VPNs to connect to outside servers, developing useful homophones, acronyms, or figures to substitute sensitive wording to evade keyword filters, and producing political satires as network connections.[81] But China's cyber sovereignty is still, almost certainly, the strongest in the world. It effectively mixes authoritarianism with neoliberalism as guiding principles to provide citizens with values and life goals that are supposedly good for them.[82] The enormous censorship apparatus has also collaborated seamlessly with the equally strong propaganda apparatus, cultivating the cultural pride and nationalist sentiments of the people. The strong sovereignty the PRC has enjoyed clearly owes much to this effective control of internet communication. But there are also cracking moments, such as the 2022 "A4 Revolution," whose spontaneous and nationwide nature seems to suggest that there could still be possibilities of large-scale cyber coalition breaking down the seemingly perfect cyber-security apparatus.

———

I have tried to illustrate how the different Chinese regimes have been eager to identify, interpret, manage, or combat different external and internal threats of the times to safeguard their sovereign integrity. Repeatedly we observe how the different regimes opted out from internal federalism and external alliance to develop a strong and unified state over a plural people inside and outside its border. Internal and external others are to be silenced or annihilated instead of negotiated with. But at the same time the "threats" that they represent are also amplified and constructed for the ruling regime to legitimize its sovereign power. Sovereignty and otherness are intimate partners.

These factors are hardly unique to China. The statist ideologies of socialist nationalism in Germany in the 1930s, for example, would not have gained such wide popularity without the threat of complete social disintegration experienced by many people in the Weimar Republic. Thomas Hobbes would not have written such a powerful theorization of the Leviathan state in 1651 without the immense devastation of the Thirty Years' War (1618–1648). It is often in the moment when the people feel least secure about their political institution and the wellbeing of their collective life that they most intensely desire sovereignty, to look for not only comfort but also possibilities. Naturally, sovereignty also seeks out these moments of collective hazard in order to generate a sense of urgency and room for exceptions.

We now shift our attention from the myth of spatial unity to the belief in temporal continuity and explore the dialectic between permanent sovereignty and radical political change in China's modern sovereign logic.

Three

Revolution as Foundation

The PRC presents its sovereignty as a fait accompli willed by the people, and the most powerful proof, supposedly, is the many revolutions conducted in the last century that paved the way for this regime. This teleological account is most characteristically presented in the PRC Constitution. While constitutions around the world vary in their degree of emphasis on tradition and break with the past, the Chinese constitution is unique in the very heavy emphasis it places on history. In the most recent Constitution, which dates from 1982 and was written to correct the radical Maoism that had held sway the previous two constitutions, identifies a running tradition of revolution from the late Qing era to now. The current constitution was written to show that the PRC is a legitimate heir to this legacy of revolution: revolution manifests the modern mandate of Heaven.

The first line of the 1982 Preamble reads: "China is a country with one of the longest histories in the world. The people of all of China's nationalities have jointly created a culture of grandeur and have a glorious revolutionary tradition." The Preamble then dates this "glorious revolutionary tradition" back to the 1840s; since then, the Chinese people have successively conducted struggles and revolutions for national independence and democracy. This Preamble situates the current PRC sovereignty within a running Chinese culture that is constantly renewing itself, often through violence. Thus, while the 1949 revolution created a break in history, it was at the same time an organic part of this internal historical dynamic.

In principle, 1949 was supposed to represent the end of this history of revolution; the Preamble does not elaborate on the violent political unrest that continued after 1949. From the radical economic ambitions in the Great Leap Forward to the thorough uprooting of class enemies in the Cultural Revolution, the unrest brought to society and the political establishment was no less destructive than the 1949 revolution. Although it is never stated explicitly, the 1982 Constitution was written partly to acknowledge yet criticize the destructive forces unleashed by Maoism. The new Constitution of the Deng regime now stood on the threshold of a new era of perpetual peace and prosperity, opening to and reconciling with the world. The Preamble also shows the reason for this revolutionary tradition, in which the cycles of changes promoted by the series of revolutions manifest the sovereignty's lasting creativity.

Much has changed in the roughly four decades since the 1982 Constitution was ratified, but this logic holding the chain of revolutions as evidence of the legitimacy of the current sovereignty remains honored. In today's China, sovereigntism is an ideology of order and permanence, but such a grand, and imagined, unity cannot be sustained without a parallel logic of aggression and destruction paving the way. If the external and internal threats constituting China's modern state sovereignty discussed in the previous chapter are elements that the state navigates, annihilates, or even creates in order to maintain its discourse of unity, revolution is not external to China's sovereign power but resides at its heart. As Nobel Prize laureate Liu Xiaobo has observed, there is no word in communist China more sacred or richer in moral force than "revolution."[1]

Revolution as Heaven's Mandate

As mentioned in chapter 1, the idea of Heaven's mandate is both beyond humans and in their best interests. However, there is no way for humans to decipher Heaven's mandate until it reveals itself. As such, the concept of *Tianming* can conveniently be appropriated by different political powers. The intimate relation between revolution and sovereignty in China's imperial history is undergirded by this philosophy.

To be more specific: this myth of Heaven's mandate is often used by the ruling regime to support its authority and to condemn all challengers. At the same time, it has also been appropriated by revolutionaries to legitimize their actions of usurping sovereignty. Those who conduct the revolution (*geming* 革命) successfully claim to have received the mandate (*shouming* 受命) to become the sovereign. As Elizabeth Perry observes, China's history is full of rebellions and revolutions, which are central elements in Chinese political culture: "In Imperial China, one who managed to wrest the throne by force thereby gained Confucian sanction for his rule: as the proverb put it bluntly, 'He who succeeds is a king or marquis; he who fails is an outlaw.'"[2]

The term *geming* 革命, which first appeared in the ancient oracle *Book of Change*, refers to a judiciary and seasonal new beginning. If done in ways that follow the propensity of Heaven and humans, *geming* would lead to the restoration of universal order.[3] This ancient wisdom of propriety, then, means the human world is following the unfolding of a transcendental mandate of Heaven. This traditional definition complies with the original meaning of the term *revolution* in Europe, which signifies the eternal motion of the heavenly bodies and also suggests a motion of restoration swinging back to a preordained order. In both cases, we observe how revolution and order are always already intertwined: revolution both upsets the status quo and restores a larger order. Revolution is considered a necessary act of correction in the eternal cosmic order. It does not need to link to the change of political regimes; it is just a natural law.

Entering modern times, the term *revolution* gradually came to refer to those violent acts and large-scale schemes intended to topple a government. This modern political concept also arrived in Asia. It was Japanese scholars who first used the ancient Chinese term *geming* to translate the new Western concept of revolution. It was this Japanese version, in turn, that was then picked up by late Qing Chinese scholars and politicians to describe the strong urge of the time to radically transform the political structure of the nation.[4]

Confucianism is not historical materialism, and it neither predicts nor theorizes the occurrence of revolution based on specific social or economic factors. Instead, successful revolution is read retroactively as a moral event, and it is the duty of the new sage-king to provide the balance of the universe when it is disturbed by a corrupted regime. While *Tian* implies a natural order of morality that grounds the behavior and activity of the human world, *Tian* will only bless those who are fit to rule. Human beings have no choice but respect the supremacy of *Tian*, but each of us also has the responsibilities as a moral subject to help *Tian* to realize its mandate. In turn, Heaven's mandate bestows instant legitimacy upon successful rebel leaders, encouraging those who are politically ambitious to prove that they are the chosen ones.

Confucianism is a conservative ideology, encouraging the people to submit to the structure of the dominant power. Yet it is also an ideology that considers education, through both self-cultivation and emulation, to be equally important, promising ordinary individuals that they can one day become a part of the ruling elite. Confucianism, particularly Mencius, does not deny the people the political wisdom and the right to act—indeed, it affirms that their political actions and decisions, if cultivated correctly, would coincide with Heaven's mandate.[5] Generations of Confucian scholars revered their Emperors on the one hand and followed Mencius's teaching on the other hand, believing that popular revolt against a despotic rule could be just.[6] Confucian scholars believed that it was their responsibility not only to fathom Heaven but also to use their intellectual ability to teach the Emperor and the ordinary people alike to align themselves with the ideal moral universe. Revolution could be a last resort.

Revolution is central to the Chinese dynastic structure. What made the late Qing revolutionaries more radical was their rejection of the entire imperial system and traditional thinking, including Confucianism. With the increasing popularity of Social Darwinism, the newly educated began to replace the circular dynastic logic with linear teleology, assuming that China would follow European countries to progress from authoritarian monarchy to liberal democracy. Such radical change, it was believed, could only be achieved through revolution and violence.[7] This revolution was also probably the first in China's history driven primarily by an intellectual discourse of national dignity instead of hunger or the material interests of concerned parties. These violent roots of China's modernity continue to inform the sovereign powers that came after.

Revolution and Democracy in the Republican Period

Sun Yat-sen's revolutionary party proudly presented the new Republic of China as the first republic in Asia. In this version of events, the ROC, representing the spirit of innovation and determination, was the most politically progressive body of the time. But the 1911 Xinhai Revolution did not achieve much of what it promised. In 1923 Sun Yat-sen solemnly announced in the KMT Party Assembly: "The revolution has not yet succeeded, and comrades still need to work hard." Two years later, Sun reiterated this in his will. Indeed, it is clear that the idea of continual revolution was central to Sun's political career until his death. Sun compared himself to Lenin, seeing both men as the major revolutionary leaders in Asia overthrowing old and ailing regimes.[8] He also developed close connections with the Soviet Union to assist the KMT to fight the northern warlords. This collaboration corresponded to the Soviet Union's own policies of subsidizing revolutionary parties around the world to engage in their own national revolutions. Sun welcomed the Soviet support also in the name of carrying on the revolution. With Yuan Shikai and different warlords holding onto their political power, Sun was convinced that revolution had to continue, and it was this revolutionary discourse that sustained the legitimacy of the new sovereign state.

After Sun's death, Chiang Kai-shek presented himself as the legitimate heir to this continuing Chinese revolution. Chiang immediately launched the Northern Expedition (1926–1928), or the so-called "Second Revolution," against the Beiyang government, as an act to continue Sun's unfinished revolution. But, as Brian Tsui argues, Chiang also decoupled national revolution from social revolution, making sure that while this new revolution continued to mobilize the populace and pursue China's independence from the West, it was not meant to attack social hierarchies and inequalities.[9] Ironically, conservatism was summoned to assist the discourse of revolution, while the KMT government tried to replace the iconoclastic May Fourth Movement with the nationalistic New Culture Movement.

This discourse of national revolution continued after the success of the Northern Expedition, and in 1927 KMT's enemy was shifted from the warlords to the communists. Now the CCP was portrayed as the major block to China's successful revolution. The KMT government launched the Shanghai massacre in 1927 against CCP members, and the wounded oppositional party was forced to move inland and establish its own sovereign areas first in Jiangxi and Fujian, and then in the remote Yan'an region, which ultimately led to KMT's defeat two decades later. China might have forged a very different path if the KMT had decided to live with the oppositional party and to find ways to develop an enduring parliamentary system that could incorporate a plurality of voices into its governance.

While Sun Yat-sen and his followers asserted that revolution could bring about democracy, Chiang used the same revolutionary discourse to delay democracy. Sun delivered a nation-building blueprint in 1924 that delineated the development of the political structure of the new nation-state in three different stages: military government (軍政 *junzheng*), tutelage government (訓政 *xunzheng*), and constitutional government (憲政 *xianzheng*).[10] To Sun, military government could only be exercised during revolution. He hoped that whenever a province became stabilized, then tutelage government could begin, and the duty of this government would be to teach the people how to exercise democracy and establish constitutional government. The third period could begin when all the counties in the province were ready to exercise self-rule, so full democracy should commence. In other words, to Sun there were two roads leading to democracy: in a top-down way, the government should teach the people how to exercise democracy; in a bottom-up way, democracy begins with the local county level and gradually moves up to the province and the national level. According to this blueprint, the first military government period had begun in 1917 when Guangzhou's Nationalist government was first established. The second stage was to begin with the establishment of the national government in Nanjing in 1928, which hopefully was a short transition period for the implementation of constitutional government.

However, despite the repeated pleas of party members and intellectuals, the Chiang Kai-shek government kept refusing to enter the phase of constitutional government. Chiang insisted that decades after the Xinhai Revolution China was still caught in a revolutionary period, that the Chinese citizens were not mature enough to rule themselves, and that they needed the KMT's tutelage to learn to practice democracy.[11] The third period did not officially begin until two decades later, in 1947, during the midst of the civil war. Chiang was aware that the KMT was on the verge of complete dismantling, and it needed to gain the support of the populace by offering democracy. Between 1927 and 1947, Chiang exercised revolutionary rhetoric by infinitely extending the authoritarian tutelage government period, allowing the state of exception to suspend the constitution in the name of revolution. Revolution is indeed core to KMT's sovereign logic.

Ironically, in a speech in 1947, Chiang complained that the revolutionary spirit of his party had almost completely dissipated because the high officials, only interested in protecting their own interests, had refused cooperation.[12] One year later, at the verge of KMT's final defeat, Chiang Kai-shek addressed his military commanders and civilian cadres:

> To tell the truth, never, in China or abroad, has there been a revolutionary party as decrepit [*tuitang*] and degenerate [*fubai*] as we [the KMT] are today. There has been never one as lacking spirit, lacking discipline, and even more, lacking standards of right and wrong as we are today. This kind of party should long ago have been destroyed and swept away![13]

For Chiang, the main cause of the fall of the KMT, which continued to call itself the Revolutionary Party, was the party members' betrayal of the original revolutionary spirit. They were only keen on protecting their self-interest, sacrificing the original revolutionary promise of serving the entire population and building a strong nation. But Chiang, as Mao later would, failed to notice how detrimental it was to buttress a new state sovereignty with the revolutionary spirit, which always challenges state building efforts.

Like Sun, Chiang also asserted that both 1911 and 1927 revolutions led by his party were meant to realize democracy in China. But his delay of constitutional government was also based on his insistence that China was not ready for democracy. He never clearly explained whether it was the KMT's demand for continual revolution that halted democracy, or the Chinese people's incapacity for democracy that forced revolution to go on. We only know that the KMT never delivered on the promise of democracy until absolutely necessary as a tradeoff to buy back popular support. Direct election of the National Assembly was initially allowed, and the one-party state was ended to allow other parties to compete for the rulership. On the verge of losing its sovereign power, the KMT was finally ready to experiment with a democratic institution. Revolution, democracy, and sovereignty were the political missions of China's first republic, yet these high ideals were lost in the maze woven by threads of political rhetoric and realpolitik.

Most of the revolutions that have happened in modern times have been presented as means to achieve democracy. Such rhetoric dates back to the French Revolution but was reinvigorated by Marxism, which propelled many successful revolutions in the twentieth century. But most of them did not lead to democracy, with the Arab Spring a recent and sad example: after the change in the sovereign in certain countries, many of the countries involved in the Arab Spring have suffered from socio-political instability and economic challenges.[14] Democracy might be a crucial factor to propel revolution around the world in modern times, but successful revolutions do not always deliver genuine democracy as promised.

Looking back at recent world history, democracy happens, but those sustainable democracies are often not the direct results of revolution.[15] Instead, effective democratic changes are usually brought about by slow institutional reforms, involving meticulous coordination of political institutions and actors. It is obviously important that the citizens must first demand change and show enough mutual respect among themselves. But at the same time, the state must also be ready to share power. In Europe, those states willing to undergo reform are often based on actual interests in terms of, for example, conscription, taxation, and economic development.[16] More recently, those authoritarian regimes in Asia, such as Japan, South Korea, and Taiwan, were willing to embark on democratic reforms when they were confident that they would fare well in democratic elections.[17] Periods of sudden rise and decline of great powers also create powerful incentives and opportunities for sweeping international waves of domestic transformation.[18] While definitions of democracy make for a perennial academic debate, it is beyond doubt that democracy has not yet reached China, despite the many revolutions already taken place. Instead, democracy is often a pretext—or a false hope—for revolution.

The Fetishization of Revolution in the Socialist Period

We tend to imagine revolution as a political event organized by oppositional or underground forces inside the country, which represent the anger and frustration of an exasperated people against their sovereign power. But actual revolutions are much less pure. Sovereignty changes are usually the result of particular alignments of different internal and external events. Domestic unrest often happens when the state is strained by wars, which then leads to full-scale revolution and new sovereignty. This is shown, for example, in the 1917 Bolshevik revolution that followed Russian losses in World War I. We also see that internal revolutions follow quickly on the heels of fallen empires, which was observed repeatedly in the twentieth century. The collapse of the central empires in Europe in 1918, the fall of the British Empire after World War II, and the disintegration of the Soviet Union in the early 1990s all led to revolution and the establishment of new sovereign countries all over the world. Interested foreign powers also often intervene in civil wars, supporting specific revolutionary powers for their own interests. This was observed in China's civil war in the late 1940s, when Stalin supported both the KMT and the CCP strategically, remaining on the fence to observe and take advantage of the ways history would unfold.[19] It was CCP's imminent victory in late 1948 that convinced Moscow to commit entirely to its communist counterpart.

The revolutionary tradition central to PRC's sovereign discourses also involved many external factors. Yet these were often omitted from the mainstream narrative. To the PRC, all socialist revolutions are the results entirely of the people's own initiatives, wisdom, and courage. But in reality, socialist revolutions, including those of the PRC, are intertwined with external forces. The Soviet Union was a particularly important player in promoting and instructing these revolutions, while Maoist China would soon rise and consider the exportation of revolutions to other countries one of its central missions.

To understand the ultra-sovereign dimensions of socialist revolution, let us go back to the founding ideologies of the USSR. In order to develop a proletarian internationalism that would ultimately bring all of humankind to communism, the Communist Party of the Soviet Union (CPSU) considered the exportation of revolution to be one of its main duties starting in the 1920s. The party did so by inviting revolutionaries around the world to become dependent on the Soviet Union for their material military support.[20] The export of revolution was central to this Soviet internationalism, both due to ideological convictions and real concerns for sovereign safety.

In time, the Soviet internationalist revolutionary spirit was happily adopted by the new PRC sovereign state, at least on the surface. When Sino-Soviet relations began to sour in the mid-1950s, China developed a new Maoist international alliance to compete with the Soviet internationalism by providing material and spiritual support to revolutionary allies all over the world. The PRC offered food and money to many independent and decolonizing Asian, African, and Latin American countries, and it also connected with the oppressed peoples in Western countries, such as African Americans in the United States.[21]

The internationalist mentalities and policies of the PRC also won the sincere friendship of major intellectual figures in the West, ranging from W.E.B. De Bois in the United States to Julia Kristeva in France.[22] Indeed, communists around the world traveled to China from the 1950s to the 1970s to acquire political training. They toured the country to be impressed by the model factories and agricultural collectives, and they met the friendly and charismatic Chinese leaders. The personal stories of these travelers to China formed the basis for the creation of a counter-narrative to the dominant Soviet narratives when they went back to their communities. They helped to construct the myth that the Chinese revolution was the best model of world revolution, in contrast to the one in the Soviet Union which had already been proven to be revisionist, as they claimed.[23] These international Maoist intellectuals considered themselves both instructors and messengers, providing the masses in their own countries with the political enlightenment they needed to become revolutionaries.

These international Maoists were so keen on telling the PRC story largely because they believed the 1949 CCP revolution was indeed an emancipating one. But how to carry the revolutionary force forward into the state building project was another matter. In Maoist China, the state tirelessly upheld the revolution as the expression of the nation's popular sovereignty. But such veneration of a past revolution forestalls a living popular sovereignty, denying any new sovereign expressions of the people by consecrating the 1949 spirits as eternal. The nation was also left with a strong feeling of restlessness. The impulse of permanent revolution against anything static characterized Maoism.[24] It was believed that when society began stabilized, a new elite class would be formed, and social hierarchy would become rigid, so class struggle must again be called upon to protect socialism. In Socialist China, revolutionary discourses could be found everywhere; almost anything done in the name of the revolution could be considered righteous and justified.

To be more precise, Mao first fully theorized his idea of continual revolution in 1956 to encourage constant class struggle and renewal of political energy for the young republic.[25] While the revolutionary mentality in the 1950s was still contained within the state-building project, Maoists waged the 1966 Great Proletarian Cultural Revolution to show the Maoist regime's determination to sacrifice sovereign stability for political regeneration. To prevent the socialist state from falling into the alleged revisionism that had recently manifested in the Soviet Union, Mao rekindled the revolutionary spirit to destroy all the institutions he had helped to build in the previous two decades, so the people could erect the country anew. Mao was determined to plunge the new sovereign country into chaos, with the purpose of revolutionizing both the socialist institutions and the socialist citizens, clearing the way for a utopian communist end.

Mao's continual revolution differs from Trotsky's theory of permanent revolution in the latter's emphasis on international social revolutions, that revolutions must happen across the world in order to effectively combat global capitalism, while Mao's concept is directed at the nation itself. But the results were tragic: not only did this attempt at internal continual revolution destroy many lives and families, but it invited capitalism to settle in China after Maoism's own blatant failure. Revolution could both destroy and sustain the sovereign institutions, and the Cultural Revolution showed the most profound manifestation of this dilemma: that the most radical socialist revolution also destroys a young and aspiring socialist country.

In stark contrast to many liberal democratic countries that rely on learned professionals, a predictable bureaucracy, and accountable institutions to propel social change, Socialist China depended on the "mass line"—the Maoist method of pulling the wisdom of the masses together and encouraging them to participate in politics directly in order to allow extensive and intensive changes to happen quickly. The PRC's first Constitution already stated that the new state practiced a "people's democratic dictatorship" (人民民主專政). In this, then, the PRC again followed the Soviet Union by bringing democracy and dictatorship together, so that it was the people who warranted the state's authoritarianism and continual revolution. With such a close connection, while the party was authorized by the people, the party also instructed the masses to steer social campaigns at the local level, which created pressure within villages and work units, so all had to conform. Political campaigns tended to be effective—and indeed, wave after wave of fundamental social change were achieved in Socialist China through such mass campaigns. But many of these campaigns were carried out with tremendous social violence, and the party was not always in control of the agitated masses it had whipped up.

The most "violent" dimension of the Maoist revolution might rest on its ultimate goal of creating not only a new socialist society but also new individuals. It was the soul that was the eventual concern. Individuals were classified into groups according to their class background and revolutionary consciousness, but ultimately each of them would have to become the same communist subject. Emphasis on self-cultivation and self-correction, theoretically initiated by oneself, could become extremely coercive and exploitative, submitting one's entire private life to the ideological scrutiny of the sovereign state.[26] In the name of revolution, the self-reform demanded of intellectuals might be the most intense, with many ending up taking their own lives to avoid facing the "dictatorship" exercised on them.

Such levels of fetishization of revolution in Maoist China also explained its doom. Chiang Kai-shek had lamented that it was the failure of the KMT to maintain its revolutionary spirit that caused the party to lose the country. Ironically, Mao lost China by holding too tightly onto his continual revolution rhetoric. Many ordinary citizens were exhausted by the overall revolutionary milieu infiltrating people's lives, witnessing some of the catastrophic outcomes. Sadly, similar rhetoric was again detected in the recent COVID pandemic control, hoping that the lockdown surveillance could be initiated by the masses themselves, which, unfortunately, only created conflicts and tensions within communities.

Not all revolutions resort to large-scale physical violence to derail a sovereign, and there are other ways to encourage the ruling regime to dole out its power relatively peacefully. This is shown, for example, in the arrest of the "Gang of Four" in 1976 and Deng Xiaoping's resumption of power in 1978, which together marked China's transition to its postsocialist stage. Whether the "peaceful" transition from Mao to Deng should be described as a revolution or a reform is of incessant debate. As Deng's post-1978 governance was fundamentally different from Mao's and was made possible by unseating the ruling unit, I would consider it an event akin to a revolution. This is particularly clear if we adopt the Marxist framework to understand this transition from Mao to Deng and from socialism to postsocialism. Regardless of the term used, it was here that the determining factor of China's economy shifted back to the market, and it involved radical qualitative changes rather than fine-tuned quantitative improvement. This peaceful transition might also prove Marx and Engels partially right: they approved of the use of armed revolution to achieve socialism but also saw the possibility of a peaceful transition to socialism.[27] What happened in China in the late 1970s could be seen as a typical peaceful revolution, although it reversed the historical trajectory that Marx and Engels prophesied. And it was this peaceful revolution that opened the door for the PRC to become a major contributor to the new phase of global capitalism.

Statism in the Postsocialist Period

Both Chiang Kai-shek and Mao Zedong were devoted to building a powerful and centralized state along the model of Leninism.[28] Under their leadership, the KMT and the CCP inevitably displayed an affinity with the Bolshevik model of party-building, mass mobilization, and, more subtly, the Leninist belief in the reign of violence, which was also echoed in the dictatorial practices of many of their monarchic predecessors. The Chiang regime suppressed peaceful protests violently throughout its reign; Mao also famously argued that political power grows out of the barrel of a gun.

But the revolutionary narrative was gradually overtaken by the modernization narrative in the 1980s and 1990s, due to both the official repudiation of radical Maoism and the growing influence of the ideology of Development that considers modernization a gradual and teleological process. With Cultural Revolution identified as a historical mistake, the celebrating of revolution based on class struggles fell out of favor. Instead, modern culture is increasingly seen as a result of the complexity and multiplicity of social changes under different circumstances.[29] Therefore, China's modernization could no longer be easily understood as the natural result of a succession of revolutions, and the sovereignty also shifted its focus from revolution to modernization as the mark of its legitimacy.

Entering the Xi era, revolution was once again highlighted. Revolution is both openly celebrated and implicitly denounced in the current statist environment. Let us look at an example. As part of the celebrations of the CCP's 100th anniversary, President Xi gave an important speech in 2021 in which he perpetuated a rhetoric very similar to the one in the Preamble discussed earlier. But the critical undertone against Mao's fanaticism found widely in the Deng era could hardly be detected now, and revolution became all sacred. In this speech he celebrated China's legacy of revolution as the reflection of the Chinese people's determination to stand up to foreign pressure and commit to national rejuvenation.

> After the Opium War of 1840, however, China was gradually reduced to a semi-colonial, semi-feudal society and suffered greater ravages than ever before . . . To save the nation from peril, the Chinese people put up a courageous fight. As noble-minded patriots sought to pull the nation together, the Taiping Heavenly Kingdom Movement, the Reform Movement of 1898, the Yihetuan Movement [Boxer Rebellion], and the Revolution of 1911 rose one after the other, and a variety of plans were devised to ensure national survival, but all of these ended in failure. China was in urgent need of new ideas to lead the movement to save the nation and a new organization to rally revolutionary forces. . . .
>
> Through the Northern Expedition, the Agrarian Revolutionary War, the War of Resistance Against Japanese Aggression, and the War of Liberation, we fought armed counter-revolution with armed revolution, toppling the three mountains of imperialism, feudalism, and bureaucrat-capitalism, and establishing the People's Republic of China, which made the people masters of the country. We thus secured our nation's independence and liberated our people.[30]

Xi's words, widely echoed in other state discourses, highlight a chain of armed struggles (except the 1898 Reform Movement) from 1850 to 1949 that are deemed "revolutionary": from the Taiping Movement and the Boxer Rebellion, which wreaked havoc in late Qing, to the Northern

Expedition and Anti-Japanese War, led primarily by the KMT. By labeling these moments "revolutionary," Xi praised them as crucial contributions to the ultimate 1949 liberation. All of these political events are presented by Xi as reflections of popular sovereignty. Thus, they each represent part of a tradition of courage and determination of the people to usher China to its current stage of pride and prosperity.

This historical narration differs the most from 1982 Preamble in the subtle refutation of the pacifying policies of the Deng era, and now the Xi government encourages the people to embrace the mentality of struggles again. While the establishment of the PRC in 1949 is here presented as the culmination of this revolutionary history, Xi continues in the speech afterwards to celebrate the revolutionary tradition within the party after Liberation. Unlike the 1982 Preamble, which described the transformation of the revolutionary energy into development and reform in the new era, Xi is here enthusiastic about keeping the revolutionary spirit alive: "We will continue to promote our glorious traditions and sustain our revolutionary legacy, so that the great founding spirit of the Party will always be kept alive and carried forward." The revolutionary tradition continues, although it is now repackaged as the people's determination to show the world that "China's national rejuvenation has become a historical inevitability."

Xi also included in this historical narrative the notion that "we must continue working to promote the building of a human community with a shared future. Peace, concord, and harmony are ideas the Chinese nation has pursued and carried forward for more than 5,000 years." In the same speech, we are told that the Chinese people can "put up a courageous fight," while they also "do not carry aggressive traits in their genes." This dialectical depiction of the Chinese people being both aggressive and amicable facilitates the PRC's governance to meander between struggles and peace, confrontation and reconciliation, as demanded by the situation.

Xi has expressed his admiration of Mao Zedong on several occasions, and he is clearly the Chinese state leader in the postsocialist period most committed to the idea of revolution. But underlying Xi's revolutionary consciousness is also a statism, which is supported by a different set of philosophical discourses, including Confucian-Legalism and Carl Schmitt's political theory. Both have been selectively used to hold up a sovereigntism that celebrates national unity, state authority, and perpetual peace, which is also anti-revolutionary.

With the new Republic established in the early twentieth century, China advertised itself as a modern nation uprooting the entire traditional political philosophy. Yet traditional ideas have continued to exert enormous influence. Chiang Kai-Shek never shied away from his belief in Confucianism; indeed, his ill-fated New Life Movement was primarily a Confucian-Legalist movement with a sprinkling of Christian flavors.[31] Mao also had a complicated relationship with Confucianism and Legalism throughout his life. His early essays show his interest in traditional Chinese thought, which would continue to resurface in different forms in his intellectual and political life.[32] Overall, Mao was very critical of Confucianism, condemning its feudalist and conservative components; he held Legalism in greater esteem. Mao criticized Legalism as serving the elite class, but he also found it a more progressive Chinese traditional thought. This was particularly the case in the last years of his life, when Mao praised Legalism's emphasis on law and the present over the past—unlike Confucianism, which fetishized the past.

The postsocialist period shows a reversed tendency: while Confucianism has increasingly been reemphasized,[33] Legalism was not much mentioned in the official discourses due primarily to its traditional association with monarchic dictatorship. But the current Chinese "rule-by-law" system could clearly be seen as a manifestation of Legalism. The Xi regime repeatedly emphasizes the importance of Sinicization of Marxism, and Legalism is clearly referenced in the development of a socialist rule of law with Chinese characteristics. Xi's new governance principle has been described as a new type of Confucian-Legalist statecraft, emphasizing both social harmony and fear of law, giving the party both the authority and the tools to consolidate and reinforce its power.[34] Xi also seems to have a high regard for the Legalist master Shang Yang 商鞅 (390–338 BCE), whose efforts to gain the trust of the people are held by Xi as a most important principle of the Chinese version of the rule of law.[35] Xi also refers to Shang's courage in following neither a fixed principle nor the idealized tradition to rule the country as a cultural root of the PRC's current reform project.[36] What has not been directly mentioned is Shang Yang's demand for the people's complete obedience to the Qin state.

At the same time, there has been increasing interest in Schmitt's writings since the 2000s.[37] Scholars are attracted to Schmitt primarily due to two of his fundamental positions, anti-liberalism and a strong state, which come down to two central arguments of the current PRC's sovereign ideology: that liberalism destroys a harmonious polity, and only a strong state can lead China to prosperity. The Chinese statists refer, for example, to Schmitt's ideas of an absolute constitution to justify the leadership of the CCP, the friend-enemy political structure for continual national struggle, and the historical failure of Western parliamentary politics.[38] As Schmitt believes that sovereignty presupposes the need for homogeneity, many PRC statist scholars find Schmitt instructive.[39] Schmitt is clear that the people are heterogeneous, but as the subject of democracy they must be treated as a homogeneity corresponding to the singularity of the state. The logic of state sovereignty rests on the identity of rulers and ruled, governing and governed, subject and object of state authority.[40] Contemporary Chinese scholars find these ideas attractive to support the state's efforts in prioritizing national security over individual liberty.

But Schmitt is often read in China without a full contextualization of his thought. The Weimar Republic was legitimized primarily by the Weimar Constitution, which for the first time gave the German people a bill of rights and a normative frame for public life. It was under this condition that Schmitt theorized the superiority of the absolute constitution as a means to protect the unity of the nation.[41] He was most critical of the bureaucratization of Weimar's legal apparatus and aspired to sustain a "genuine" form of rule of law, which could truly reflect the will of the people. Although Schmitt emphasizes the power of sovereign authority to decide whether to suspend the application of its law during times of emergency, the end of such acts is to retain the superiority of the constitution. But in modern China, the law is always a direct instrument of the state. There is no pretense that the law can be independent from the ruling party. There were eleven central government constitutions and constitutional drafts written between 1908 and 1982, but China has yet to attain constitutionalism.[42] As legal scholar Jerome Cohen argues, when one compares the uses of law in traditional China, the ROC, and the PRC, "significant differences of course appear. Yet one major similarity stands out—law and legal institutions still serve principally as instruments for enhancing the power of the state and for disciplining the people to carry out its policies."[43]

Moreover, Schmitt's idea of the totality of the state is supported by the premise of the state's neutrality. Facing factional conflicts in the parliament and the invasion of commercial interests of public power, Schmitt argues that the state must represent the people in making decisions, but on the condition that it is neutral and impartial, speaking and acting for the largest interests of society.[44] In contrast to this condition of neutrality that Schmitt finds essential for the state to legitimize its political authority, the CCP holds a large stake in China's society. In the 1950s, the socialist government nationalized most private property. Entering the postsocialist period, the gradual transformation of state ownership to private ownership facilitated the state to accumulate a large amount of capital, benefiting not only the state treasury but also leaders at all levels privately. It is problematic to assume the impartiality of the state and its representatives when capital and power are circulating so intensely within the party. If China adopts Schmittian statism without a vigorous legal consciousness and the state's committed neutrality, what remains could only be brute force as well as incessant power struggles and clandestine negotiations.

The current PRC interest in Confucian-Legalism and Schmitt's philosophy tends to be largely cherry-picking. But this also demonstrates some fundamental contradictions within the PRC sovereign discourses, particularly the simultaneous disavowal and acknowledgment of revolution. Legalism, for example, is decidedly against revolution. Han Feizi 韓非子 (280–233 BCE), one of its founding masters, was explicit about his disagreement of Mencius's approval to remove a despotic ruler. Han Feizi believed that a plurality of political views in society always existed. If this option of revolution were given to the people, it would create confusion and give an excuse to would-be usurpers to bring havoc to society.[45] Legalism was primarily a school of authoritarianism, teaching the monarchy how to maintain perennial sovereignty by all means.

But we must also recognize that the earliest form of Legalism, initiated and implemented by Shang Yang's reforms (356 BCE and 347 BCE), was meant to take power away from the aristocrats to the monarchy in the Qin state, and it also fundamentally restructured society by challenging the powerful lords. Although the main purpose of Shang Yang's

Legalist reform was to strengthen and support the ruling regime, there was an implicit revolutionary dimension of this political philosophy. This remotely reverberates with Xi's celebration of continual revolution in to-day's China, in the sense that Legalism is also reinstated to combat a corrupt political status quo. Xi justifies his centralized power by assert-ing that after decades of Open Door Policy, the CCP is under threat from corruption and liberalism.[46] Legalism is adopted by the Xi government to revamp the party, as a part of the "revolutionary spirit" emphasized in Xi's political discourses, although such spirit can only benefit the ruling regime.

Schmitt also disapproves of revolution. He was critical of the French Revolution in particular and political revolutions in general—which, as he writes, tend to be result of romantic sentiments and subjectivism.[47] To him, an emotion that does not transcend the limits of the subjec-tive cannot be the foundation of a community, and the intoxication of sociability is not a basis of a lasting association.[48] The seemingly om-nipotent Volk theorized by Schmitt occupies only a passive role in his political world, as they, being the source of the sovereign power, are only capable of responding with a simple "yes" or "no" to the state ap-paratus.[49] To Schmitt, a powerful and strong leadership rests with the state apparatus, and the role of the people is to endorse or reject it. The current PRC sovereigntism might depict the people as more active. But their popular support of the sovereign is simply assumed, which echoes with Schmitt's theorization.

Schmitt's rejection of political romanticism is clearly not compatible with Maoism, but there has been an academic trend in recent years precisely to compare Schmitt and Mao in the PRC, with the purposes of explaining Schmitt's instructive value in China's governance. For ex-ample, legal scholar Zheng Qi suggests that the Chinese can learn from Schmitt's celebration of the people's free will. She argues that both Mao and Schmitt demanded the people's commitment to the leader-ship and unity of the sovereign state, but Mao privileged the role of the authorities in identifying the enemy and in constructing homogeneity, whereas Schmitt's conception of the state is based on people's funda-mental political choice under constitutional laws.[50] Liu Xiaofeng, argu-ably the most important Schmittian scholar in the PRC today, seems to suggest the opposite, that Schmitt does not fetishize the masses as Mao does. When he compares Schmitt's reading of guerrilla warfare with Mao's, Liu observes Schmitt's praises of the guerrilla's moral integrity and their commitment to the local, which is in accord with Mao. But Liu also argues that Schmitt is ultimately critical of the guerrillas, because they are not part of the state and lack the mandate of the sovereign.[51] Liu here contrasts Mao's anarchistic tendency with Schmitt's emphasis on institution. Zheng emphasizes Mao's authoritarianism, while Liu focuses on Mao's political voluntarism. In both cases, Schmitt serves the purpose of correcting Mao, lessons of much value to contemporary China.

Since the Deng period, the rhetoric of revolution has maintained a low profile. But over the last few years, the Maoist revolutionary vector has started to return. On the one hand, Xi's Chinese Dream preaches a harmonious society; on the other, the CCP also asks its members never to forget the idea of struggles in their everyday execution of the party's will.[52] Xi also keeps reiterating the importance of the CCP to undergo "self-revolution" incessantly to ensure that the people do not abandon the party.[53] This demand for incessant struggles, resurrecting Mao's continual revolution, has been emphasized in all aspects of Xi's governance, particularly under the general anti-corruption, anti-Western, and later anti-virus rhetoric. Clearly, Xi only wants a limited revolution that is completely under his control. Still, the national involution caused by such rhetoric of struggles against the external and internal threats is straining the people to a dangerous point. We will return to this in chapter 6.

Revolution and Sovereignty

While many people in the West harken back to their founding revolutions, specifically the French Revolution and the American Revolution, as events of the distant past, revolution is much closer to the people's memory in China, as is also the case in Russia, Turkey, Iran, and many postsocialist or postcolonial countries. In China, the successful revolutions in 1911 and 1949 introduced not just new ruling regimes but also political structures and ideologies never seen in China before. The resultant regimes, the ROC and the PRC, in turn considered their revolutions sacred, to the extent that at some point they both emphasized a mentality of permanent revolution. In an opposite way, the capitalist turn witnessed in the 1980s could be considered both a revolution on its own and a direct result of the failed Cultural Revolution, which was launched precisely to prevent the state from taking up the capitalist road again.

Most existing regimes gained their power—and thereby their sovereignty—by overthrowing the previous ones through rebellions or civil wars. For example, the utter destruction and traumatic experiences unleashed by the French Revolution were considered by some as a structural necessity to destroy the old and enter a new era. With the king beheaded, the people were shown definitively that they were now the new heads of state.[54] Not only in China but around the world revolution is placed at the core of sovereignty, as seen in national holidays around the world commemorating the uprising of the current regime against the previous one.

Revolutions also often provide those precious moments of collective solidarity and self-rule for the people to experience an authentic sovereign will. Close to each of our memories might be the local rallies in which we have taken part, or even participation in a sporting event in a large stadium. In these and other instances of solidarity, a unified "us" is constructed, a sublime sociability is experienced, fashioning a sense of collective sovereignty achieved neither in our everyday life nor in our bureaucratic political institutions. Revolution often provides some "authentic" moments of sovereignty, when the participants encounter an intense experience of presence, connection, and solidarity.

But violence necessarily begets violence, and the state must prevent the use of violence against itself. Revolution is also the sovereign power's most profound fear, and the state is permanently driven to the eradication of all revolutions. As Jacques Derrida reminds us:

> What the state fears (the state being law in its greatest force) is not so much crime or *brigandage*, even on the grand scale of the Mafia or heavy drug traffic, as long as they transgress the law with an eye toward particular benefits, however important they may be. The state is afraid of fundamental, founding violence, that is, violence able to justify, to legitimate . . . and so to present itself as having a right to law.[55]

Universal to all state sovereign power is, first, the celebration of its own revolution that brings it to power and, second, the suppression of any causes that might introduce new revolutions. Violence is therefore dichotomized into one that threatens order (in the form of revolution) and one that protects order (in the form of sovereignty), and the two contradict and legitimize each other. Meanwhile, there is a widespread romanticization of the revolutionary spirit. However much the state monopolizes violence and punishment, the people continue to fetishize revolutionary violence and glorify those who resist, and the rebels are lauded in folk and popular culture all over the world. They remain the undercurrent of sovereign logic.

Hannah Arendt points out the pertinent tension between foundation and revolution, both of which are central to modern sovereignty:

> If foundation was the aim and the end of revolution, then the revolutionary spirit was not merely the spirit of beginning something new but of starting something permanent and enduring; a lasting institution, embodying this spirit and en-couraging it to new achievements, would be self-defeating. From which it unfortunately seems to follow that nothing threatens the very achievements of revolution more dan-gerously and more acutely than the spirit what has brought them about.[56]

To Arendt, foundation and revolution in any political regime are equally important, although they also contradict and destroy each other. All sovereign powers need to come to terms with this tension, and the state, idealistically, should bring both to fruition. Arendt believes that these constituting but contradictory dynamics can be productively internalized by the state, so that it constantly seeks the endorsement from the people, while also responding to their changing needs. However, reality always falls short of such high expectations. She laments that most post-revolutionary thought fails to remember and continue the revolutionary spirit that drove the revolution, which reminds us of Chiang Kai-shek's lament of the fall of the KMT. She also points out that most revolutionaries fail to build a lasting institution after their success, echoing the way the Cultural Revolution unfolded. If we, like Arendt, un-derstand revolution and institution together as each other's task and spirit, then the people should fear neither revolution nor institution, in the sense that the institution should always seek its own rejuvenation, and the ultimate purpose of revolution is to construct, not to destroy. As

Arendt explains, revolution provides the foundation of the new regime by realizing the potentialities of political actions and new institutions. Idealistically, while the institution should never forget the revolutionary spirit that both destroys and rejuvenates, the institution is also meant to function and last.

Nurtured by the opposite sets of sentiments submitting to and rebelling against the state, the current Chinese government legitimizes itself by tapping into the violence unleashed in its revolutionary history while celebrating harmony and compliance as the correction of the former. We could argue that the current PRC government is also struggling with the Arendtian dialectic between institution and revolution. But if revolution and institution are orchestrated only to maintain and justify the present power structure, it would be hard to anticipate how the sovereign can continue to grow with the people and respond to their changing needs. Indeed, measured against this Arendtian idealism, the sovereign history of modern China is clearly wanting. The late Qing revolutionaries believed that only revolution could bring about new foundations, but the republican revolution did not nurture lasting institutions, and the KMT failed to construct a democratic apparatus that could realize the popular sovereignty it had promised. The current postsocialist state also appears to have forgotten its revolutionary promises, indirectly shown in the slogan "Don't forget the original intentions" (*wuwang chuxin* 勿忘初心) that has flooded the official propaganda culture in recent years.[57]

The pairing of sovereignty and revolution could, as Arendt contends, realize healthy political institutions that both persist and welcome change. But there is also a tragic dimension of political reality that all institutions are prone to corruption and invite revolution, engendering the vicious circles of distrust and fear. If revolution is at the core of sovereign power, the latter could be extremely brutal. Overall, China's Long Twentieth Century can be characterized as much as a period of collective longing for sovereignty as a period of incessant revolutions, and they condition each other.

———

As shown in modern and contemporary China, the more the country has been shocked by revolutions, the more the people want order and authority. The opposite is also the case: many Chinese people have been drawn to the idea of radical change precisely because they find China, as one of the oldest countries in the world, conservative and prone to maintaining the status quo. Through the lens of revolution, we see sovereignty constantly caught in the dynamics between change and stagnation, resistance and authority, as well as political fanaticism and the urge for order. But most importantly, this historical review also invites us to comprehend the logic behind the current PRC government's seemingly contradictory discourses around revolution—revolution is both glorified and feared. This government legitimizes its increasing authoritarianism in the name of protecting sovereign security, but the draconian controls also inevitably summon grievances and resistance.

Democracy could be a key to resolve this impasse. Revolution is often considered a means to achieve democracy, as Zhang Taiyan and Sun Yat-sen argued for the anti-Manchurian revolution, as well as Mao Zedong and his communist comrades for their communist revolution. However, instead of realizing the democratic promises, the sovereignty achieved through revolution could quickly become authoritarian.[58] We could argue that it was Mao's "democratic" revolution that directly made his latter authoritarianism possible. It is not easy, as many have claimed, to demarcate democratic revolution and *coups d'état* because the latter are often conducted in the name of the former, and the former can easily slide into the latter.

But it does not mean we should give up our democratic visions. In China, both the ROC and the PRC have tried different ways, barring universal suffrage, to maintain their sovereignty after their successful revolutions. Democracy is more often presented as rhetoric instead of conducted as difficult human praxis. As shown in the experiences of many other countries, democracy is the most effective way to prevent new revolutions to take place. The biggest regret of the 1911 and 1949 revolutions might indeed be their inability to fulfill their original promise for democracy. Maybe we should give democracy a chance to break the vicious circle of revolution-sovereignty.

Part II

Culture and Representation

Four

Popular Sovereignty and Republican Literature

In basically all modern nation-states, state sovereignty and certain forms of popular sovereignty exist side by side. The relations between them differ substantially in different countries, but in all cases the dynamic between the pair imply neither genuine democracy (that the people are the master of the state) nor pure authoritarianism (that the state is the master of the people). Instead, each political community demonstrates complex mutual influences and the simultaneous existence of the two, depending on the different political conditions. How to conceptualize and realize the multitude of the people into a singular command is also central to many political philosophies.

The people existed prior to the state; indeed, they are the entire reason for the state to exist. In modern societies, where there is no divine force conceptualized as above and beyond the human world, the state, given so much power to rule the people, can only be legitimized by the people themselves, and all popular communities develop their own institutions to maintain order and deliberate public concerns. Modern sovereignty calls the people the master while demanding from the people their total obedience. The common tendency of dichotomizing popular sovereignty and state sovereignty, assuming the former as the embodiment of people's power while the latter is the hegemonic other, is highly problematic.

It is likely that popular sovereignty as a concept and a practice was first formulated and propagated during the French Revolution. Since then, it has been understood as an independent and autonomous power that, in theory, expresses the united will of the citizens, excluding all nongeneralizable interests and admitting only those that contribute to the common good of the people. This classical view, derived from Rousseau, is highly idealistic. Such a view assumes that unmediated consensus can be achieved among the people and that the people are so mature that each of them can be freed from their private interests and think in consideration of others.

But the reality of popular sovereignty is different. Among the people, normative consensus is rare. If such consensus ever happens, it is often secured in advance through tradition and ethos[1] or if there is an obvious common enemy jeopardizing the nation. Instead of a "consensus of all," what we see in most self-proclaimed popular sovereignty is either the "tyranny of the majority" or the propaganda of the dominant group, which might create graver inequality and grievances. Another problematic dimension of popular sovereignty is the assumption that the people are the master of themselves and of everything within the sovereign territory. This might cultivate an exclusive logic of possession as well as encourage the people to believe in their capacity to solve all their problems (sometimes at the expense of others).[2] Such logic inhibits the development of a consciousness of global commons to protect common-pool resources.

We must also remember that the consensus assumed in popular sovereignty can be achieved not only by participatory or representative democracy but also by the public sentiments mobilized by diverse means, such as nationalism and fascism. However much they are related, popular sovereignty is not democracy. Even though universal suffrage can be a method to attain popular sovereignty, so too are populism, the cult of personality, religious identification, and so on. Politicians and regimes of all kinds have relied on their interpretations of popular sovereignty to justify their illiberal policies. Populists are particularly keen on, and capable of, invoking popular sovereignty to describe themselves as "true" democrats owing to their supposedly direct connection to the people.[3] We need not enter a debate about universal definitions. But popular sovereignty has been widely appropriated to support political structures of different kinds, including countries labeled as authoritarian in the West, such as the Islamic Republic of Iran.[4]

The term *popular sovereignty* (*renmin zhuquan* 人民主權 or *zhuquan zaimin* 主權在民) has not gained much currency in twentieth-century China. That said, the related concepts—particularly the term people (*renmin*) as an abstract, unified, and powerful entity—is central to basically all major modern political events and discourses in China. All sovereign regimes or challenging parties claim that they represent and receive their legitimacy from the people, i.e., they are constituted by popular sovereignty. But considering the pluralistic nature of the people and the statist tendency of both the ROC and the PRC, the idea of popular sovereignty might be one of the biggest myths in China's modern politics, where universal suffrage has never been allowed (except in certain exceptional moments such as the Hunan warlord period, when a form of parliamentary democracy was tried out), and the majority of the people never give their direct consent to the ruling regime.

In this chapter we focus on China in the first decades of the twentieth century. When the Qing dynasty transitioned to the new republic, many people found popular sovereignty much more abstract than monarchical sovereignty had been. The people were asked to dramatically transform their political consciousness such that they could form a unified political mandate to designate their own ruler. They were told that they were no longer plebeians to be ruled but the deliberative public called upon to rule themselves. Liberalists like Yan Fu supported the popular sovereignty modeled on Rousseau's social contract theory, and he also argued that state sovereignty must be established on the basis of the endorsement of individual citizens.[5] But constitutionalists such as Kang Youwei and Liang Qichao were more skeptical about the idea of popular sovereignty, as they argued that ordinary Chinese citizens were not up to performing the necessary duties. They promoted a more centralized state sovereignty, emphasizing the importance of central authority in holding the disintegrating nation together.[6]

Here I provide three different sets of intellectual responses to the brand-new idea of popular sovereignty at that time. First, I explore how Sun Yat-sen himself articulated this imported political doctrine within China's own social context. To prove their sovereign legitimacy, both Sun and the Republican warlords had to appropriate the "people" as their political foundation. Second, social scientists also tried to investigate the identity of the Chinese people, who could then be sutured into modern society and became their own rulers. The scientific articulation, which could be considered a form of cultural discourse, was essential as much to modern governance as to citizenry formation. Third, I discuss the representation of the people by the May Fourth writers. Disillusioned by the 1911 Revolution and the poor performance of the new state, these writers, representing the opposite tendency of the former two, questioned whether the people were capable of becoming modern citizens and forming popular sovereignty. The writers even indulged in a self-expression of impotency, blaming China's political predicament on the people's failure to be master of themselves. This might be the most powerful protest challenging the new sovereign logic during this period of disintegration and possibilities.

Sun Yat-sen's Popular Sovereignty

Popular sovereignty, in theory, cannot be substantiated without a people that is capable of expressing collective opinions, exercising solidarity, and participating in political processes. While in reality we can say that this can only be a myth, as a concept it was invented during the eighteenth century by European thinkers. All of Europe was then run by monarchies, which needed only to secure the support of the nobility, the clergy, and the social elites; as such, they did not develop a common culture with their mostly illiterate subjects, who however came to be imagined as the owner of sovereignty.

The "people"—as a unified entity composed of bonded individuals with shared cultural background and political destiny—is clearly a modern invention. It was constructed through heavily edited historical narratives, interpretations of dominant moral-political ideology, or pure fictions, often in the service of nationalism. This modern concept of the people, which first appeared around the time of the French Revolution, has since been employed around the world, endowed with a unified, dignified, confident, and primarily masculine identity. A conjecture equating the people, the nation, and the state became a modern assumption in the twentieth century, allowing the state to further mold the production and enforcement of normative practices among the people. Operating in the name of the people, the state legitimizes itself as the apparatus of the people's self-ruling.

The ruling regime (or the competing forces) is often the most enthusiastic promoter of the idea of the sovereign people, and they need the intellectuals for such discursive construction because it is they who describe, narrate, and explain. Overall, popular sovereignty is less an institutional design than an ideological presentation, although the former cannot be absent. It is in the realm of culture where we can detect most prominently how popular sovereignty is a discursive disarray, where hegemony and contingencies, control and resistance, big words and everyday life meet and clash.

In China, the new Republican and Socialist states, established in 1911 and 1949 after successful revolutions, presented themselves as the expressions of the general will of the people, which existed prior to the states and gave the mandate to the revolutionary parties to build a new apparatus. But the other way around is probably more accurate: that Sun Yat-sen and Mao Zedong conjured the state first, and it was the duty of the state to deliver the nation to the people and the world.[7] The people were obviously there, but the new regimes had to define the people in a way that speak in one voice and support their sovereign state. After the successful revolutions, they both had to invent a popular sovereignty to legitimize the power they now gathered. Indeed, most new sovereign states engage in two activities at the same time: they both prescribe and describe the people, which is both a discursive construction and an empirical reality.

In the previous chapters Sun has been treated primarily as the embodiment of the revolution and the KMT party; here I want to emphasize him as an author, particularly his role in authoring China's first popular sovereignty theory. In 1905, Sun Yat-sen first formulated and advanced three principles—nationalism (*minzu* 民族), popular sovereignty (*minquan* 民權), and people's livelihood (*minsheng* 民生)—as the guiding principles of his state-building blueprint. Since all three terms begin with *min* (people), it was known as "Three Principles of the People" (*Sanmin zhuyi* 三民主義), and it is still the official political doctrine of today's KMT in Taiwan. Some scholars translate *minquan* as "democracy." But in his deliberation of *minquan* he describes it as the successor of *shenquan* 神權 (divine sovereignty) and *junquan* 君權 (monarchic sovereignty), and

I believe popular sovereignty is the most appropriate translation.[8] In Sun's formulation, nationalism and popular sovereignty are closely connected, as they are the pillars of the modern nation-state as it originated in Europe. But he also introduced the third idea of people's welfare to correct the social inequality that he observed in the West. He admitted that he learned all these people-related principles from the West, but he also believed that China could practice them in a way that avoided the problems the West had experienced. Sun also raised the idea of "Division of Authority," differentiating sovereignty (*quan* 權) from power (*neng* 能), asserting that sovereignty belongs to the people, while power belongs to the government.[9] These two concepts can be seen as Sun's rendition of *pouvoir constituant* and *pouvoir constitué*, respectively. Together, the "Three Principles of the People" and the "Division of Authority" formed China's first theory of popular sovereignty.

It is clear that not only Sun but many of his compatriots believed that popular sovereignty as a political ideal could be realized with the right institutional arrangement. According to historian Xiaowei Zheng, the ideas of the renowned constitutional scholar Minobe Tatsukichi 美濃部達吉 (1873–1948), who taught at Tokyo Imperial University but was invited to give lectures specifically to the Chinese students studying at Hōsei University, were instrumental in introducing the philosophy of popular sovereignty to China through these Chinese students studying in Japan.[10] Minobe was among the few major thinkers in Japan at that time who denounced the centralized state and showed a commitment to liberal democracy.[11]

But it would be a mistake to assume that these Chinese revolutionaries considered popular sovereignty only a philosophy. Sun also presented it as a form of folk sentiment that could be mobilized and exploited to achieve specific popular purposes. In a lecture, Sun elaborated his popular sovereignty idea by telling the story of the Gelao Society (Gelaohui 哥老會), a patriotic secret association composed of former members and supporters of the failed Taiping Kingdom. Sun recalled that in the mid-1870s, General Zuo Zongtang 左宗棠 (1812–1885) was given the task of crushing an insurrection in Xinjiang. He failed at first because his army did not listen to him. Most of the soldiers were members of the Gelao Society and identified with its leader, who happened to lead the insurrection Zuo had been asked to stamp out. Upon the advice of his secretary, General Zuo was finally able to gain the trust of his subordinates by himself joining the Gelao Society. Sun argued that the success of General Zuo was due entirely to the power of the Chinese nationalism that the Gelao Society represented.[12] This nationalism was not a state-directed, top-down propaganda; instead, it was made up of the bottom-up voluntary devotions and collaborations among the people for the people. Zuo's final victory proved that state sovereignty must pledge allegiance to popular sovereignty, and this folk nationalism is the powerful sentiment that the state must connect to, cultivate, and promote.

At a time when Sun was advancing a progressive mass politics, this story shows that Sun's concept of popular sovereignty was not constructed out of a pluralistic polity comprising emancipated and autonomous citizens. Instead, Sun's "people" came from the popular masses, bonding with each other via their common nationalist sentiments and urge for collective prosperity. Telling Zuo's success story of appropriating and manipulating the folk sentiment, Sun identified that as the key to his sovereign project. For a similar purpose, Sun also praised Hong Xiuquan 洪秀全 (1814–1864), the leader of the Taiping Rebellion, as an outstanding leader who practiced centralized wealth distribution and brought wealth to his people.[13] Historians have pointed out that the nation-state developed in nineteenth-century Europe was more the outcome of the will of the revolutionary elites to concentrate political power than any political consciousness emanating from below.[14] We might say that Sun and his fellow revolutionaries were also keen on developing their own political power by manipulating the sentiments of the people.

As these accounts show, Sun did not see popular sovereignty as the product of strenuous efforts of mutual enlightenment; rather, it was raw energy already existing among the common, masculine folks to which the state had to gain access and then seek to shape. Sun's sovereign ideology sought to establish both an empirical knowledge and a political design of the people: once we gain knowledge about them, we can shape them. In his telling, the Gelao Society and its members already existed, and General Zuo's tasks were to tap into this popular sovereignty and then steer it to modern state-building. To the new sovereign power, "the people" was not an empty signifier. Instead, the people were both a new regime of knowledge and the most important source of power.

After resigning as Temporary President in 1912, Sun immediately traveled all over China. He went to the country and listened to all kinds of people. But Sun also gave many lectures, hoping to influence those he met. He wanted both to know about his people and to turn them into modern citizens useful for the new republic. Sun was particularly concerned about the development of a national railway system, not only to promote trade but also to develop a modern national community in which people could develop better communication, break down parochial borders, and establish a national identity.[15] To Sun, the railway was as much an advanced technology as a symbol of the unity of the Chinese people which must be built.

It is true that the Warlords period was characterized by political instability. But I have argued that it was also a time of trial and error, projecting many possibilities. There were vigorous discussions about different political systems, and there was a common commitment, even if in name only, to popular sovereignty. For example, though often an empty signifier, the term "the people" was employed by very different narratives for sovereign legitimacy. When the new republic was first formed, Sun announced that "the national citizens comprise the body of the republic, and we cannot forget this principle."[16] In his "Declaration of the President of the Republic of China," delivered in 1913, Yuan Shikai also claimed that the body of the Republic was now the people, whose general wish for happiness was Yuan's prime governance objective.[17] Compared with Sun, Yuan was more interested in Constitutionalism than Nationalism, but common to both ideologies was the central position of the people. Chen Jiongming, the leader of the Guangdong area during the Warlords period, also asserted his full confidence in the Chinese people and considered them capable of creating a truly democratic state.[18]

Many politicians stressed their commitment and loyalty to the people in order to legitimize the new era as more advanced than the imperial dynasties. Yet this exaltation of the people also reflected the new political reality, where popular support, which cannot be proven and remained empty, was the only legitimacy they could claim. But overall, intellectuals during the period were much less interested in discussing an institutional arrangement that would allow popular sovereignty to develop in China than upholding classical Enlightenment concepts such as liberty and equality as well as the contesting ideologies such as socialism and liberalism competing around the world. Many of them actually used the two terms *minquan* and *renquan* 人權 (human rights) as if they were the same.[19] Among Sun Yat-sen's three concepts of the people, popular sovereignty might be the least discussed and developed.

The People: A Fact, a Design, or Simply a Saying?

Popular sovereignty also implies an epistemological order, which must be deciphered for both an effective modern governance and the citizens' self-recognition. First, the modern state must learn to govern the people in such a way that would lead the people to be satisfied with and trust the government. Second, the subjects themselves also need to gain knowledge and an awareness of themselves to exercise popular sovereignty. To achieve these goals, Republican scholars began to introduce new techniques of social survey research that they had learned from the West to develop a knowledge of the Chinese people. But most importantly, it is also the "claim" of such scientific knowledge that marks the modern times. The social sciences might be primarily methods, but in the context of governance they are also a declaration to convince both people and the government of the sovereign legitimacy.

This was particularly obvious after 1927, when the KMT finally united the country and set out to build a modern sovereign state. At that time, an enormous volume of social statistics was being published.[20] The new social scientists seized the opportunity to develop a new epistemological order by producing facts about Chinese society.[21] Sociologist Franklin C. H. Lee (Li Jinghan 李景漢) (1895–1986) and others initiated the "Chinese Social Survey Movement" (*Zhongguo shehui diaocha yundong* 中國社會調查運動) in 1927.[22] The term *social survey* was used to differentiate itself from the institutionalized sociological studies emphasizing objectivity and methods of behavioral sciences. The goal of social survey, according to Li and his peers, was to serve social needs and to obtain useful information to develop better governance. They emphasized direct observation of social life, and the researchers tasked themselves with offering practical recommendations to the government on family, welfare, population, and other social problems. Their overarching goal was to understand the actual living conditions of individuals and communities.

These initial studies were driven primarily by missionary and American funding. But soon the KMT government became much more active in supporting this research. Textbooks were written and university curricula were standardized, and the media also publicized related research and ideas. The state also founded the Academia Sinica, the major assignment of which was to implement large-scale social research for the benefit of policymaking.[23] Competitive methods and philosophies were also developed. Lee and his followers developed a new type of research named "community survey" (*shequ diaocha* 社區調查) to emphasize targeted studies of discrete communities, particularly those in rural areas, to contrast with macro sociological studies. Major intellectuals such as Liang Shuming 梁漱溟 (1893–1988) and Fei Xiaotong 費孝通 (1910–2005) were keen supporters of this movement, and their works were particularly influential among young intellectuals with leftist inclinations, some of whom would then contribute related knowledge and discussions to the development of the Communist Party. There were also many investigations and surveys designed to understand ethnic minorities.

To achieve a new multicultural sovereignty, the post-1927 government was compelled to create a new epistemology about its ethnic citizens. Some scholars explained China's current difficulties as partly the result of its "racial problems." The state therefore commissioned studies about the cultural and biological makeup of the different ethnic groups.[24] The abstract idea that race is a system of modern knowledge drove many concrete efforts to establish new knowledge precisely to support that abstract idea. They believed that China needed to gain a knowledge of the racial bodies, defined by scientific descriptions of bodily features and intellectual aptitude, and advanced ways to improve the quality of the Chinese people as a whole. Eugenics was central to this discussion, and birth control and population improvement were widely held among intellectuals as central to the modern nation-state building.[25]

Others emphasized the urgency of the state to construct the modern citizenry so that the population of China could match, or exceed, the achievements of those in Western countries. The state believed that modern nationals needed to be strong in modern knowledge, physical capacity, and collaborative skills. It was widely shared among intellectuals that the only way for China to survive the international competition was to improve the civil and professional quality of the population through education. The traditional curriculum had to be completely replaced with modern syllabi and knowledge. On top of the regular subjects, students were taught a variety of other topics, including hygiene, scouting, etiquette, and military skills as parts of the comprehensive modern citizenship training.[26]

If the new knowledge regime described above was still anchored primarily in rational thinking, there was also much discussion about more abstract cultural manners and civility: what the Chinese should wear, how they should greet each other, what kinds of everyday expressions should be used, and so on. By observing the new rules of apparel and etiquette, individuals could present themselves as members of a modern community.[27] For the first time in China's history, the state also entered the people's private sphere of childbirth and childrearing in the name of cultivating desirable citizens to rule the country. Motherhood was a particular concern, to make sure women could reproduce a new generation of the modern Chinese people. There was also the emerging discourse of separation of work and home under industrialization, so the urbanite was fed with the rhetoric of a "culture of domesticity," which indirectly allowed the state and the public to enter homes to supervise the reproduction and parenting process.[28] Instead of inviting individuals to leave their private sphere to enter the public political realm, this new citizen movement encouraged the state to police the domestic sphere.

Such knowledge of the people, and the expectations that derived therefrom, were so important to a new republic whose legitimacy could only come from the people. For the first time in China's history, the ordinary people were considered both the subject and the object of sovereignty. The state had to gain knowledge about its people, which was presented as source of its sovereign legitimacy, while the people also needed to become aware of themselves.

Literary Representations of the People

However much the discourse of popular sovereignty dominated the mainstream political rhetoric in China at the beginning of the century, the concept was already highly controversial in Europe. The anxiety about popular sovereignty was particularly evident in late nineteenth- and early twentieth-century Germany, which witnessed the difficult transition of the nation from the formation of the German Empire in 1871 to the establishment of the Weimar Republic in 1919. The many political problems produced by new and experimental parliamentary politics during this period prompted major thinkers—from Leopold von Ranke to Friedrich Nietzsche to Max Weber to Carl Schmitt—to cast doubt on popular sovereignty. Regardless of their own aims, these thinkers agreed that such sovereignty seemed to encourage herd instincts and blunt clashes of interests instead of engendering the promised democracy.[29]

Republican China could not avoid these problems, and many critics began to doubt the ability of the people to be the sovereign owner. As the Chinese government transitioned from imperial rule to partial democracy, some republican politicians and thinkers began to detect the latter's political ineffectiveness and re-emphasized the importance of leadership and authority, advocating a greater role for moral reform.[30] Many intellectuals, from Zhang Dongsun to Hu Shi, were also suspicious of popular sovereignty, and they were skeptical—if not downright cynical—about the political readiness of both the state and the people to enter the modern world. But most of them still promoted democracy over dictatorship and believed that the Chinese people could learn through the practices.[31]

Core to the political predicament was the quality of the people. There were incessant debates about whether it was government or culture that was most crucial for promoting modernization and reform. Many believed in institutions more than they did culture: Chen Duxiu, for example, abandoned his earlier May Fourth belief that the transformation of culture was a prerequisite for the transformation of the political order, and in 1921 he co-founded the CCP with the conviction that the most urgent task for China was the formation of a new communist state led by the working class.[32] But many more emphasized culture, and they believed that what China needed was not a new political regime but rather the re-engineering of the Chinese "soul." To many prominent Chinese thinkers, the human mind is more important than socio-political structure for achieving a genuine democracy. There was an enormous drive of iconoclastic energy in the field of culture with the hope of improving the populace to qualify for popular sovereignty

The New Culture Movement could be dated back to the establishment of new literary magazines, by Liang Qichao and his peers, in Japan and China at the turn of the twentieth century. These magazines promoted the use of vernacular Chinese language to depict and discuss the modern lives of the Chinese people. Their supporters believed that a new language was essential to bring the new nation into being.

The May Fourth Movement, which could also be seen as the second phase of the New Culture movement, was a spontaneous cultural revolution. It was initiated primarily by widespread protests spearheaded by university students after China signed the 1919 Treaty of Versailles that ended World War I; this act transferred a part of China's Shandong territory from a defeated Germany to Japan, rather than returning the territory to Chinese administration. In other words, the May Fourth Movement emerged directly out of a sovereignty concern, although the critical energies quickly moved to the realm of culture to locate the deep-rooted cause of the political crisis.

The New Life Movement in the 1930s was also politically driven—but this time by the ruling regime. The Republican government, worried that the national culture was increasingly dominated by left-wing thinkers, promoted its own civil campaign that aimed to steer the national culture toward its right-wing position. The New Life Movement was primarily a conservative project, with an agenda to protect traditional Chinese morality while synthesizing Christian values, hoping to provide China with a modern moral and social order.

These three cultural campaigns differed in content and form, but they all invested utilitarian values in culture. Cultural revolution was considered so important because it contributed to the important political projects: anti-monarchic revolution, anti-imperialist struggles, and anti-leftist campaigns. It was also believed that the people had to acquire a new mentality and worldview, without which a genuine popular sovereignty could not be achieved. But generally speaking, the Republican government had little success in appropriating culture for its own use.

The KMT also had some interest in using art and literature to mold the desirable modern nationals and to galvanize their identification. This was especially true after national unification in 1927, when the new Nanjing government wanted to cleanse the communist ideology already spreading throughout the culture. Like the left, the right also fostered a nationalist art and literature that cultivated national belonging and appealed to the people. The KMT cultural apparatus, modeling itself after fascism, denied class differences and promoted a national spirit that demanded one heart and one voice of the entire people.[33] It also launched a cultural campaign promoting the "Arts of the Three Principles of People" and implemented a national censorship apparatus directed against those cultural products deemed unwelcome by the regime. But this KMT cultural campaign did not gain much traction among the public. The idea of the "Arts of the Three Principles of People" was used primarily by state media, such as *Central Daily News* (*Zhongyang ribao* 中央日報), and it did not succeed in attracting cultural workers to produce any propaganda works. Instead of promoting a new Republican literature that supported the state, the campaign ended up focusing on attacking left-wing authors and their works.[34]

In fact, by the time the KMT finally gained nominal control of the entire nation in 1928, it was too late—too late to launch national propaganda campaigns effective enough to turn the tide. By that time, the cultural scene had already been widely penetrated by anti-KMT sentiment. A new generation of intellectuals influenced by left-wing thinking came of age in the late 1920s, and many were completely disillusioned by the ruling regime. Instead, they were attracted to a loose sense of international socialism. Here, I want to shift the focus from state-engineered projects to responses of these intellectuals, and I discuss how the cultural milieu of the 1920s constructed a sturdy barricade preventing the KMT sovereign ideology from infiltrating the more progressive young intellectuals.

The unreadiness of the people for democracy was a common conviction among intellectuals across a wide cultural and political spectrum at that time. Predictably, conservative writers argued that the popular political discourses of the time, which included the masses in the political process, were dangerous. They believed that there had to be a long process of training for the Chinese citizenry to be able to participate responsibly in the democratic process, and China's modernization must first rely on well-educated elites.[35] The progressive side also distrusted the masses. The May Fourth iconoclasts were doubtful about both the elites and the ordinary people. These writers did not seem to care much about state sovereignty, probably because the state was too weak, and they were mostly concerned about the people. However, the people were not depicted as innocent masses waiting to be rescued; instead, they were blamed for the current political desperation. If the May Fourth Movement was motivated by the urgent need to re-engineer the soul of the Chinese people, we might say that it turned out to be more successful at articulating their desperation instead of pointing a way out.

Before we read these Republican literatures more carefully, we should remember that this cultural and political pessimism contrasted greatly with the late Qing culture. Intellectuals in the late nineteenth century were called upon to offer their opinions by the Qing court through the various "Reform of Governance" campaigns. But many of them had given up on the earlier practice of reaching the court through high-ranking patrons. Instead, they chose the more popular form of the novel, which was published in serialized form in newly established newspapers and journals outside the court's control.[36] This led to the rise of the "political novel": while many of these novels showed their support for top-down reform, a considerable number displayed their identification with the revolutionaries.

Consider, for example, one of the most famous and esteemed late Qing novels, *Flower in the Sea of Retribution* (1903).[37] It loosely follows the life of the courtesan Fu Caiyun (who was modeled after a real person, Sai Jinhua 賽金花 (1872–1936)) to showcase major political happenings of the 1860s to the 1900s. This novel presents more than two hundred characters that echo real historical figures. Moreover, it brings together many originally unrelated political figures and events—which readers would have come across in the newspapers—in ways that relate to each other. This approach effectively reinforced the coherent unity of China as a political community. The novel also presents the political events of Qing China on an extensive world stage, punctuated by major international events and exquisite depictions of the social hypocrisy of the Qing's political upper echelons. Because of the way the novel offers an organic identity to China as a political and civic nation on such an extensive scale, we might say that this is the first fiction to present China as a modern sovereign nation, also witnessing the inevitable downfall of an ailing empire. From the prostitutes in Shanghai to Empress Cixi in the imperial palaces, from a Nihilist assassin in Russia to sophisticated Guangdong revolutionaries, everyone in the novel is, directly or indirectly, connected to the fall of a dynasty.

Another famous example that shows the direct interaction between politics and literature is Liang Qichao's 1902 "The Future of New China."[38] After the failure of the Hundred Days' Reform (1898), Liang realized that China's political reform could not be successful without the people becoming mature enough to exercise their popular sovereignty. Therefore, in 1902, he launched the literary journal *New Fiction*; in the inaugural editorial, he wrote a now-famous line "to renew a people, we must first renew their fictions."[39] He encouraged the new generation of intellectuals to use fiction for both pedagogical and political purposes. As an example, Liang published his novella "The Future of New China"

in *New Fiction*: it records the arguments between two fictional characters who support constitutional monarchy and republican revolution,
respectively. The two characters, although constantly contesting their
political differences, were also deeply connected by their common devotion to reviving Chinese culture and the Chinese nation.

Such direct reference to politics found in late Qing novels would
soon fall into oblivion. Instead, the new May Fourth writers cared more
about whether the Chinese people could rescue themselves from their
suffocating culture and depraved society. The "quality" of the people
became the nexus of many discussions and representations during the
Republican period. Some critics argued that there was already an advanced culture developing in the urban area. Timothy Tingfang Lew, a
famous intellectual who had just returned to Shanghai after spending
ten years in the United States, expressed his awe at the sophistication
of Shanghai's culture in 1921. One evening, roaming through the city, he
collected forty-seven magazines. "I found that there were more up-to-
date things discussed and a wider range of opinions expressed in those
magazines than any combination of forty-seven magazines picked up
from an American newspaper stand would contain," he wrote.[40] It might
have been an exaggeration, but there was an optimism among some Chinese people that they were capable of becoming modern citizens.

But the dominant view, I must say, was less rosy. Many writers blamed
Chinese culture for the allegedly second-rate people. We can find such
implications in the works of major republican writers, from Fu Sinian
傅斯年 (1896–1950) and Pan Guangdan 潘光旦 (1899–1967) to Lu Xun 魯迅
(1881–1936) and Hu Shi. They were able to find many ways to explain
in their essays or novels the selfish and uncooperative character of the
Chinese people, and they attributed such servile personality traits to
the circular historical structure of traditional monarchy and even China's regional weather and geography.[41] Many of them also criticized the
Confucian culture as the root cause of the failure of Western democracy in China. For example, Hu Shi criticized the way Confucianism was
transformed from a philosophy into a religion, such that the individuals
had to be totally obedient to their family and ancestors.[42] Overall, it was
widely agreed that the kind of citizenship idealized in the West could
not be cultivated within a Confucian society, which China still was.

Such pessimism was particularly widespread among the May Fourth
writers, who were often described as the "Romantic Generation"

because they were heavily influenced by Western romantic literature, and their works were saturated with the sensuality of self-pity and self-indulgence. In the West, the Romantic writers rebelled against the Enlightenment by privileging passion over reason, nature over culture, human desire over technological advancement. We certainly can find similar traits in their Chinese counterparts. As Leo Ou-fan Lee describes the May Fourth writers, "The many high-sounding abstractions such as freedom, beauty, and truth are but emotional ideals springing from ebullient minds seized in the delirium of action."[43]

Compared with their late Qing predecessors, the May Fourth writers were disillusioned by the political idealism and rationalism of the previous revolutionaries. Instead of directly commenting on the current political structures and debates, many new writers conceptualized politics in more private terms, focusing on how the deep structure of Chinese culture had been internalized in individual characters. There was an unspoken frustration that popular sovereignty was a lie and that the people were simply incapable of democracy. For example, Lu Xun wrote, "I thought I was the slave before the revolution. Quickly after the revolution, I realized that I was cheated by the slaves to become their slaves. To me, many citizens of the Republic are in fact the enemies of the Republic."[44] Many May Fourth writers were deeply agonized and shared Lu Xun's revelation: not only had the revolution betrayed the people, but the people had also not lived up to the expectations of the revolution.

Let us take a closer look at the works of Lu Xun and Yu Dafu 郁達夫 (1896–1945). Both writers exemplified the generation's widely shared doubts about China as a modern sovereign state and the Chinese people as modern citizens.

Representations of Political Impotence

Instead of portraying heroes, Lu Xun, particularly in his early novellas, was devoted to characters who are weak, frustrated, indecisive, and incapable of change. They are mostly victims of the oppressive Chinese culture, humiliated and injured, indirectly reflecting the overall May Fourth sensibility. They include Ah Q in "The Story of Ah Q" (1921), Xianglin's wife in "Blessings" (1924), the Hua family in "Medicine" (1919), Kong Yiji in the story of the same name (1919), and the narrator and Runtu in "My Old Home" (1921). These docile and unfit citizens reflect Lu Xun's desperation over China's democratic future. Unlike the young intellectuals who aspire to lead the country to modernization found abundantly in late Qing novels, or the "people" to be seen in the socialist literature who are masters of the new nation, Lu Xun's commoners are too trapped—within their social hierarchy and their personal suffering—to enter modernity. They tend to be narrow-minded and selfish, indifferent and timid. They prefer to be spectators instead of actors, and they choose to follow and not to lead. Cursed by their culture, they are members of the herd, or they live simply to continue a dead ancestry. For those few capable of self-reflection, they are incapable of action and do not have the courage to fight back. Their existence explained and signaled the backwardness of the culture and the people, who must undergo drastic reform in order to be qualified as modern citizens: the legitimate representative of popular sovereignty.

For example, "Medicine" depicts Little-bolt, a young man suffering from tuberculosis whose parents try everything they can to cure his illness.[45] Their last resort is to buy a steamed bread roll, which costs them a fortune; it has been soaked with the fresh blood of the young revolutionary, Xia Yu, who has just been executed. The bun does not save Little-bolt's life; instead, at the end of the story, Xia Yu and Little-bolt are found buried next to each other. The two young men, although they have never met, are mirror images of each other. This is most clearly shown in the last scene, when their mothers meet each other during their visit to their sons' graves. Xia Yu is killed by his own uncle, who informed on him, while Little-bolt is so sick that he could only be manipulated by his parents. They are not able to be masters of themselves, because the older generation simply suffocated them to death. In a most direct way, they are victims of the adult world, and they are too frail to be the hope of the nation.

We can find another pair of young men in another famous short story "Hometown."[46] The narrator is the kind-hearted son of a landlord, who developed a genuine friendship with his plebian friend Runtu when they grew up together. Many years later, he realizes he has the chance to go back to his old home, and he looks forward to meeting Runtu again. But the narrator is quickly overwhelmed by the unbridgeable distance between them once they meet. In the narrator's memory, Runtu was a happy, knowledgeable, articulate, and lively figure. But the adult Runtu has become dull, burdened by his heavy family responsibilities and his daily struggles to make ends meet. Since the narrator has imagined

Runtu as representing the best part of his "old home," he is completely disillusioned. Now he can find no anchor to connect himself with his homeland, or even his nation. Again, both the narrator and Runtu, like Little-bolt and Xia Yu in "Medicine," are condemned by their society. Where is the bright future promised by the revolution?

As some critics have pointed out, Lu Xun's literature is characterized by the incessant process of self-negation and self-renewal.[47] Through his writing, Lu Xun calls attention to the political uselessness of literature and his characters. We might call him cynical, but his core condemnation could be interpreted as attempts to de-fetishize popular sovereignty and discourage vested parties from appropriating the abstract idea of the people to serve their purposes. The depiction of these useless figures, in other words, could also be a highly political act, revealing the hypocrisy of the popular sovereignty claims in the ruling ideology. His writings often reference an uncontaminated childhood, attesting to the Romantic tendency of his thinking. In contrast, he is clearly angry with the adult world. His writings might not suggest how China could be otherwise, but Lu Xun encourages readers to reflect on their own impotence. As literary expressions, his outcry of desperation is clearly more powerful than any easy articulation of hope.

It is true that many late Qing/early Republican intellectuals preached an "elite nationalism" to the common people, suggesting a clear epistemological hierarchy between the teachers and the taught.[48] But the May Fourth writers did not necessarily see themselves as elite; they tended to be unsure of themselves, crippled by their sense of impotency to lead the masses. While Lu Xun did not superimpose himself directly on the characters, many of his fellow writers did. We can observe much regret and shame in those figures that functioned as embodiments of the authors themselves. At that time, many May Fourth writers were newly exposed to psychoanalysis. This explains why many were obsessed over psychologically dissecting themselves in their attempts to articulate the Chinese individual, who is both a prototype of the race and a radically irreducible atomic human. These self-depictions, perhaps, demonstrate even more powerfully how these writers were not convinced of the new sovereign power. In this vein, the most representative fiction might be the famous novella "Sinking" (Chenlun 沉淪) by Yu Dafu, which—like Lu Xun's "The Story of Ah Q"—is considered one of the founding modern works of fiction in China.

Yu wrote the piece in Tokyo in 1921, and the work became vastly popular and controversial once published. The protagonist of the novella is a twenty-one-year-old Chinese student studying in Japan, with clear autobiographical echoes of the writer himself. This is primarily a psychological story, featuring the inner struggles and self-dialogue of the male protagonist. His father died when he was three, and his education was constantly disturbed by all kinds of political unrest. He was finally sent to Japan for education by his elder brother, himself a struggling official. Thinking about sex all the time, he dislikes his Japanese and Chinese schoolmates in Tokyo and only wants to read literature on his own. The sentimental protagonist hates himself and everyone else, and he is particularly angry at the Japanese for looking down on him, although the racist humiliations are mostly the result of his thoughts rather than concrete experiences. He then moves to "City N" for college. In a motel, he masturbates and spies on the daughter of the motel owner as she takes a shower, while his psychological state deteriorates. He breaks with his brother, settles in a remote cottage, and visits a brothel. Yu ends the novella with the protagonist's agony: "O China, my China, you are the cause of my death! . . . I wish you could become rich and strong soon! . . . Many, many of your children are still suffering."[49] Yu connects the character's debasement with that of China, and the suicide of the narrator is a protest against a failed nation.

Yu the writer seems to be both sympathetic to and critical of the protagonist in "Sinking," who keeps connecting his own deprivation with his national identity, attributing his personal failure to the weakness of his own country. The protagonist craves sex and love, but he is shameful of the ways that he satisfies his need for the former and is too timid to pursue the latter. He is both egoistic and so self-abased that he becomes frustrated about life in general. He seems to keep asking if he is to blame or if his country is to blame.

The reality faced by the character and Yu was disappointing indeed. Yu was very critical of the corrupt political world in post-revolutionary China, as seen in Yu's other works, such as the short story "Kongxu" 空虚 (Emptiness) (1922) and the essay "Guangzhou shiqing" 廣州事情 (Matters in Guangzhou) (1927). There are connections between the character's mental breakdown and the author's nationalism, while the anemic nation is also associated with the inability of the male figure to survive.[50] If Chinese sovereignty is always presented in masculine and patriarchal terms, Yu's male anxiety of impotency could be seen as a direct challenge to the prevalent sovereign discourse.

In "Sinking," the protagonist is aware of both his personal self and his national self, overwhelmed by his intense emotions while also struggling to be in control of both. We do not know from the story whether or not the protagonist commits suicide, and his mumbling monologue can be seen as a poetic response of himself to himself. But it is this deep anxiety to reach one's inner self through aesthetic means that makes Yu's work so politically ambitious. By choosing death through a poetic voice, this act can also be read as an indirect celebration of the will of the individual. This could also be an alternative project to the state-engineered popular sovereignty by highlighting not only the uniqueness but also the inarticulation of the individuals involved.

The May Fourth writers did not show much interest in the "Three Principles of the People," nor did they directly challenge the discourses of nationalism, popular sovereignty, and welfare. Most of the May Fourth writers were nationalists, due mostly to China's vulnerability to Western imperialism and partly to their own experiences of racism abroad, as many of these writers studied in Japan and felt discriminated against due to their Chinese identity.[51] But they were most disappointed with their people and their government in a failing democracy. They believed that the conservatism of this ancient country naturally cultivates ailing citizens. Their simultaneous identification with nationalism, individualism, and romanticism did not reconcile, and this partly explains their frustration about the mutual corruption between the individual and the collective, shown most desperately in the protagonist in "Sinking" who chooses suicide as a way out.

To me, though, what characterizes these examples of May Fourth literature is less a cultural determinism (that the Chinese people were inherently depraved) than a political consciousness of the urgency of the birth of genuine popular sovereignty. Like their revolutionary predecessors, the May Fourth generation suggests a sense of gravity that if the Chinese people cannot become proper citizens quickly enough, the culture and the country will disappear forever. But their political consciousness was also decidedly new to the time. For the first time, Chinese intellectuals and writers assigned ordinary individuals, instead of the Confucian scholar-officials or revolutionary elites, with the role of guiding their sovereign. For the first time, they also viewed ordinary people as responsible for the political wellbeing of the state. The Chinese people might not qualify for such a task yet, but this awareness was clearly revolutionary. Variations of this same set of questions would continue to surface again and again, becoming one of the most central intellectual questions in modern and contemporary China. Such deep self-reflection was, and has remained, indispensable for China's continual political modernization.

———

Although not clearly articulated, popular sovereignty was certainly a key political concern of the late Qing and Republican period. Although Sun Yat-sen's theory of "Three Principles of the People" consecrated popular sovereignty as the ruling ideology of Republican China, it was more rhetoric than reality. Intellectuals responded to this empty promise of popular sovereignty by providing knowledge and criticism. On the one hand, the social scientists aspired to educate the people and the state along an Enlightenment path. More soberly, the writers realized its impossibility through the depiction of utter desperation. We observe a genuine anxiety about sovereignty in their literature, in terms of the ability of both the self and the state to attain the common good. We can hardly find any characters that measure up to the Rousseauian political actors; instead, in the May Fourth literature we see the abundant portrayal of the impotency, idiosyncrasy, and noncompliance of the Chinese individuals.

Such distrust of popular sovereignty put two social tendencies of the time on display. First, the writers were disappointed with both the political reality and their fellows, and they also displayed a lack of political will. The negative and critical positions held by the modern Chinese writers concurred with the self-assumed social roles of their Western counterparts, showing a radical departure from the traditional utilitarian ideology assumed by Confucian scholars. But the writers' frustrations should not be seen as a complete rejection of popular sovereignty; hope is the most powerful when people are in genuine desperation.

Second—probably against the intentions of the authors—this distrust in the people directly sanctioned statism, since the state could always claim that it was the people who had refused to become the masters of the country. The writers displayed their pessimism about the willfulness and capacity of the general people to provide political leadership and to solve difficult political problems together. While this awareness is what makes this literature so powerful, it also sanctions the state to appoint itself the task of bringing a new citizenship under its tutorage. With a people that presumably failed to enter the public realm, the state justified its role as the shepherd in an extended presence, as already discussed in chapter 3.

This gloomy atmosphere would change when a new generation of leftist writers came of age in the 1930s; they would enthusiastically support radical social change and express their best hopes for popular sovereignty.[52] This progressive cultural milieu would be reinforced after 1949 and move to the next level, when popular sovereignty would become the mass line. In turn, the socialist intellectuals would effectively be incorporated into the propaganda machine celebrating the new sovereignty, also depleting the critical power of the May Fourth writers.

Five

Territorial Sovereignty and Socialist Landscape Paintings

In the future China will remember Mao Zedong not only as an epoch-making political leader but also as an influential Romantic poet. Instead of following his May Fourth compatriots by writing in modern Chinese, Mao dwelled in the classical lyrical style, which he found more powerful in glorifying revolution and depicting the beauty of nature. Consider the first lines of what is probably his most famous poem, "Snow, Adopted After the Tune of Chin Yuan Chun" 沁園春·雪 (1936):

North country scene	北國風光,
A hundred leagues locked in ice	千里冰封,
A thousand leagues of whirling snow.	萬里雪飄。
Both sides of the Great Wall	望長城內外,
One single white immensity.	惟餘莽莽;
The Yellow River's swift current	大河上下,
Is stilled from end to end.	頓失滔滔。
The mountains dance like silver snakes	山舞銀蛇,

And the highlands charge like wax-hued elephants,	原馳蠟象，
Vying with Heaven in stature.	欲與天公試比高。
On a fine day, the land,	須晴日，
Clad in white, adorned in red,	看紅裝素裹，
Grows more enchanting.	分外妖嬈。
This land (jiangshan) so rich in beauty	江山如此多嬌，
Has made countless heroes bow in homage.[1]	引無數英雄競折腰。

This poem depicts the beauty of northern China, adorned by the glistening snow and ice on the mountains and the river flowing down the hills, so our imaginations can wander from the Great Wall to the Yellow River, transcending mountains and plateaus. These breathtaking scenes of *jiangshan* 江山, which literally means "river and mountain," are so diverse and spectacular that they "made countless heroes bow in homage." From here the poem goes on to narrate that it is due to such incredible territorial beauty that major founding monarchs in China's history, such as the First Emperor of Qin, Emperor Wu of Han, and Genghis Khan, were induced to fight for sovereign power. Implicitly, these countless heroes also include Mao himself, who was then a forty-three-year-old CCP leader who had just successfully led his army to settle in Yan'an after the dreadful Long March.

Thirteen years later, Mao finally fulfilled this "widely shared" dream of conquering the *jiangshan*. Accompanying the CCP's ascension to sovereignty was the political demand for both a new national art and a new way to present its sovereignty. This chapter is about the depiction of this new socialist *jiangshan*, which was both a personal fascination of Mao's and an enormous sovereign project. I examine a new genre of national painting developed in the 1950s and 1960s, which I would call "socialist landscape." It is a modern version of *guohua* 國畫 (national painting), infusing the traditional genre of landscape, or *shanshui* 山水 (mountain and water), with the ideology of socialist realism. It was a period when many experiments took place in the art world, featuring different genres, from figures to history, from comic strips to posters, adopted as propaganda. To answer the call of the time, artists made an enormous effort to reshape the style of their art. Due largely to the high esteem *shanshui* has enjoyed in Imperial China since Song, the socialist landscape was a most representative artistic project in the new era, supporting and also defying key ideological missions of the new state.

In the following I focus on exploring the many contradictions embodied in this genre. The genre is unique in a few aspects. First, the painters were cultural elites still powerful as experts and connoisseurs capable of shaping and commanding popular sovereignty, and the new state was attracted by their cultural capital. Another unique feature of this genre is its direct implication with sovereign power, and much effort was devoted to the methods of presenting the new beauty of the sovereign territory. Under the contradictory demands of materialism and romanticism, concrete physical details and revolutionary spirit must be both presented and glorified. Also, it bore both the Maoist mandate of incessant struggle and the sovereign task of providing enthusiasm and optimism.

While the previous chapter focused on popular sovereignty, my emphasis on territorial sovereignty here is meant to remind us of the importance of territory in modern sovereignty—bearing in mind that the people and their land do not need to overlap. I also use this case study to illustrate how the popular voice during the socialist period was effectively appropriated by the state through the mediation of intellectuals. In the previous chapter I illustrated how the May Fourth writers positioned themselves with a distance from both the state and the people. Here I want to show how the socialist intellectuals were assigned the role of aligning the state and the people completely. With the mediation of these cultural workers, state sovereignty and popular sovereignty seem to overlap. The new *jiangshan* depicted by these artists provides us not only with visual access to the spirit of the time, but it can also be a window to understanding the continual success of the PRC propaganda until today.

Let us begin with the idea of Socialist propaganda, which was decidedly new to China.

Art as Propaganda

Jiangshan, or "river and mountain," is a term that has been used in China for thousands of years to refer to both the Chinese territory and the ruling power, a resonant reminder of the inherent connection between sovereignty and territory.[2] *Jiangshan* could be understood as the Chinese version of territorial sovereignty, although the implication of state power in the Chinese term is more subtle. In 2021, when celebrating the CCP's one-hundred-year anniversary, President Xi Jinping said: "People are our *jiangshan*. The CCP fight for the *jiangshan*, guard the *jiangshan*, with the aim of protecting the heart of the people, so that they can lead good lives."[3] Xi's use of *jiangshan* here directly links the state with territory and people, aligning state sovereignty and popular sovereignty.

In both Mao's poem and Xi's speech, *jiangshan* is the national territory aestheticized, moralized, and politicalized. It is primarily a trope, a literary construction referring to a certain aesthetic and political sublime embodied in the topography of the broadly defined Chinese areas. For the modern state, the bounded national territory is its most important fixed asset: while people might come and go, every inch of the sovereign land is rigidly marked and guarded within the current nation-state system. While *jiangshan* also implies the political regime controlling the territory, it describes a looser sense of space beyond political borders, bearing upon the wonder of Mother Nature, which does not necessarily honor artificial boundaries and human-made meanings. The term vividly demonstrates the many meanings associated with the aestheticization of sovereign territory in the Chinese context.

The PRC was not the first modern regime in China to aestheticize its territory for political purposes; its immediate predecessor, the Republican state, had already engaged in similar attempts. Having learned from other fascist governments' efforts how to galvanize the people's nationalist identification, the KMT government also understood the political values of aesthetics. Despite its deep entanglement in internal and external wars, the government made an effort to promote a new imagination of a unified country as strong and beautiful.

Such efforts can be seen, for example, in state-sponsored projects such as "South-eastern Scenic Tours." Artists, writers, and photographers were invited to take part in national sightseeing tours to produce artworks depicting the beauty of the picturesque landscape and the latest accomplishments of the nation in transportation—particularly the railway.[4] When the Dunhuang caves art was first discovered, the KMT government—despite being occupied with fighting the dreadful Second Sino-Japanese War—expended the extra effort to set up the Dunhuang Academy at the edge of the Gobi Desert and organize artists and critics to travel to the northwestern hinterland.[5] The purpose was to showcase China's historical grandeur and territorial immensity. But these efforts remained scattered and failed to generate a larger movement to impact society.

The CCP, following up on these initial attempts and also learning from the Soviet example, relied heavily on propaganda to aestheticize the new nation and gauge identification. Needless to say, the wholehearted participation of the artists and writers was particularly important in such tasks, which largely explained the far better effects the socialist propaganda achieved than its Republican predecessor could.

The CCP Central Committee's Publicity Department (or Central Propaganda Department, *Zhongxuanbu* 中宣部), which was set up in 1924, was modeled after its counterpart in the Soviet Union. In 1941, during World War II, the CCP officially assigned the Department the tasks of leadership and censorship related to theory, opinion, education, culture, and the arts as parts of its war efforts. Entering the socialist period, the tasks of the Central Propaganda Department expanded further. It began to supervise not only activities directly related to ideology and culture but also all kinds of mass organizations in China, ranging from trade unions to artists' associations, as well as the party branches in state and non-state bureaucracies. The Central Propaganda Department became a central organ of the mass line policy, and the nationwide networks of its different levels functioned as bridges between the party and the people.[6] Unsurprisingly, it enjoyed extensive powers and reach within society, while the artists and writers became the paramount tools of the party's ambitions in directing the people's "thought reform."

Under the direct guidance of the Propaganda Department, hierarchical networks of cultural workers' associations were quickly formed, headed by the China Federation of Literary and Art Circles (*Zhongguo wenlian* 中國文聯). Most of the artists and writers were compelled to join at least one of the branches. The state also successfully incorporated almost all existing cultural enterprises into its apparatus, providing cultural workers with stable incomes and working environments. A few remained independent. But since almost all publication and exhibition venues were now controlled by the state, all cultural workers had to yield to the new political demands if they wanted to remain active.

The state also proactively commissioned artists and writers to produce works of different genres to glorify the new country. The socialist landscape might be the most symbolic in this regard because it embodies the successful socialist reform of a supposedly regressive artform. In the first decade of socialist rule, the new regime oscillated between rejecting the socialist landscape altogether as reactionary and relying on it as the most effective means to glorify the grandeur of the new sovereign power. This indecision reveals the general predicament of many new sovereigns: how to use the traditional form that appeals to the masses to sanction the new power without conferring the old ideologies that they are intended to replace?

In the early 1950s, many critics were indeed negative about the *guohua* style of painting.[7] At first, it was historical oil paintings (following the Soviet Union) that were chosen to represent the new nation. Many works were commissioned by the state to record the major events and battles leading to CCP sovereignty. However, as the Sino-Soviet relationship soured in the mid-1950s, Mao became eager to develop China's own national path. Major campaigns began to promote the readoption of traditional arts as a venue for propaganda. Critics started to assert that Chinese artistic styles were capable of depicting modern social relations after all. In fact, some began to argue that all cultural forms could be credited as socialist arts as long as they conveyed the right messages. Thus, the traditional art form was retained, but it had to go through a major reform in which the arts were reinvigorated through Marxist materialism.[8]

An epitome of this project was the "New *Guohua* Campaign" 新國畫運動, which tasked painters to modernize traditional literati paintings by portraying the new landscape of the new republic.[9] As the name of this campaign suggested, the idea of "new *guohua*"—an art form belonging to the new Chinese people—was put forward to be differentiated from old *guohua*, which had belonged exclusively to the old ruling class.[10] While the May Fourth writers felt urged to express one's inner voice and sense of impotence as an allegory of the dysfunctional polity, the socialist painters could only be the chorus of the state singing in unison. Praise for the new political regime and messages of national pride flooded these arts. The traditional landscape form and techniques were largely retained, but new elements and messages were added. We see, for example, the profuse use of the color red and the sporadic inclusion of modern objects, such as modern vehicles and cable lines, with the purpose of conjuring a new socialist—and aestheticized—sovereignty. We also find opposite sentiments, such as the ancient Daoist human-nature harmony and the new Maoist ideology of struggles, coexisting in these paintings, presenting the national territory with the new sovereign ideology through traditional media. Many of the works produced then are now considered "Red Classics," attracting record-high prices.

This movement had two waves. The socialist reformation of *guohua* was advanced as early as 1949,[11] and it was the painters themselves who played an active role in the first phase. One of the most important events undertaken by the painters themselves was the 1954 Jiangnan painting tour and the resulting exhibition by painters Li Keran 李可染 (1907–1989), Zhang Ding 張仃 (1917–2010), and Luo Ming 羅銘 (1912–1998).[12] This exhibition attracted a flurry of essays, written by prominent artists, critics, and art collectives.[13] Their opinions differed, and they criticized each other as not sufficiently revolutionary. But overall they endorsed the capability of *guohua* to depict life in a way that honored materialism. Many critics were truly excited by these landscape paintings, which experimented with color, shading, still life, and linear perspectives not commonly found in traditional literati paintings. The critics also took this opportunity to discuss how the new socialist visual art could benefit from merging the Chinese styles and the materialist worldview.

The propaganda heat initiated by the Great Leap Forward conjured a second wave of the New *Guohua* Campaign. This time the state was much more proactive, encouraging the *guohua* painters to produce magnificent landscape paintings to promote the nationalist spirit, agitating and justifying the hugely demanding production projects occurring all over the country. Having already gone through a turbulent history of criticism and reformation in the early 1950s, the new *guohua* finally qualified as both modern and Chinese and thus useful to the new sovereign.

Selected paintings were quickly appropriated by the state for propaganda purposes.[14] Critics commented on them in major newspapers and magazines; many high-profile nationwide exhibition tours were organized; and they were also published widely as propaganda posters. These paintings were taught at schools, hung in museums, and served as backdrops at major state events. Fu Baoshi 傅抱石 (1904–1965), for example, was not only given leadership positions in major art institutions, he was also appointed a representative of the Chinese People's Political Consultative Conference (CPPCC) and invited to give a keynote speech there, which was in turn published in major newspapers such as the *People's Daily* and *Xinhua Daily*. His works became a major component of a new art institution: high-profile academic workshops were organized to discuss and praise his works, and artists had to learn from his works to justify their own.[15] With such noisy trumpeting of the state bureaucratic apparatus, these works also entered the people's everyday life. Citizens were invited to identify with the new nation through these spectacular visions.

Most importantly, the artists, through their aesthetic labor, could also cleanse their bourgeois background and traditional training by savoring the revolutionary spirit of the new nation. Holding fast to the state's campaign of "Going up the Mountains and Down to the Villages," the art institutions in the mid-1950s began to encourage the artists to embed themselves among the people, in order to understand the new social relations.[16] But between "Going up to the Mountain" and "Down to the Village," most of the master artists preferred the former over the latter. While mountains and villages are two relevant, if not equivalent, geographical categories in the state discourse, their differences were more obvious to the artists, as they pertained to two different destinations and genres. Going down to the villages, artists were required to depict the new rural life of the people realistically, and they had to ruminate what the new political environment had brought the people. Instead, by going up the mountain, the traditionally trained *guohua* artists could indulge in the aesthetics they enjoyed.

Most of the elite *guohua* painters, unless they were identified as rightists, did not need to be sent down to the villages but retained the rights to continue their practices. They had to show their reform by depicting the new socialist landscape, mostly as advancement from the largely traditional landscape of mountains and waters. Overall, most artists appreciated the opportunity to draw in the mountain areas so they could leave their—often over-politicized—institutions and focus on their art. The landscape was indeed considered a "safer" genre.[17] By dwelling in grand landscape, many of the artists succeeded in avoiding the criticisms directed at them in their work units as much as they could.

There were plenty of peasant paintings, which were guided, touched up, or sometimes entirely produced by "sent-down" professional artists as part of the popularization and politicization of art.[18] But they were always presented as the peasants' own productions, with the aim of celebrating the people's native creativity now realized and unleashed in the new Maoist environment. These paintings demonstrated the way the peasants were thriving and approving of the new sovereignty in turn. Such self-realization and self-apprehension of one's full potentiality is presented as the greatest proof of popular sovereignty, in which the intellectuals, theoretically, had no role to play.

However, it was also a time most difficult to detect the voice and taste of the people, as both the market and the criticism were largely controlled by the state. Most of the mass media created space to encourage their readers and audience to voice their opinions, supervise the governments, and comment on larger cultural and social issues. Many letters were indeed sent to various art journals penned by ordinary citizens commenting on artworks and trends. For example, the most important art journal of the time, *Meishu* 美術 (Arts), featured an important column "Qunzhong yijian" 群眾意見 (Opinions from the people), which pledged to collect discussions to guide national art development. But a majority of them evaluated pieces and phenomena closely aligned with the official ideology. The political intent of these so-called people's opinions was so obvious that we do not know how much they represented "the people" or even who exactly "the people" were. We must not equate propaganda with popular sovereignty, but in Maoist China propaganda was indeed so carefully crafted by the state to both fake and resemble popular sovereignty.

Concreteness and Abstraction

Compared to medieval Europe, where there was a complicated visual and spatial economy to substantiate royal sovereignty,[19] the Chinese iconography of the imperial power was much less elaborate; instead, they relied primarily on localized rituals and Confucian teaching in oral form to maintain the political hierarchy. Traditional landscape paintings, infused with both Daoist transcendence and Confucian propriety, might be the only visual tool available to help visualize the dynamics between imperial prowess and the larger cosmic order that nature embodies.

As mentioned, the traditional *Tianxia* imperialist sovereignty is very different from that of the modern sovereignty based on the nation-state, in the sense that the former does not refer to a concrete national border. Instead, such a traditional Chinese ideology, like those of many other premodern empires, operated within a vast geopolitical world, and not all the claimed regions were directly controlled by China's political center. Even in the Qing dynasty, where cartography was already rather sophisticated, the court deliberately kept certain external borders unspecified, partly to imply continual expansion and defense.[20] The Manchu rulers also deliberately allowed the semi-autonomy of certain border areas, with the aim of discouraging the different ethnic groups to mingle and maintaining the mutual distrust among the groups to prevent them from collaborating to fight the Manchu.[21] But entering the modern times, core to state sovereignty is a fixed state border, allowing those inside to exercise jurisdictional independence while preventing outsiders from interfering with their autonomy.

The aestheticized idea of modern *jiangshan* could be seen as one combining both the loose *Tianxia* structure, in which the border is vague, and the modern nation-state, in which the border is fixed. In Mao's poem, the "*jiangshan* so rich in beauty" refers to both the *Tianxia* imagination of the imperial borderless world and the modern nation-state. The abstraction of universal beauty, the concreteness of the national border, and a cultural China inherited from the past are all implied in both Mao's poems and these socialist paintings. Describing sovereign territory, *jiangshan* also implies an object status, as a thing constantly luring individuals and parties to fight and possess, attracting and legitimizing the ambitious to lay hold of it.

One of the most representative paintings in this regard is *The Land So Rich in Beauty* (江山如此多嬌 *Jiangshan ruci duojiao*) (1959), commissioned by the Central Government to decorate the newly constructed Great Hall of the People in Beijing (Figure 5.1). Fu Baoshi and Guan Shanyue 關山月 (1912–2000), the two master painters representing the mid-region Jinling School and the southern Lingnan School, were tasked to incorporate the scenery of different regions all over the country into one painting, which could visualize the essence of that famous poetic line by Mao. As Fu recalled, many leaders gave advice during the production process, and Vice Premier Chen Yi instructed the two artists that the painting must include:

> Scenes inside and outside the Great Wall, top and bottom of the Yellow River. It also needs to show the East Sea, the snow mountain of the frontier, the verdant and lush land south of

Yangtze River. Geographically it must include scenes of the
East, West, South, and North, as well as the seasons of Spring,
Summer, Autumn, and Winter . . .[22]

With such clear instructions, the two painters assimilated iconic images
of different parts of China into one composition, with the southern
landscape in the foreground on the right and the sublime mountains
and snow scenes in the background on the left, supervised and bright-
ened by the sun—embodying Mao—in the upper righthand corner. Iconic
images of the different regions of the country, such as the Great Wall,
the Yellow River, the Yangtze River, Mount Everest, and Mount Tai, could
be identified. The ways in which they are depicted are also so abstract
that transcends all sovereign boundaries.

While most socialist landscape paintings tend to emphasize realism,
this painting is quite particular in the genre in trying to so abstractly,
within one frame, assemble discrete elements that are physically very
remote from each other. It was probably due to the impossible political mission given to the painters that they had to render the national
jiangshan at such a high level of abstraction. But the coexistence of the

FIGURE 5.1:   *Fu Baoshi and Guan Shanyue,* Jiangshan ruci duojiao
江山如此多嬌 *(The land so rich in beauty)* (1959), guohua

concrete and the abstract is central to the Chinese traditional aesthetics. This traditional style coincidentally facilitates the state's highest propaganda apparatus to edit China's key landscape symbols to become a new sovereign landscape.

The Chinese landscape has in fact been oscillating between realism and spiritualism. When the genre was first developed during the Tang dynasty, artists emphasized both the observation of physical reality and their personal expression.[23] But gradually attention shifted to the spiritual dimensions, and Chinese painters rarely left their studios to produce landscape paintings. Many of the Ming and Qing artists were more interested in capturing or mimicking the spirits of nature and the previous masterworks instead of creating new pieces based on the changing reality.

The new collective quest of modernity reversed this tendency, and the emphasis on science and objectivity drew many late Qing and early Republican artists and educators to return to drawing from life (*xiesheng* 寫生), in contrast to the free expressions (*xieyi* 寫意) tradition that the *shanshui* genre had privileged.[24] A new generation of *guohua* painters, some of whom had received extensive training in Western painting, began to adopt drawing from life to produce new landscapes as a way to challenge the stagnant academic style and to visualize a new modern state. While it was generally believed that sketching from life was a central part of Western painting in line with modern epistemology, some Chinese artists also believed that there was a tradition of outdoor painting in China that had disappeared and that the Western art methods could help them to revive this lost legacy.[25]

Entering the socialist period, a dominant national aesthetics gradually came into being, meant to fulfill different missions. On the one hand, the traditional aesthetic power of *xieyi* was deemed effective to gauge the identification of the people, particularly the educated; on the other hand, socialist realism was poised to become the dominant ideology, emphasizing representations as real. Between the two forces, life drawing of landscape seemed to be able to meander between the realistic approach and the aestheticization of politics. A comparable set of tensions can be detected in socialist photography, which was utilized as eyewitness testimony of the revolutionary achievement but was also tirelessly staged to exhibit the "correct" and "beautified" history.[26] Given the task of merging aesthetics and politics, the abstract and the concrete, both the conceptual *guohua* paintings and the photographs struggled to incorporate their opposite. While adding performances to the journalistic photographs helped the medium to become effective propaganda, the new landscape paintings conveyed the political sublime by combining concrete *jiangshan* details and the transcendental spirit of revolution.

Touring around the major scenic and revolutionary sites for observational drawing became a politically correct way to produce modern Chinese landscape, elevating the artists' political consciousness while giving them opportunities to escape the political criticisms directed at them in their work units. Local governments or official art institutions were eager to organize such artist tours, while other artists went their own way. Almost all major *guohua* artists participated in one or more of these trips, and they praised observational drawing as a more "scientific" method to approach all subject matter. They toured the country during the Great Famine, producing splendid landscape paintings to celebrate the regime; today, critics condemn them for turning a blind eye to people's suffering, which they must have observed everywhere.[27] During the most intense period of politicization, the majority of the people—including the master painters—tried to escape politics.

Two master *guohua* painters—Li Keran and Fu Baoshi—were instrumental in promoting these artists' tours. Between 1954 and 1959, Li took four extensive trips and traveled both inside and outside the country.[28] These four trips took seventeen months, and resulted in more than two hundred single-sheet inkbrush sketches as well as numerous pen-and-pencil sketches.[29] Li argued that the reform of *guohua* must begin with the artists' deep immersion in human life (*shenghuo* 生活). But he was clearly more interested in nature than human life. We seldom see human beings interacting among themselves or with the environment in these paintings. When he mentions life, he seems simply to anthropomorphize nature: Li made the famous statement that, as an artist of the new China, he vowed to produce biographies of the country's mountains and rivers (為祖國山河立傳).[30]

Fu Baoshi began to promote drawing from life tours in 1953. At the peak of his career, he also organized a very high-profile artist working tour in September 1960, following the inauguration of the Jiangsu Chinese Painting Institute, of which he was the director. Over the course of three months, this group of thirteen *guohua* artists engaged in the so-called "Twenty-three Thousand Li of Life Sketching," visiting more than a dozen places in six provinces: Henan, Shaanxi, Sichuan, Hubei, Hunan, and Guangdong. The sites the artists visited included famous mountains, grand and modern construction sites, and the sacred revolutionary areas with the aim of aestheticizing and monumentalizing these sites with revolutionary spirit. In May 1961, the works produced were displayed in a major exhibition, *New Faces of Mountains and Rivers* 山河新貌, in Beijing's National Art Museum of China. It was widely considered the zenith of the New *Guohua* Movement, also consecrating Fu's leader position in the Chinese art world. Ironically, this movement ended up endorsing the elite position of the master painters, in contrast to the popularization of arts that were the main theme of the current cultural policies.

The 1954 trip by Li Keran, Zhang Ding, and Luo Ming covered the Jiangnan area, which has long been one of the most prosperous regions in China and features many favorite sites of literati painters historically. Fu's "Twenty-three Thousand Li of Life Sketching" tour in 1960 also began in the Jiangnan area, though the painters this time traveled further away, to Yan'an in the Northwest, Chongqing in the West, and Guangzhou in the South. But neither trip reached the borderland, and the scenery depicted was still mostly the standard transcendental borderless beauty of *Tianxia*, symbolically "modernized" by scattered images of modern objects such as factory buildings and the national red flag of the PRC.

A set of works that tellingly reveals such dialectics between aesthetic universalism and territorial materiality is Li Keran's *Wanshan Hongbian* 萬山紅遍 (Redness all over ten thousand mountains); its title again was taken from another of Mao's poems, "Changsha, adopted after the tune of Chin Yuan Chun" 沁園春·長沙. Portraying different parts of the country that he visited—the first two were painted in Conghua, Guangdong, while the other five depicted Beijing's Western Hills—Li produced seven versions under the same title in the 1962–1964 period (Figures 5.2 and 5.3). All seven works were directly or indirectly commissioned by the state, and the artist was provided with the best conditions to produce the art, including being stationed in resorts reserved for state leaders. The last painting was commissioned to celebrate the fifteenth anniversary of the state's formation, establishing a direct relationship between state sovereignty and the monumental landscape.

Although these paintings represent two completely different regions of China, their compositions and styles are strikingly similar: in each,

FIGURE 5.2: *Li Keran, Wanshan Hongbian 2* 萬山紅遍 2 (*Redness all over ten thousand mountains 2*) (1963), guohua (*produced in Conghua, Guangdong*)

FIGURE 5.3: *Li Keran, Wanshan Hongbian 7* 萬山紅遍 7 *(Redness all over ten thousand mountains 7) (1964), guohua (produced in Beijing)*

the entire scene is saturated with different layers of redness crowded with mountains and trees, punctuated by the running stream on the left and scattered houses on the right. We find hardly any empty space in this set of paintings, in contrast to traditional landscape painting, which emphasizes the dynamics between materials and emptiness, between the visible and the invisible. The painter also introduces the effects of sunlight, techniques borrowed from Western paintings, to give a spiritual aura to the scene. The central layers of the mountain are designed to produce a sense of height competition, increasing the grandiosity of the landscape. With the trees in the front, houses in the lower middle ground, and the mountains shooting up in the back, the entire scene becomes a monument, composed of strong vertical patterns yet comfortably anchored on the ground. The running stream maintains the traditional Chinese spirit and provides enlivening dynamism, while the blurring background suggests an infinite space. The saturating use of redness cannot be politically naïve, and the painter's celebration of the ownership of the landscape by the "red" regime is beyond doubt.

Being described as "life-paintings," these paintings, however, were driven by a strong mindset of design, such that the concrete physical details could be abstracted into a generic form that represents the new socialist landscape. Li was clearly following the traditional Chinese aesthetics that emphasized abstract spirit more than concrete forms. But in the political atmosphere of the time, he also needed to proclaim his commitment to materialism, which the method of "drawing from life" was able to realize. In these paintings we observe his efforts of creating a universal rendition of the Chinese revolutionary spirit in dialectical terms. By combining his actual presence and observations of the visible landscape and the invisible revolutionary spirit endowed by the new ruling power, Li fulfilled the demand of his times both to be loyal to the theory of dialectical materialism and to produce effective propaganda.[31]

We should note that both Li Keran and Fu Baoshi were originally famous figure painters, but they gave up on figure painting and focused on landscape upon the state's call in the mid-1950s. There were painters interested in people's everyday life, such as Lin Fengmian 林風眠 (1900–1991), Feng Zikai 豐子愷 (1898–1975), and Huang Zhou 黄冑 (1925–1997), and there were also portrayals of the scenery of the frontier, most famously the oil paintings of Dong Xiwen 董希文 (1914–1973). But the traditional landscape masters, who were given the highest state honor both in the imperial times and in Maoist China, were decidedly devoted to the traditional style of *shanshui*. The genre's symbolization of power persists until today. Consider the huge landscape paintings hanging in the Great Hall of the People in Beijing: they witnessed and presided over the most important meetings of the state in the name of the so-called "mountains and rivers of the ancestral nation" (*zuguo shanhe* 祖國山河). Along the imperial tradition established since the Song dynasty, the landscape was tasked to glorify the sovereign power.

We might say that socialist artists trod the same path of their imperial predecessors, producing monumental landscape paintings as symbols of the power of the ruling regime. While Marxist materialism was the *de jure* ideology, the aura of romanticism and glorification of power dominated these Red Classics, with almost no mention of the class struggle or real social conditions. Many of the *guohua* painters titled their works with lines from Mao's poems, and Fu Baoshi reportedly produced more than two hundred paintings based on Mao's lines. Legitimized by Mao's poems, *guohua* painters could maintain a clear distance from the people's everyday life and be submerged in the abstract and the transcendence of nature and revolution.

Struggles and Harmony

The landscape is attractive not only because it is beautiful but also because it is a significant part of our lives. For centuries, the Chinese artists revered the mountains as spiritual: larger than life, the mountains provided the Chinese people with a sense of visible spirituality. Down the hill, the Chinese farmers considered their farmland their most important asset. They developed a deep corporeal connection with the land, which provided them with food and shelter. Their cropland also symbolized the connection from their ancestors to their offspring, which most directly manifested the family's sovereignty, which was particularly important in China.

Historically, the landowning families had always enjoyed the right to exploit, and the duty to sustain, the natural resources within what they considered to be their communal territories. Moreover, these rights to land and resources, based more on an individual's ancestors than birth or residence, demarcated the insiders from the outsiders.[32] As an agricultural nation, China has bred a social system based largely on the integrity of extended families, in which land is passed from generation to generation, and the land includes not only the soil but also the associated natural resources such as water and weather. Most importantly, the land provided people not only with food and shelter but also with a lineage: the land buried their ancestors, nurtured them, and witnessed the birth of their offspring. Ancestor-worship could easily be translated into a vague form of land-worship. After all, the land was the most powerful symbol of one's descent.

This economy was radically challenged by the new socialist ideology, replacing the family with the state as the property owner. Generally speaking, the modern state has a right to territorial jurisdiction, so it can make laws within its territory to regulate the people and the things there, according to what supposedly are the best interests of the people. Often, the state also claims resource rights, so it can profit from the resources in their territories.[33] This engenders an exclusionary logic, denying non-citizens access to both the territories and the natural resources situated there.[34] This idea of state sovereignty is further reinforced by socialism, which sanctions the state to appropriate, manage, or alter the environment within its territory in the name of the people. While the liberal state confers property rights to the citizens, the socialist state masters all economic activities. Ironically, there are striking similarities in the socialist logic of state sovereignty and of property rights: the state has all the rights to determine what can be done with its possession.

Mao, following orthodox Marxism, argued that the state would ultimately wither away when China reached a state of communist utopia. But the state apparatus was considered essential during the socialist period, for it could lead the people and steer history to the right track before reaching utopian communism.[35] Only the socialist state, benefited by the scientific knowledge of historical materialism, could represent the total interests of the people in a neutral, objective, and comprehensive manner. As such, the socialist state assumed the sole power in distributing and redistributing the wealth of the nation among the people, and it also possessed the power to coordinate the economic activities within the state.

The sovereign should not be understood simply as the authority that exercises power over a territory and a people, but it coordinates the two domains of land and population sophisticatedly so that they are mutually intertwined yet not completely overlapping—consider extraterritorial-ity, such that the sovereign power is exercised at the point of connection between the physical environment and the human species, allowing one sovereignty to legitimize the other.[36] Let us examine more carefully the case in Socialist China. The state was founded on the violent land reform campaigns of the 1950s, usurping land from landlords through aggressive mass movements and redistributing them land to the poor. This redistri-bution process allowed the new state to gain access to and shape the social structure in this huge country down to the village level.[37] These activi-ties fulfilled the party's promises for wealth redistribution through class struggle, galvanizing the identification of many people and also usurping the political power that had been possessed by the original landowners. While countless ordinary peasants now had their land to plow, the state's influence also successfully reached the vast rural population.

After the Land Reform came the Agricultural Cooperative Movement, which organized individual rural households into larger and larger co-operatives so that the government could more effectively control the village economy and coordinate the economic activities of the entire nation. The Great Leap Forward also became possible, as the state could now extract as much as it could from agriculture to finance the industri-alization of the nation. In the name of benefiting the entire population, this policy was clearly discriminatory against the rural population. The "poor and blank" Maoist subjects were agitated to perform the most fe-rocious struggles to make the most impossible historical changes.[38] The culmination of this collectivization project and idealistic modernization operation was the Great Famine (1959–1961), which according to various estimates led to tens of millions of premature deaths.[39] This "difficult period," according to the official account, was caused primarily by a na-tionwide drought. While the actual death toll continues to be debated fiercely, it is now generally agreed that the famine was linked to the many policies and political mistakes made as part of the Great Leap Forward.[40]

On the other hand, the socialist state sometimes treated its land and environment as its enemy, engaging in many ill-conceived engineer-ing projects that resulted in deforestation, desertification, and river damage.[41] The emphasis on growth has indeed been a prominent fea-ture of the PRC sovereignty, particularly in the socialist period when the land was considered an instrument to be employed, or a resource to be exploited, to assist the Chinese people as a whole to flourish. The *jiangshan* was thus not only an aesthetic site of transcendental identification but also a reservoir of resources to be exploited so that the people could be elevated from poverty.

In the new socialist landscape paintings, we seldom see human struggles. Indeed, the traditional *shanshui* tends not to emphasize human actions, aggrandizing the sublimity of the landscape by minimizing or trivializing human activities. The abstract principles of traditional arts such as *qi* 氣 (air), *shen* 神 (spirit), or *yun* 韻 (tone) tend to understate human activities. But these modern paintings, despite the premise that they are highly critical of idealism, do not explore how we constitute and inhabit the world in a corporial sense. These so-called materialist works do not present the ways in which we take part in an intimate space that we share with other human beings, living things, and objects. The landscape exists in aloofness, and we do not easily observe a sense of human spatial connectedness.

In their own lifeworld, the *guohua* painters had their own share of political struggles. On the one hand, chaos was everywhere in people's lives, while class struggle was also at the center of the sovereign ideology. Asked to depict contemporary political life, the socialist artists struggled to come to terms with the meanings of struggles. On the other hand, socialist realism, which was motivated more by the sovereign interests of promoting people's submission than by the Marxist ideology of class struggles, tends to celebrate the bright side of society. This is, ironically, reinforced by the traditional Daoist-Confucian themes of serenity and consonance, which have been so central to the genre of landscape.

As a result, while the landscape is the site of concrete physical struggles, the socialist landscape paintings also present the land as a source of pure, inexhaustible spiritual value, where the people live with each other in harmony. Trying to come to terms with such conflicts, some painters chose to handle the struggles by depicting them as humans' efforts to overcome nature. In these new landscape paintings, the land is portrayed as both a source of sublime beauty and a site of resources that can be extracted by the Chinese people, while also injecting transcendental socialist and nationalist sentiments to turn them into effective propaganda.

The most interesting example in this regard might be Fu Baoshi's *Meidu zhuangguan* 煤都壯觀 (Spectacular view of the coal capital) (1964) (Figure 5.4), one of the two paintings he produced for the Fushun Coal Mines.[42]

FIGURE 5.4: *Fu Baoshi*, Meidu zhuangguan 煤都壯觀 (*Spectacular view of the coal capital*) (1964), guohua

In 1961, Fu Baoshi was invited to tour the northeast to produce paintings of the region. One of the sites he visited was the Fushun 撫順 mine, the most productive coal mine in the country. Fu produced a few sketches of its West field during the visit, and the painting was finalized in 1964. When he was first shown the scene by the local party secretary, Fu admitted he was reluctant to paint what he saw because he found the scene "not paintable" (*buruhua* 不入畫, basically means ugly). But he was touched when hearing the party secretary cry, "Look at the coal, how beautiful the color is!" Fu was astonished by this comment, and he decided to paint and capture this sentiment.[43]

Fu's job was to turn this idealistic exclamation into materialist art. But he explained that, despite the extensive experimentation he undertook with the ink to capture the texture of coal, it was difficult to portray the robustness of the coal mine and the grandeur of the mining enterprises. He found it very difficult to produce the layers of blackness with the black ink, and he was not satisfied with the final product. This painting captures the scene from a distance, with carts on the bottom roads following one after the other to carry the coal away. We also see the roads circling up the coal hills, which echo the secluded cold mountains featured in traditional landscape. There are basically no people, and the vehicles and machines depicted are clearly dwarfed by the grand landscape. As Fu wrote in the caption, "The most touching part [of this scenery] is that while there are supposedly over ten thousand workers working in the field, I do not see many people from this perspective. Really spectacular."[44] Following his landscape painting predecessors, Fu tried to demonstrate how the heroic landscape dominated and outshone the individual human beings.

The Fushun Coal Mine, which had been in operation since the late nineteenth century, was taken over by the Japanese army after 1905. The mine, along with all of Manchuria, was returned to the KMT government in 1945 after World War II, and it quickly became the most productive coal mine in the country. But decades of destructive mining techniques also caused frequent landslides that threatened to sink the city. There is reason to believe that the Maoist style of mining, which cut dangerously steep angles into the ground without refilling, was an ecological disaster.[45] An observer recalled his first impression of the mine when he was first sent there to work:

> When we first arrived the South field [of Fushun Coal Mine], the entire hill was composed of barren rocks, and there was no single grass. Not even mosses and lichen can be found. We could only see smoke coming out from the shale, with sparkling flames here and there. Being a child who grew up in the countryside, I was so sad seeing how the land was destroyed by industrial exploitation.[46]

Although this man recalled his first impression of the South field of the mine, not the West field Fu portrayed, it is interesting that he came away with the opposite impression of Fu's. Instead of echoing the unpleasant feeling of an ordinary worker, Fu's painting aimed to capture the Party Secretary's exclamation of the "beauty" of coal. But Fu also indirectly admitted that such industrialization projects produced a scene disagreeable to most definitions of beauty. Arguably, Fu did not romanticize the scene and turn it into a spirited mountain; rather, he used crude brush strokes to present the truncated smoke lingering along the slope, and he presented the roads in ways that cut the mountain into pieces. Overall, the relative murkiness of the vision and the uneven texture of coal fields do not put one in the mind of traditional Chinese aesthetic concepts. Fu produced an ambiguous landscape that could hardly be called "beautiful." In fact, he admitted that he expended much effort in painting the mines without producing a work that was to his satisfaction. This unique style was not followed up by Fu or other painters. As such, this painting remains peculiar artistic testimony of this ambitious state project.

The dominant ideology of Maoism emphasizes antagonism and struggle, which were embodied in those paintings celebrating industrial achievements and humanity's conquest of nature. But most of the paintings in the genre were also expected to follow the traditional Chinese aesthetics with transcendental values of tranquility, spirituality, and harmony, on the one hand, and socialist realism that portrays the bright side of society, on the other. Being the propaganda of a young regime, these paintings were tasked with presenting the people's struggle as the means to achieve social harmony embedded in the utopian socialist end without any hint of criticism to current society.

Privileging the state project of development, these paintings also reveal the unfortunate fact that the meanings of use value and reification in Socialist China were never fully explored; instead, the discourse of development dominated Chinese Marxism as a political ideology. Such sovereign desire prevented reflection on the complex relation among human, nature, and society. An exclusive logic of territorial sovereignty also blinded society from seeing how we might share our common goods not only with outsiders but also with future generations, both in China and other places. While we might not be able to do away with the idea of sovereignty, we could develop a fairer version: we might learn to see, among other things, the Earth as living space instead of a field of beautified and commodified natural resources waiting to be exploited. We are entitled to have sovereign rights to the land we occupy, but the rights should not be totalistic. We also have a duty to cultivate and preserve the land as a universal good for common flourishing.[47]

Landscape and Power

Both in China and the West, landscape painting is entangled with power: the scenery being drawn could be conceptualized as the possession of those who commission or own the painting. Or the works are political allegories produced by the artists in lieu of their direct expression of political loyalty. We could also read the formal aspects politically, reflecting how they are meant to glorify and justify the sovereign's power.

In Europe, linear perspective in visual arts was developed in the fifteenth century, around the same time that the rudimentary modern nation-state began to take shape. The political logic of modern sovereignty supported—and was supported by—such single-point perspective of spatial organization of land. These paintings suggested precision of spatial control and unity of territory with a central locus of power.[48] They also engaged a subjective response of those who observed the featured scene.[49] In these seemingly tranquil landscape paintings, both the representations and the referenced physical world are full of political values, synthesizing the landscape into a singular possession.[50]

In China, landscape is also a highly politicized genre. During the Northern Song dynasty (960–1127) the genre of landscape painting rose to its historical peak, driven partly by the court, which actively appropriated the symbolic power of the landscape to glorify itself. This was also made possible by the loyal support of the literati painters. Grand paintings of enormous size were commissioned and placed in specific sites of the court, designed to support its rites and regulations.[51] Meanwhile, the literati also produced landscape paintings on their own, depicting the spirits inherent in a landscape that acquires life and power beyond the human world.[52]

We can say that there have been two opposite, but highly related, strains of ideology attached to Chinese landscape painting since the Song. On the one hand, the literati created paintings to emphasize their own autonomy from the court and therefore their independent critical and intellectual power. On the other hand, the court also appropriated the transcendentality and monumentality of these paintings to glorify the emperor. While the landscape painting was clearly infused with Daoist values, stressing the transcendence of nature over human control, its ideology was also at the same time Confucian, with nature and the human world in their proper place. The seemingly oppositional Daoist literati and Confucian imperial perspectives were two sides of the same elite patriarchal world, displaying either the worlds seen by the literati disillusioned by sovereignty, or the worlds seen by those in power. Needless to say, consolidating the sovereign and the literati perspectives of the landscape was also the male space, as travel and outdoor leisure were restricted to upper-class male members of society, whereas elite women stayed home and, if fortunate enough to be allowed to paint, were restricted to the subject matter of flowers and birds.[53]

Similarly, the Socialist regime gave the *guohua* painters a comparable task, to conjure a beauty that could be used politically, and its aesthetic of grandiosity is clearly masculine. Basically all of the established landscape painters were male, and they spoke the same language of power and heroism. For example, Li Keran vowed to produce biographies for the country's mountains and rivers. Despite this idealism, what we see is only a one-sided political appropriation of the landscape. Lacking any sincere reflection on the interaction between human activities and nature, Li can only depict them in consonance. If these new socialist artworks could be more profoundly materialist—liberating our senses to experience the world anew—they might be able to further open up our sensibility to nature that traditional *shanshui* has already professed and encourage us to reflect on our sovereign desire to control the environment.

But we should not deny that many fine works were produced during this period, characterizing a unique and awkward moment of *guohua* renaissance in modern China, witnessing new techniques and innovative modes of communication. The enormous support of the state played an important role, as it sincerely sought the collaboration of artists, critics, and readers to produce effective propaganda. Indeed, the Maoist state took the arts very seriously. In addition to Mao's true artistic talent and deep affection for the arts, there was an army of intellectuals in the upper Maoist echelon ready to defend the meanings and beauty of the arts along with the sovereignty of the new republic. Senior scholar-officials such as Hu Feng 胡風 (1902–1985), Guo Moruo 郭沫若 (1892–1978), He Qifang 何其芳 (1912–1977), and Wang Zhaowen 王朝聞 (1909–2004) might have been political enemies at times, but they all found ways to interpret the state-sponsored arts as cultural treasures in their respectively convincing ways.

This new socialist intelligentsia, not structurally unlike their Confucian predecessors, formed a strong cultural-political establishment to articulate the splendor and glory of the new nation. But it is an oversimplification to view socialist arts solely as propaganda. This Chinese art establishment was not only statist or socialist; it also inherited the traditional literati connoisseur tradition. As shown in their essays, many of these scholar-officials were sincerely delighted in arts for its own sake, as the arts produced aesthetic enjoyment which might not lead to other purposes. Many of them are also convinced that a new China had already been built, and therefore demanded a new form of aesthetic organization and judgment. However much the art circles were monopolized by state ideology, this consolidated cultural echelon was very effective in promoting arts in the vast country. Art was both propaganda and an end of itself.

———

This chapter and the last are devoted to popular and territorial sovereignty respectively, but I also want to analyze the relations between sovereignty and intellectuals. The previous chapter showed how writers during the Republican period critiqued not only the state but also the Chinese people, doubting their quality and ability to be the master of the new sovereign state. These socially conscious, thoughtful, and independent intellectuals served the role of both criticizing and representing the plural populace of the time. Entering the socialist period, however, the dominant social roles of the intellectuals shifted dramatically, moving from the social edge to the center of power, supporting and glorifying the state and mainstream society.[54] Compared to the ROC, the authority of the new Maoist state was much more secured across society, partly due to the groundwork laid down by these intellectuals and cultural workers, providing the kinds of public opinion and collective sentiments that were congenial to the new political regime.

In both cases, intellectuals were crucial to the formation and articulation of popular sovereignty, whether they are opposed to or sided with state sovereignty. These two chapters show that political power is not only in the hands of those who rule; the intellectuals also hold, convey, and transform power in ways that the sovereign must try to appropriate. While power exists everywhere and flows among people, intellectuals are trained to manipulate and retain power and turn it into productive or destructive energy for others to use. The intellectuals could use the power to secure their own interests, or they could fight power, to create new sites of resistance against social injustice and create new possibilities. The May Fourth intellectuals have largely been considered more respectable than the Socialist intellectuals because of their criticality and social marginality compared to the latter's submission to power. Entering the postsocialist period, the people finally found the means to express themselves directly and massively. In the next chapter we will take leave of the cultural mediators and explore the expression of popular sovereignty in cyberculture.

Six

Economic Sovereignty and
Postsocialist Digital Culture

The CCP has presided over China from 1949 until now. The same party has engineered two completely different, if not opposite, econo-political systems. Before 1979, Socialist China asserted its sovereign legitimacy through its membership and leadership in socialist internationalism, providing the Chinese people the supposedly correct scientific worldview and knowledge of historical development. The same Communist Party in postsocialist China, however, no longer emphasizes its ownership of the universal truth but instead highlights its capacity in providing wealth and peace to the Chinese people. Since the Deng era, the party no longer holds to its knowledge of dialectical materialism, but it emphasizes the PRC state's pragmatism for the benefit of the people. Exercised by the same political party, the PRC's sovereign ideology shifted from politics to economy, from truth to interests.

This de-ideologization was again revised at the dawn of the Xi period. After three decades of constant reorientation and the resultant sea change in people's lives and viewpoints, the current Xi government prioritizes certainty and tradition, which does garner a lot of support. Now the state highlights the sacredness of sovereignty, also asserting the superiority of the Chinese civilization, while continuing to promise economic prosperity to the people. The security of the state and the wealth of the people are now emphasized as mutually constitutive. While neoliberalism is characterized by the retreat of the state in many parts of the world, the Chinese state enters every corner of society, developing pervasive mass surveillance systems to reinforce social norms and collaborating with tech companies to regulate digital communications. At the same time, different kinds of decentralized capitalist activities thrive in society under the supervision of the state.

Today's PRC seems to be able to incorporate the seemingly mutually contradictory neoliberalism and statism, actively intervening and shaping both the market and society while providing peace and prosperity to the people. In return, the people present themselves as increasingly docile and compliant, seeing how the power of the state and the market feed each other. The linchpin of the social contract between the people and the state is economic development. Some might conclude that after 150 years of political modernization in China, state sovereignty seems to be able to line up with popular sovereignty most agreeably.

In the previous two chapters, I discussed how cultural elites responded to the sovereignty constructed by the ruling regimes in the republican and socialist periods. Here, my attention shifts to the ordinary people of today and their responses to the current sovereign power, however indirectly, through their participation in the digital culture. If the former Maoist regime legitimized its sovereign power primarily through mass politicization, and Deng through depoliticization, the current Xi government has shifted back to politics again. But this is a politics promoting both atomization and collectivity, encouraging individual subjects to strive for their economic wellbeing in a neoliberal fashion, while at the same time to be an active political subject supporting the state.

To explore the new dynamics between popular sovereignty and state sovereignty in Xi's China, I present a case study that demonstrates how the people can still express themselves in spite of the state's wishes. Specifically, I focus on a meme that has spread rapidly among Chinese internet users in the last few years: "garlic chives" (*jiucai* 韭菜), an edible plant that grows widely in China. This metaphor is used in contemporary China to refer to those ordinary Chinese people who are constantly induced to participate in all kinds of economic activities but whose investments are destined to be consumed by the establishment. Corresponding with these garlic chives is the sickle (*liandao* 镰刀), a farming tool for harvesting the *jiucai*, as a term to describe the economic and political forces feeding upon the fortunes lost by individual investors.

This popular meme and code word, which has now become a part of the Chinese people's everyday lexicon, shows how Chinese citizens reflect on their social conditions and respond to the ways in which the power of biology, economics, and politics converge on the self. On the one hand, this metaphor suggests a form of self-commodification. In the current neoliberal environment, individuals do not just invest their labor in the market; they also commodify their entire selves—knowledge, creativity, saving, and debt—as forms of capital. Capitalism effectively absorbs the people's energy in their self-thriving, and this energy is then harvested by the paternalistic-biopolitical state for its own growth. On the other hand, the increasing self-commodification also intensifies alienation, which might awaken the people's self-sovereignty, shown most uniquely in the cultural expression of *jiucai*. On one side, then, is sophisticated postsocialist economic sovereignty, and on the other is the people's own awareness and expression of this structure. Together, the *jiucai* metaphor exposes the economic and political meanings of individual Chinese bodies as the foundation of the current PRC sovereign state. The associated tensions offer a new window to enable us to understand popular sovereignty—if it exists—in contemporary China.

Economic Sovereignty and Biopolitics

Given that it is concerned with exchange and circulation, economics tends to traverse national boundaries, and such transnational movements have been further reinforced in the age of globalization. Today, it is impossible to understand economic sovereignty along the lines of territorial sovereignty, as the latter is defined by the state's complete sovereignty within its border, while economic sovereignty could not be possible without recognizing the transnational nature of capital.

The postsocialist PRC has exhibited a special approach to economic sovereignty at a time when communist ideology was systematically replaced by what has become known as state capitalism. Its exploratory form was developed in the 1980s when Deng Xiaoping abandoned Maoist politics. The Deng regime was exceptionally venturesome, and was widely lauded, for its embrace of and adaptability to change. It pioneered the statecraft of "crossing the river by touching the stones," which allowed the state to morph along new challenges. Pragmatism became the state ideology, encouraging the people to meet the world and experiment with new methods.[1]

But the Deng government was also careful not to loosen the party's grip on economics, so China refrained from giving up its state capacity in controlling the financial market. Critics credited Deng's policies for facilitating the PRC to sail through the shock therapy of the 1980s, allowing the socialist economy to be transformed by the market while preventing complete price deregulation and wholesale privatization.[2] The most important legacy Deng left behind might be his 1992 Southern Tour—following three years of Western hostility in response to the Tiananmen Square crackdown—which was widely considered a commitment to developing a Chinese style of capitalism.

Indeed, the PRC is not the only state emphasizing its capacity in protecting itself from the predatory global market. The economic success achieved by East Asia in general since the 1950s has been celebrated as a form of developmental statism. Critics praise the state's capacity for welcoming and engineering global capitalism, without losing the capacity to resolve internal social problems.[3] Many critics are also encouraged by the fact that despite the strong sovereign control, democracy still find room to develop in some of these countries.

During the Jiang Zemin period (1993–2003), China was poised to develop a flexible economic sovereignty, balancing between transnational capital flows and state control. The major event marking the advent of the PRC's comprehensive economic sovereignty policy was China's accession to the World Trade Organization (WTO) in 2001, after fifteen years of negotiation. It was also during this period the term *jingji zhuquan* 經濟主權 (economic sovereignty) first appeared widely in China's news media to demonstrate the state's promise and ability to protect its national economic interest along its accession to the WTO. Willing to change plenty of its socialist policies to adhere to the WTO's regulations, the PRC also recorded tremendous growth in both commodity exports and foreign investments. But the numerous restrictions it placed on capital flows—particularly outflows—also saved China from the unpredictable impacts of the changing world economy.

As is well documented, China has embraced and benefited from global capitalism, while the world economy also makes the most of

China's world factory capacity.[4] The PRC has also been very vocal about its success in protecting its economic autonomy. It proclaims that the country was able to sail through the 2008 global financial crisis because of its strong economic sovereignty, severing itself from the volatile global finance market due to its effective protective system. The term *economic sovereignty* became popular again in the 2019 Sino-US trade war, in which the PRC state accused the United States of invading China's sovereignty by demanding a structural change to its economic system. Ironically, we have also observed how the term has recently been used around the world to criticize the expansionist policies of the PRC in investing in the key industries of other countries. Australian critics, for example, also demand that their state defend its own economic sovereignty against China.[5]

Many of these discussions understand economic sovereignty in terms of territorial sovereignty, that the state has all the power to control the economic activities inside the state border. But this approach is problematic not only because of the transnational nature of capital; the studies of economics, I believe, require an analytic framework featuring facilitation instead of prohibition. For a more effective theoretical investigation, maybe we can learn from "biopolitics."

Biopolitics is a concept that describes how modern governments are legitimized by their ability to promote the prosperity of the people in general; it also reminds us that economic growth and biological growth are highly related. Karl Polanyi was the first to demonstrate that the liberal capitalism developed in the late eighteenth century already assumed a close relationship between the sphere of economics and human's biological nature: biology and economy are governed by the same sets of natural laws, and they are separated from the political sphere.[6] Michel Foucault further theorizes that the biopolitical state not only manages people's lives but it makes each of the lives of the individuals proliferate, giving the subjects the impression that the state serves their natural desire to prosper. This is made possible by the new technology of power over population (such as new social survey methods and techniques to understand and communicate with the national population), such that the government can better establish norms and practices to articulate its alliance with the people.

Biopolitics is so powerful because the state follows and propagates an economic rationality emphasizing freedom and competition, which are supposed to be parts of human nature, turning the sovereign power into an economic-juridical ensemble that aligns with individuals' desire for wealth. This new governmentality, according to Foucault, is nourished by the existing dominant ideology of liberalism and the expanding nature of capitalism. The most important purpose of the state is to support economic growth, while civil society exists to provide the missing social dimensions.[7] Foucault also indicates that this biopower conjoins different existing regimes of power, i.e., sovereignty, discipline, and security, into a new sovereign power capable of controlling the life and death of individuals and collectives.[8] As such, the biological, the economic, and the political become deeply intertwined in this biopolitical governmentality. State governance is guided by a logic of productivity and growth, encouraging the formation of a new political sovereignty that aligns with the people's general material desires. The political actor is replaced by a subject motivated by one's own biological drive, and in a capitalist society this biological drive becomes entirely economic. According to Foucault, these subjects are constantly struggling in the market for the accumulation of social and economic capital, which also facilitates the state to depoliticize them.

Foucault's theorization of neoliberalism—composed of the biological and the economic—is highly relevant to the postsocialist Chinese environment. But his devaluation of political actions also implies an overemphasis of the power of the market and the materialistic, such that the biological/biologized subject is deprived of any higher public morality. Foucault's theory is based on the assumption that the biological and the economic are both caught in a blind drive for development—to which individuals submit. It is true that a person's political consciousness is often fostered by one's own socioeconomic experiences, desires, and frustrations. But Foucault's downplaying of people's public concerns and intersubjectivity, far from providing a way out, risks endorsing the ways this system works.

A close reading of contemporary Chinese economic sovereignty might force us to find ways to expand Foucault's model. In today's China, both the Foucauldian notion of population and the Maoist notion of the people are essential components of the sovereign logic. Both are state constructions: the population is taken care of and assisted by the state for the individuals' material prosperity, while the people are the sovereign subjects who compose and legitimize the state. While the latter is increasingly displaced by the former, core to today's governmentality in China is the careful manipulation of these two notions of the people to align with the state's "Chinese Dream." But again, the individuals are silenced, and there is nowhere to start discussing a popular sovereignty other than modes that are already steered by state sovereignty.

Postsocialist Involution

In general Marxist analysis, the state is often understood as the political organization of the bourgeoisie to serve their economic interests, assuming economics as the base upon which all is built.[9] There seems to be an opposite tendency in postsocialist China: capitalism is only a means for the empowerment of the state, whose security is the be-all and end-all of all state policies.[10] While this Chinese statist neoliberalism has been very successful, we also begin to observe in today's China a unique form of involution, showing this state capitalism might be running out of steam. Economic security is emphasized to justify the inward turn of national economy.

Although the PRC continues to offer itself as the guardian of globalization in the midst of the new round of Sino-US diplomatic tension, a new term, the "great domestic circulation" (國內大循環), appears to signify a major shift of economic policy. The term was first advanced by President Xi in May 2020; two months later, he mentioned it again in a meeting with China's major businesspeople to ask them to refocus on the domestic market: "We must gradually form a new development pattern with the domestic market as the main body, while ensuring that the domestic and international circulations mutually promote each other."[11] Although international trade is still valued, Xi's emphasis on the domestic market demonstrates both his awareness of the global economic downturn and his mistrust of Western countries. China's new economic policies are shifting from globalization back to the national market, an approach some critics have criticized as undoing Deng Xiaoping's "opening up" policies. While still promoting globalization, the Xi government is aware that as certain Western countries are trying to rely less on China for supply, China must learn to rely more on itself for markets.

Observers have praised the Chinese government's pragmatic approach to economic activities. It is true that the PRC has devoted itself to raising the national research and design capacity to help the country's industries to produce high-quality services and knowledge-intensive products. But observers also point out that when it comes to the patents registered in China, these are mostly incremental improvements on previous work. Those advances praised as innovations in China are often geared to adjusting products to suit local tastes; the innovation is primarily based on consumer desires.[12] Scholars of political economy have also demonstrated that China's recent economic growth has been based largely on local competition among towns and cities. Cases of economic success in China are often the result of local bureaucrats being flexible and motivated enough to meet the needs of local firms, while domestic producers actively invest in learning and upgrading to excel in the fierce domestic markets crowded with local and global players.[13] As a result, cutthroat competition in the domestic market is extremely common in China. Such reckless internal competition is becoming more intense as China enters its "great domestic circulation" period, reflected in the sudden popularity of the term *neijuanhua* 内捲化 in China's internet world in the second half of 2020.

In his 1963 book *Agricultural Involution*, anthropologist Clifford Geertz studies the centuries of wet-rice cultivation practices in Indonesia, finding that the repeated and labor-intensive practices did not bring significant technological or political change but instead put the people under more intense labor competition without improving their skills or methods.[14] American historian Philip C. C. Huang first used Geertz's idea of "involution" to describe Chinese rural development in the Yangzi Delta in the Ming-Qing period, which was also characterized by ever-increasing labor input with diminishing marginal returns. In the Chinese translation of the book, the neologism *neijuanhua* is used for Geertz's idea of "involution."[15]

While the term has been used in China for three decades, it suddenly became a buzzword on the Chinese internet in 2020, when globalization slowed down substantially due to COVID and Sino-US trade tensions. The term is now widely used to describe the ferocious rivalry and competition Chinese citizens need to face, with even toddlers in kindergarten exposed to the rhetoric of comparison and competition. As an advertisement for a Chinese cram school warns: "We will nurture your kid if you come. We will nurture the competitors of your kid if you don't come."[16]

In the PRC, people's self-perception of their economic wellbeing is of great significance to the country's state sovereignty. Citizens are encouraged to work hard to climb the economic ladder made possible by the state, and their economic wellbeing in turn justifies their support of the illiberal government. This sovereign logic is built largely on the people's continual desire to benefit from the national and global economy while enjoying some degree of personal freedom sprinkled with a hefty dose of national pride. But the associated labor exploitation, produced by global offshoring enterprises or the domestic gig industry alike, and the enormous privacy invasion, are seldom discussed publicly in China.

The state's draconian control of the COVID pandemic directly roused the people to an awareness of their complete subjection to the state. The PRC government presents itself as the most successful in controlling the pandemic internationally, supported by data showing that China's life expectancy actually increased during the first two COVID years,[17] and many ordinary citizens also took up an active role in collaborating with the state to curb the spread of the virus.[18] According to the data collected in April 2020, Chinese citizens had an overall high level of satisfaction in the central government's performance at that time.[19] But such confidence dissipated little by little, which was observed widely by the citizens themselves (even if the trend never appeared in any official documents), as regional lockdowns, abuses of local governments, and the resultant economic hardships continued. As both the deterioration of the national economy and the curbing of citizens' personal liberty were felt keenly by the ordinary citizens, the state's continual lockdown policies increasingly fell out of touch with reality. Grievances and anger accumulated, first stirred up during the Shanghai lockdown in the summer of 2022 only to later explode nationwide in the "A4 Revolution" in November of the same year. At the same time, the high transmission of the COVID variant Omicron also broke down China's draconian network of preventive policies. Allegedly, millions died, and the youth unemployment rose so high that the state stopped releasing current data.

Involution is only intensifying, as citizens are caught in increasingly severe political control and economic competition. The Xi government, however, is sailing through the tempest confidently, and the sovereign authority seems to be unscathed by the public grievances. This state will likely persist in its centralization of power and strengthening its resolve, along with a censorship system so well-functioning that no organized oppositional voices could be raised. But no government can completely control public opinions, and the people can always find ways to express themselves. While the state is increasingly monopolizing the collective voice of the people, we can still find ways to hear their delicate utterances.

"Garlic Chives" and Economic Subjects

The Chinese people under the Xi reign like calling themselves garlic chives probably because they see a lot of themselves in this plant. The garlic chive (*allium tuberosum*, or Chinese chive) is an extremely adaptive plant capable of enduring both cold and hot weather; it is widely cultivated in different parts of China. It is basically perennial, so once the seeds are planted, they will regrow every year. It is also very easy to manage, to the extent that farmers just need to cut the plants with a sickle, or a sharp mussel shell in some places, when they are tall enough, and the stalk is always sure to grow again. Because it is both easy to plant and nutritious—rich in different kinds of vitamins—garlic chives can be found in many Chinese regional cuisines. Chinese medicine also praises its high medicinal values for treating abdominal pain, diarrhea, hematemesis, snakebite, and asthma. In the West, it is treated primarily as a herb, largely because of its strong garlic flavor and pungent aroma. It is also used in floral arrangements, characterized by its tall and vertical leaves as well as the star-shaped cream-colored small flowers. Ecologically, it is described as an invasive species.

In Chinese culture, garlic chives have long been associated with grassroots, low-end productivity. But *jiucai* first became a trendy term on China's internet around 2010: those investors/traders who lost money in the rapidly expanding stock market were termed *jiucai*. In 2011, a woman who calls herself "Ocean Star Sand" 海星沙, lamenting online how she had lost money repeatedly on the stock market, pleaded for help from fellow netizens for investment strategies. Her appeal received a wide response, with both reproaches and sincere assistance, giving her brief fame as the "Jiucai Girl" 韭菜姑娘. The term *jiucai* soon became a buzzword and went viral, widely used to refer to all those individuals who persistently losing money in investments but never learn their lesson, who maintain a blind faith in their luck or whatever inside tips they receive to beat the market.

As more and more capital floats around the country, China has become a casino, with all kinds of investment opportunities conjured up and shoved onto the markets. They include cryptocurrencies such as Bitcoin and Ethereum, the availability of ever more complex derivative and insurance products, online lending that led to the 2018 P2P crisis,[20] and the trading of a variety of fashionable commodities such as sneakers, designer bags, and even concert tickets. There might be a few lucky investors able to make a fortune, but there are many more losers than winners: many more "garlic chives," that is, than "sickles." There is also a bestselling book titled *The Self-Cultivation of the Garlic Chives*, which was published to provide psychological and strategic tips for succeeding on the stock market.[21] Evidently, the garlic chive is a metaphor of subject formation in contemporary China, used by the Chinese people themselves to mock their voluntary participation in the jungle of greed and brutality.

The term *jiucai* also quickly entered popular culture, with people making up songs and DIY music videos to be uploaded to Douyin, the original Chinese version of TikTok, and other online platforms. There was considerable interest in the "Song of Garlic Chives" (*Jiucai ge* 韭菜歌), which was adapted from a 2002 pop song titled "Endless Charm" 魅力無限 by singer Sun Yue 孫悅.[22] Because there is a line repeating the word "here" (就在 *jiuzai*), netizens turned it into a cover song, supplemented with their own videos, by rephrasing *jiuzai* to *jiucai*: those who are here are *jiucai*. As shown in these self-made videos, this *jiucai* song frenzy is clearly intended to be self-mockery. The videos are often performed by ordinary-looking people singing in a domestic location (often a kitchen) or working environment, suggesting how the ordinary Chinese people are aware of their voluntary submission to the sickles for the sake of survival. Some *jiucai* rap songs were also developed around the cryptocurrency frenzy, mocking the stupidity of the investors and the viciousness of the speculative market.

Interestingly, before the garlic chive became such a popular icon, it had also been appropriated as a human resources management method.[23] An article published in a professional journal for the power generation industries, written by someone affiliated with Zhejiang Zheneng Zhenhai Power Generation Company, promoted his company's development of a "Garlic Chives Method" in human management: it employed a reserve army of cheap trainees, and subjected the existing regular employees to constant contract renewal, so the less capable ones could duly be replaced by the trainees. This method is presumably based on the nature of the garlic chive plant, which must be cut down before it can continue to grow. Zhejiang Zheneng Zhenhai is a state-owned enterprise (SOE), and such companies once provided permanent employment; however, they gradually adopted a policy of contract employment in the first years of the 2000s as a response to the new capitalist environment.

Here, then, the so-called "garlic chives" method is promoted to justify the quick turnaround of contract workers, promising to increase a company's productivity by extracting the productivity of human labor. It is true that the term "Garlic Chives Method" does not seem to have gained popularity in China's human resources domain. But the use of garlic chives as a metaphor for rapid replacement hiring showcases the neoliberal turn of the postsocialist system and reveals the biological side of neoliberalism: human labor is still a vital source of value in late capitalism.

We cannot simply use a traditional Marxist paradigm of a static capitalist-versus-proletarian model to understand China's economy, largely due to the presence of the sovereign state above both of them. The capitalists are often condemned as sickles, but they are also sometimes lamented as garlic chives. This is particularly the case for the privately owned enterprises (POEs) that have been marginalized by SOEs over the last few years, a state policy widely referred as "the progression of SOEs and the regression of POEs" (*guojin mintui* 國進民退).

In 2002, the "Three Represents" theory, credited to Jiang Zemin, was ratified by the CCP to allow capitalists to join the party. This theory also marks the official incorporation of POEs as a legitimate part of the socialist economy. It is estimated that in 2017, POEs contributed 60 percent of China's GDP (compared with 40 percent in 2002), while SOEs only made up 23 percent of national GDP.[24] But in the same year, the Xi Jinping government began to strengthen SOEs by issuing a series of supporting policies and promoting mergers and acquisitions. The state's increasing demand for compliance has become even more obvious since the advent of COVID and the escalation of Sino-US tensions, with Xi making it clear that patriotism is the foremost criterion for Chinese entrepreneurs in such times.[25]

Critics began to describe the state's harvesting of POEs in the manner of garlic chives being cut down by the sickles, with the private capitalists having to sacrifice themselves in the face of state demands. Entrepreneurs as powerful as Jack Ma (a founder of Alibaba Group) or

Ren Zhengfei (founder of Huawei Technologies) must all be subject to the state's exacting control. Both leftists and statists can interpret these actions as responsibilities of the sovereign state to correct China's rampant capitalism and neoliberalism. However, without an independent media and civil society, the market is probably the only viable force in China powerful enough to provide counterbalance to the one-party state, the government of which, after all, is not democratically elected. The legitimacy question so central to state sovereignty is now particularly salient to today's PRC state, which has become so powerful both inside and outside China.

The metaphor of *jiucai* went viral again immediately after Youth Day in 2020. On May 4, the popular online video sharing platform Bilibili (in collaboration with a few other major mass media in China, such as China Central Television, *The Beijing News*, and *Youth Daily*) published a short video titled *To the Rear Waves* (*Zhi houlang* 致後浪), which was sensationally narrated by the famous actor He Bing. In the video, He represents the older generation, celebrating the quality, achievement, and global perspectives of the new generation.[26] As a high-profile state-sponsored campaign, the video—as expected—initially attracted many compliments, but they were quickly followed by a flurry of criticisms, including many derivative and ironic videos produced by the younger generation. Needless to say, many of them quickly disappeared under China's censorship regime. These videos demonstrate the frustrations of younger people, who are all too aware of their precarious situation they occupy: many of them are overworked, underpaid, and sent to Africa for the Belt and Road Initiative.[27] There we also see *jiucai* widely used as a metaphor to represent the younger generation, who are exploited and harvested by the establishment.[28]

Consider just one of these satirical videos, titled *To the Preceding Waves* (*Zhi qianlang* 致前浪). In Chinese, the term "preceding waves" refers to the older generation, corresponding to the "rear waves" which refers to the younger generation. The young narrator talks with direct reference to He Bing, who asserts in the original video *To the Rear Waves*:

> I'm looking at you guys with great envy.
> The wealth, the knowledge, the wisdom, and the art that people have created in thousands of years;
> They are just like gifts for you.

The prosperity of technology, the flourishing of culture, the bustling of cities, the fruits of modern civilization;
They are opened layer by layer, for you to enjoy.

In the satirical video, the narrator goes:

I'm looking at you with great jealousy.
The wealth, land, power, and rhetoric that people have accumulated for thousands of years;
They are like gifts made specifically for you.
Technological prosperity, cultural prosperity, urban prosperity, all the fruits of modern civilization;
You open them layer by layer; you enjoy them alone.

By changing only a few words and the positioning of the narrator, the work of satire turns the logic upside down. In so doing, the video highlights how the establishment manipulates the world for its own benefit, in contrast to the original video's suggestion of the older generation carving a new world where the younger generation will prosper. Moments later, the narrator makes it more explicit how the young people are exploited to support the status quo enjoyed by the older generation. He Bing says:

You are fortunate to live in this era.
But the era is more fortunate
To have people like you.

The counterpart responses by alluding to the garlic chives:

You are fortunate to meet garlic chives like us.
But we garlic chives are very unfortunate
to meet people like you.

The original video strives to show the establishment's love for and dedication to the younger generation—or perhaps it represents a biopolitical rhetoric of the sovereign power to address its subject so that the younger generation should be grateful for the auspices and protection provided by the older generation. But the satirical video thoroughly rebuked its rhetoric.

In terms of images, other than some documentary and media footage to visualize people's actual livelihoods, the producer of the satirical video also uses plenty of clips from the movie *King of Comedy* (1999), directed and performed by Stephen Chow. This is a Hong Kong black comedy that tells the story of a devoted actor who tries hard but cannot rise above the status of a movie extra. While the satirical video is full of mocking statements, this Hong Kong film occupies an especially symbolic position there. Given that it was produced in May 2020, when anti–Hong Kong sentiments flooded China's internet, this video offers a glimpse of another side of the Sino–Hong Kong relationship that could not be found in the mainstream.

Another Bilibili video uploaded in 2020 shows not the producer's but the audience's political consciousness. It was an ordinary instruction video teaching how to grow *jiucai*.[29] Since we can find similar videos from the same uploader providing horticultural instructions for other plants, we can safely infer that she did not intend this video as a political satire. But in just one year, this ordinary video received more than one million views, and it also attracted more than five thousand comments from the audience making fun of its political implications. Bilibili, modeled after the Japanese Niconico, is a platform allowing registered members to both upload videos and provide comments directly overlaid onto the video in sync. So we can see floods of comments directly responding to the script of the video narrator, like a semitransparent blanket partially covering up the image. These short comments include: "Training class for capitalists," "Harvard Business School," "Recite the entire text," "I thought this is Jack Ma broadcasting," "I am the garlic chives," "This I understand," "Political allegory." Breaking a public secret, the netizens happily participated in a fleeting online carnival, but this video was also a black comedy laying bare a taboo not intended for public display.

Despite its erratic and sometimes disastrous politics across the last three quarters of a century, the CCP has been relatively successful in securing a good part of the people's identification and endorsement. The Deng period differs from the Mao era not only in the Open Door Policy but also in the wider range of venues available for the people to express themselves. This limited liberalization was reinforced in the digital world after the 2000s. But the PRC also introduced online censorship faster and more effectively than virtually any other nation. The cat-and-mouse dynamic has been intensified in the Xi era. While the internet is monitored and censored intensely, netizens always find room to express themselves and argue with each other on approved topics, creating an atmosphere of quasi-, or pseudo-, liberalism. Those scholars studying China's online culture would likely find it problematic to describe contemporary Chinese society as "totalitarian," because propaganda and patriotism could hardly dominate its huge cyber world. As political scientist Margaret Roberts argues, "Most censorship methods implemented by the Chinese government act not as a ban but as a tax on information, forcing users to pay money or spend more time if they want to access the censored material."[30] Those who have the means and have tried hard enough can always find the materials the state does not want the people to see. However, not many people—not only in China but around the world—are willing to make the effort to explore the complicated social reality.

Mass Entrepreneurship

In China, *jiucai* has been traditionally a symbol of fertility, in terms of both its fecundity and its effects on male sexuality, and its aphrodisiac properties are supported by recent scientific studies.[31] But *jiucai* also produces a foul odor at the onset of summer. There is a common saying in northern China that "*Jiucai* in June stinks so bad that even dogs die" (六月韭, 臭死狗).[32] *Jiucai* is extremely resilient, and it cannot just be killed, as it will simply grow back again. Consider Sisyphus, who repeats eternally rolling a boulder uphill only to see it roll down again. While the Greek myth concerns the relationship between an individual and their fate, imagine the scenario where millions of clones of Sisyphus are toiling up and down the mountain, with the energy harnessed to drive the national economy and justify the legitimacy of Chinese sovereignty.

The *jiucai* meme suggests two main features of the current Chinese economic subjects: the thriving of self-sufficient and rule-abiding individuals on a gargantuan scale, and the quality of these individuals as hardworking and capable of producing wealth on their own. Here we might also see the connection between the Maoist and the neoliberal political economies. Although the Maoist collectivist mentality emphasizes self-sacrifice while the statist neoliberalism promotes personal success, the individuals in the two opposite systems are both like *jiucai*, cut to be fed into a larger power. While globalization has been a major factor behind China's recent economic miracle, the sheer size of the Chinese population is the largest asset of the national economy.

The popular meme helps us understand how these hardworking neo-liberal individuals correspond to the state's economic sovereignty, observed most pertinently in the mass entrepreneurship policy. In fact, it is also in this policy where the unique nature of PRC's sovereigntism can be observed most intimately, in the sense that it is all about survival. Knowing that China's world factory status is bound to be replaced by other developing countries that can always provide cheaper labor, then-Premier Li Keqiang, responsible for the state economy, first advocated the idea of mass entrepreneurship and innovation in 2014 and 2015 to upgrade China's economy. He advanced the slogan "Entrepreneurship of the Masses, Innovation of the Multitude" (*Dazhong chuangye wanzhong chuangxin* 大眾創業、萬眾創新) to describe the new national economic engine. This campaign rode the tide of the new information and creative economy, through which the government could upgrade its economy from low-end commodity production to high-end innovation and technology. In his annual *Government Working Report* in 2015, Li asserted that the government would "encourage people to start their own businesses and to make innovations, which will not only create more jobs and increase personal incomes, but also improve upward social mobility and social equality and justice."[33] Here Li was referring primarily to startup businesses in the digital economy, which would not be achievable without a highly developed online banking system and a strong cyberculture.

In China, youth unemployment has always been a governance challenge.[34] While the expansion of tertiary education has created many highly educated young people, China's economy is still dominated by low-skilled jobs in mass production and service industries. A lack of suitable jobs for the growing number of college graduates has been an issue for political stability. The promotion of mass entrepreneurship could lessen the burden on the state by providing young people with social security while creating room for economic growth. This neoliberal mass entrepreneurship is made possible by the rise of the new knowledge and creative economy to produce more and more new commodities and services, providing room for many people to start their own small businesses. College graduates consider their knowledge and creativity to represent significant capital. They believe they are more familiar with the tastes and desires of the young people, and they are also more sophisticated when it comes to handling the digital economic environment, from finance to retail and marketing.[35] However, some also quickly lose their investment, fall into debt, or go bankrupt: they become *jiucai*.

This promotion of mass entrepreneurship also ties into another popular governance discourse, "financial inclusion." This concept began to gain wide global attention in the early 2000s, when the World Bank identified a direct correlation between poverty and financial exclusion: those people who do not have access to banking and financial services are more likely to be poor. Financial inclusion has then been widely promoted around the world, and it has become a popular ideology in recent international policy circles as an effective way to eradicate poverty and improve human development.[36] Many international organizations such as the United Nations, the World Bank, and the International Monetary Fund diligently advise governments to facilitate individuals and small businesses to be included into the formal financial system and to access appropriate, affordable, and timely financial products and services.[37] These transnational regimes argue that by encouraging the marginalized people to have access to financial means, they can become stakeholders in the national economy, promoting and sharing the benefits of overall economic development. Upward mobility is thus made possible, and a fairer society can be created.

Financial inclusion has quickly been absorbed into the rhetoric of PRC's economic sovereignty. In 2015, the State Council issued the first national strategic plan to promote financial inclusion, which was approved by the Central Leading Group for Comprehensively Deepening Reforms (yet another group chaired by Xi Jinping himself). The document identifies financial inclusion as a key element in the realization of a "moderately prosperous society" (*xiaokang shehui* 小康社會); it also demands that market forces be led by governmental guidance.[38] Around the same time, the Chinese Academy of Financial Inclusion was established at Renmin University of China as the government think tank to facilitate the construction of a financial inclusion system. Financial inclusion became a core part of Xi's "Chinese Dream,"[39] assuming that underprivileged people can escape poverty after gaining access to finance.

Also, since the transactions are largely contained within the state, it helps buttress a vigorous domestic economy against the supposedly hostile and volatile global economy.

Financial inclusion has been further popularized in China alongside the e-commerce boom. With a consumer society so eager to buy and a microfinance system so ready to loan, individuals can become new capitalists very quickly. But since most of these new entrepreneurs lack a credit history or operate very small businesses, they turn to online banks or P2P lending platforms for easily obtainable high-interest loans. Many are quickly caught up in the web of digital loan sharks and systems of social surveillance, preparing the ground for the 2018 P2P online lending bubbles mentioned earlier. Both the lenders and the borrowers become garlic chives, and many of them are forever locked in the credit system, waiting to be harvested by the sickles.

But who are the sickles? Jack Ma's Ant Group, one of the largest players in China's booming microlending market, promised to be the world's largest IPO in 2020 but was suddenly halted by China's regulators two days before trading began. In April 2021, a record antitrust fine of 18.2 billion RMB was imposed on Ant Group's parent company, Alibaba. Its stock market price has also taken a nosedive. To many speculators, the Ant Group turned from a biggest sickle into *jiucai* overnight.

While financial inclusion has been lauded internationally as an equalizing policy, the state and capitalists collaborate to introduce the most marginalized population into the finance system, submitting everyone to debt and the credit system. The PRC's elaborate social credit system further requires Chinese citizens to comply with social norms, as any deviation can result in the deterioration of one's social credit, therefore downgrading one's position in society.

We could argue that China has now been stuck in a crisis of indebtedness, and not only in the sense of the proletariat exploited by the capitalists: the people and the sovereign state are also mutually in debt to each other. The people are told that their prosperity is based on the security of the state, and the state is also indebted to the productivity of its people. This mutual indebtedness is the gist of today's PRC sovereignty, in which the people superimpose their private interests onto those of the state. Nationalism alone does not explain the complex crisscrossing of identification and calculations; neither can idealistic concepts such as liberty or democracy easily untie the knots.

It is clear that China's national economic development has largely been driven by a process of resource capitalization through loans and debt.[40] China's recent real estate market is a representative example. Land ownership is extremely complicated in China, due largely to its socialist history. Until now, many local governments still possess much land, and both these local governments and the SOEs would finance themselves by transferring land use rights. They would do everything possible to create policies to sustain home prices, inciting developers and buyers to continue to buy. After decades of state support, China's housing sector has become "too big to fail." This explains the recent Evergrande Group crisis, which showcases how the government has been doing everything to save this most heavily indebted developer in history from going bankrupt. Even after the nationwide recession in 2022, many people are still convinced that housing prices will never fall and that government support will remain steadfast. The *jiucai*, which are indeed aware of their greedy and tragic nature, are indebted to their lenders, while the sovereign state also relies on the constant borrowing of the people to strengthen its economy. The local governments have been so invested in the local economy that the fates of the people and the state have become deeply intertwined.

Therefore, the success of the state overlaps with the success of the people. This allows the state to rely on the citizens' own industriousness to fulfill its promises to provide the people wealth and health. To encourage the people to produce wealth on their own, the state can claim its sovereign legitimacy. This logic seems to be possible only when the people are industrious enough. There has been a global scholarship trend, particularly in the late 2000s when Beijing delivered its spectacular Olympic Games, to document and prophesize the rise of the Chinese economic system to become the new world leader in a *longue durée*. Most famously, Giovanni Arrighi argued that China, with a chance to replace the United States as the world leader of the twenty-first century, would likely become a more benign economic force. This is because its development, in contrast to that of the West over the last few centuries, is not based on foreign invasion of resources and markets, domestic mass dispossession, and environmental destruction but rather on the high quality of the national labor in terms of its health, education, and capacity for self-management as well as the state's economic policies that place China's national interests first.[41] Arrighi's optimism of China's "accumulation without dispossession" may be driven by his dissatisfaction with the United States as the dominant global power, but he does not explain how to check the power of the Chinese state.[42] China pioneers a market economy under the unique condition that capital must organize around the state apparatus.[43] This makes the state particularly powerful in intervening economic activities.

Arrighi's brief mention of the "high quality" of Chinese labor was brief, but it has been magnified by many Chinese critics, and some are particularly keen on referring to Arrighi to celebrate the Chinese people's hardworking attitude.[44] But these discussions do not engage with the social conditions of this hardworking myth. Being the fuel of this "world factory," many Chinese workers have to work long hours, are assigned repetitive tasks, and are exposed to hazardous chemicals and unsafe conditions. Labor rights have been improving in some factories, but they have stagnated and even deteriorated in many others.[45] A celebration of hard work might only encourage labor exploitation. Max Weber argued that hard work is a key Protestant value, and it lies at the heart of capitalism. Similarly, traditional Chinese thought—particularly Mohism—celebrates hard work as the most essential way to improve one's living conditions.[46] This traditional "virtue" is adopted wholeheartedly by the current government, and PRC leaders have also repeatedly emphasized hard work as a most important attribute and virtue of the people.[47]

In fact, being hardworking is a major part of the Chinese Dream discourse, most obviously observed in the state-led propaganda campaign of "Chinese Dream, Beauty of Labor" (*Zhongguo meng laodong mei* 中國夢勞動美), which began in 2013. Under the new "Chinese Dream" discourse, the Propaganda Department re-engages in a "model workers" selection campaign and celebrates these workers as hardworking and innovative, ready to contribute and sacrifice but indifferent to fame and financial gain.[48] This campaign can be observed most clearly in the six-part CCTV television production *Laodong zhujiu Zhongguo meng* 勞動鑄就中國夢, *Labour Casting Chinese Dream*, 2015). Each episode is devoted to the positive effects of hard work. The first five episodes focus primarily on the benefits hard work brings to the individual: upgrading one's life, accumulating wealth, gaining wisdom, improving the quality of one's work, and attaining happiness. The final episode announces that hard work is the inherent spirit of the Chinese race.

This racial/cultural attribute of the Chinese people as hardworking was a handy and useful discourse for the state to explain China's capital accumulation. Currently, when the national economy is deteriorating rapidly with a rise of youth unemployment, the state again uses this discourse to urge the young people to work hard instead of complain.[49] It indirectly shows why *jiucai* is such a pertinent metaphor to describe the Chinese economic subjects. Under the grand narrative of national competitions, the Chinese people's humble productivity justifies China's global rise and differentiates it from that of other world powers, the ascendancy of which is viewed as the result of invasion and robbery. According to this discourse, China is destined to be the new global leader because the Chinese people are more diligent and orderly, in contrast to the people in the West, who are individualistic and intractable—most obviously witnessed in the recent COVID dramas.

It is true that China's economic success should—if only partly—be credited to its hardworking, flexible, and compliant population. But some have benefited much more than others, exacerbating social inequality. Moreover, this "world factory" economy has particularly benefited from its demographic dividend, resulting from the growth of its working-age population over the last three decades. But China has also entered a new phase, with fertility declining to below replacement level. The workforce will have to be even more hardworking to support an aging nation, which is also reflected in the involution anxiety. The virtue of hard work veils the structural injustice caused by large-scale privatization and corruption. Likewise, the social mobility of individuals is celebrated to conceal the enormous social inequality.

A most interesting development in this regard is the recent popularity of the term "lying flat" (*tangping* 躺平) on the internet, describing those who have been so exhausted by the social involution that they choose an uncooperative and resigned attitude in the face of immense pressure and a toxic work culture. This attitude of lying flat can be seen as a passive revolt against both the Chinese hardworking culture and the neoliberal entrepreneurial subject. What remains to be seen is whether the individual lying flat sees others doing the same, therefore creating a collective consciousness. A new version of "lying flat" is indeed the young people's pronouncement of refusing to have children, which is considered by some as the young people's most powerful challenge to the PRC state's legitimacy.

———

In China's imperial period, Heaven granted its mandate to the chosen sovereign rulers not on the condition of liberty, equality, or democracy but rather on morality and materiality, whoever could create a society of harmony and wealth. Socialism fundamentally challenged this ideology by introducing and privileging equity as the most important value in China. This project failed, and the collapse of socialism invited one of the most spectacular booms in capitalism in human history. Liberalism also re-emerged, generating widespread curiosity and nostalgia for the Republican period. In the last decade, a new version of statist neoliberalism develops and finds affinities with China's traditional values, celebrating individual diligence and family-based interests. Neoliberalism also helps the postsocialist state to shape liberalism to become a depoliticized economic drive.

However much the dominant socio-political system changed, the emphasis on development—entangling the individual and the national—is the red thread tying the republican, socialist, and postsocialist periods together into a continuous sovereign promise. The Chinese citizens also voluntarily subject themselves to this economic sovereigntism. This subject is hardworking and will likely persevere, but it is also perpetually forgetful, obedient, and submissive to its biological drive. Worse, the *jiucai* constantly mistakes itself as the sickle, believing it will be the ultimate winner. The intense economic competition subjects the *jiucai* to the mercy of the system, whose desire to thrive is similarly involuntary.

Gaining self-awareness is the first and most important step for *jiucai* to break away from the fate of eternal harvesting—of being only bare life. We can detect such self-awareness in another buzzword in China's internet, "human mines" or "huminerals" (*renkuang* 人礦), which describes human subjects as raw minerals to be mined and used. This is considered an updated version of *jiucai*: while *jiucai* still has a life, minerals are completely inert, lonely, meant to be exploited and discarded. The term *jiucai* has never been censored, but the state quickly banned this code word of *renkuang*, probably due to its strong dehumanizing connotation.[50]

I do not want to romanticize the *jiucai* agency, particularly in reference to the "forgetfulness" again demonstrated among many Chinese people after COVID. But I still find garlic chives a more provocative political metaphor than huminerals precisely because the former still has a life with the potential to initiate change. Biopolitics refers to the life of the human species in its totality, which is then reduced to the most rudimentary survival drive. The state is so keen on appropriating biopolitics precisely because of the enormous power of the people's survival drive. But the *jiucai* metaphor reminds us that biopolitics cuts both ways, that the political subject being nullified might wake up to reclaim one's life, and this awareness might lead him or her closer to true emancipation.

Ultimately, the most peculiar feature of *jiucai* is its massive scale. We tend to see depoliticized neoliberal subjects as singularized and solitary, yet *jiucai* can also be seen as a life force representing a collective. The life of *jiucai* has been appropriated by the dominant regime, but it can also be an incredibly resilient force if it can gain intersubjective awareness through its continual becoming. All these memes and code words characterize an internet culture with so many people participating, with so much censorship, and with so few actual political effects. But they do demonstrate how some individuals can still indirectly express themselves in an ironic, carnivalesque, yet morbid way, which in turn makes light of the people's living conditions.

While survival is an essential drive of political action, we must also consider politics more than simply individual subjects struggling for their needs. Needs often drive politics, but politics cannot continue with needs as the sole condition. We should consider biological survival a minimal (rather than maximal) purpose for the lives of individuals and collectivities.[51] Real political actions will only happen after survival is fulfilled, or transcended.

Conclusion

Sovereignty, as the source of power over a body politic, is an indispensable concept in both world realpolitik and the practice of democracy. Instead of debunking state sovereignty, this book puts it on the table and initiates a responsible conversation in the context of modern China.[1] In the name of autonomy and unity, China's changing sovereign logic has produced a range of positive and negative outcomes and repercussions, from democracy to xenophobia, germinating both solidarity and suppression. While we probably can never do away with sovereignty in the political world, we must remind ourselves that any attempts to develop a permanent and fixed sovereignty is bound to fail, precisely because sovereignty represents the self-ruling power of a group of living people, whose differences and constant mutations are irreducible. Our challenge is to realize a collective sovereignty that does not sacrifice plurality and changes in the name of representation or a desire for permanence and unity. As Derrida claims, "the choice is not between sovereignty and non-sovereignty, but among several forms of partings, partitions, divisions, conditions that come along to broach a sovereignty that is always supposed to be indivisible and unconditional."[2]

Not long ago, critics of both the left and right expressed concern about the triumph of transnational capital and global finance over sovereign autonomy, and they pointed out, often convincingly, the importance of weaker states asserting their sovereignty. It is true that capitalism traverses state borders and accentuates global inequality. It is also true that the polarizing social media and the democratization of knowledge have destabilized all hard-won normality and authority. Many peoples are losing their capacity to work together as a polity to exercise and gain collective wisdom to solve political problems. Many argue that state sovereignty is the answer.

However, the strong sovereignty discourses rising around the world seem to fall short of such high expectations. As the allure of globalization wanes, many people around the world desire a sovereign power that is not built from the bottom up through difficult negotiation, but one composed of collective emotions and exclusive pedigree, one that provides permanent security. At the same time, many political leaders also take advantage of such sentiments to encourage their citizens to identify with them and follow their version of order. In the name of unifying the people, resisting external threats, or handing down a prosperous nation to the next generation, many state leaders, democratically elected or not, are busily absolutizing an essentialized us and others.

Sovereignty is a political structure that provides the stability and identity that many people need and desire. But bracketing situations where sovereignty is indeed endangered or lost, such as the cases of certain indigenous groups, I would say the flagging of sovereignty as state principle does not provide a useful guideline or ideal for the government and the people to navigate internal and external politics. We vividly observe the deterioration of the global political and ecological environment, and we are also caught in the doomed prospect of the ever more intense competition promoted by late capitalism. Many of our most urgent tasks in contemporary politics are transborder and cooperative in nature, such as solutions to climate change, methods of alleviating global inequality, and the best ways to continue to develop artificial intelligence. Situated in a world drenched in ideological clashes and economic competitions, we must safeguard deliberation and empathy. We also need to make arduous and risky decisions supported by elaborated discussions and strenuous debates via plural, and contested, perspectives. Sovereignty tempts us to bypass these difficult processes. Engaging political decisions only through the calculations of self-interest and natural bonding would push us further away from partnership and responsibility.

While this is a book about China, the underlying concerns are universal. The unpredictability, systematic breakdown, and disobedience found in modern Chinese history happen in many other places too. The ways these ruptures have been both the pretext for the sovereign to demand unity and the evidence of the chimerical nature of such demands are also observed worldwide. There is an intimate relation between fear of change and desire for sovereignty. The more political and social changes people have experienced, the more they crave certainty, organization, and safety, and the more attractive a strong sovereign logic becomes. This also explains why a survival anxiety can so effectively hold the people together under the vague promises of sovereignty. Modern sovereignty in China was initiated by the late Qing anxiety about the survival of the Chinese race. Although China has now become such a powerful country and it is no longer a concern that the entire people would be wiped out as it was 150 years ago, the discourse of "survival" continues to thrive—though now in the name of individuals and families. The people have continued to consider survival and prosperity the main, if not sole, purpose of politics.

This kind of survival-based sovereignty is clearly not unique to China. Indeed, politicians around the world are exploiting such rhetoric. But the survival threats we are now facing are increasingly planetary in nature. We must reconceptualize survival not in terms of competition but entanglement. We do not need a sovereign logic that is washed over by the anxiety of the fall of a state because what is falling is all of humanity. The more meaningful political project is to implement collective wisdom to promote the diversity of lives; only this can guarantee the continual survival of humankind. Instead of being overwhelmed by the fear of death, we should try to affirm life and the changes it brings. This book does not propose to give up state sovereignty altogether, but it challenges us to develop a more porous, multi-layered, and communicative sovereignty that can engage with and benefit the people and things outside and inside the state border.

Undeniably, the sovereign states are now the most important players determining the future of our planet. On the world stage, sovereign states are likely to be even more aggressive in wanting to clash with each other on behalf of the people. Within the states, we might also expect more frequent and assertive uses of the sovereign logic by those in power, in the name of the people but actually targeted against the people. Living in such a political reality, our duty is to loosen up the concepts of unity and autonomy that define sovereignty. Sadly, the COVID pandemic showed an intensification of such parochialism and contestations. Instead of experimenting with new global cooperation and fairer vaccine distribution, national borders were quickly closed and states rushed to develop their own vaccines, not only as medicine but also as a source of national pride. A strong sovereign might have protected the lucky and obedient majority, but it is also more than ready to punish those who are not in compliance.

Realistically, no state can make decisions based solely on national situations, being inert to the influences of international players and national oppositional forces, in the same way that no national public spheres are genuinely inclusive of all citizens.[3] The territory-based sovereignty that considers the state border as the sole delimitation of the reach of power can only disappoint. Witnessing how the pandemic, climate change, and wars of aggression are unfolding and deteriorating in front of us, it is now a decisive moment for us to develop a new sovereign logic through which we can really see each other as distinct individuals. Indeed, no state can succeed in completely desensitizing our awareness of the actual multitude of the people and serendipity of history. There are always incidents or events that call people's attention to the social discord and power imbalance that the state aims to prevent us from seeing. While many sovereign subjects are docile, there are also those who insist on living under their own heterogeneous and resilient existence. However controlling the sovereignty is, the stubborn and unassimilable existence of these individuals could still become the agents for change.

The representative democracy practiced in many Western countries encourages us not to solve our own problems but displace them for future generations, and the market-based capitalist competitions only spawn disparity and do not help us to build solidarity and protect our commons. But neither is an unchecked authoritarianism nor a paternalistic state that impedes plurality and creativity a viable alternative. Instead of reducing difficult political practices into one identification, we can foreground the people's intersubjective relation toward a spawning life power. We can also experiment with new concepts of ownership and mastery that are regenerating rather than ossifying, appreciating both the importance and limitations of borders. Solidarity is not a given. A lasting solidarity can only be constructed based on the efforts of constantly opening up to the uniqueness of each individual member as well as the accidents of history. Constructing and protecting an embracing political community that respects the individuality of each member and embraces the potentialities the world evinces is a very difficult political project. But it is one that deserves our continual efforts. With our commitment and a streak of good luck, each of us and all of us could contribute to a more livable world together.

Notes

Preface

1. Xiao et al., "How a Chinese Doctor."

2. According to one media report, in the period from 9:30 p.m. on February 6 to 6 a.m. on February 7, Weibo recorded 670 million pageviews and 740,000 discussions of #李文亮醫生去世# (Dr. Li Wenliang passed away); 230 million pageviews and 209,000 entries of hashtag #李文亮去世# (Li Wenliang passed away), as well as 2.86 million pageviews and 10,000 discussions related to #我要言論自由# (I want freedom of press). See Lu, "Observing the Public Opinion."

3. To Girard, the act of scapegoating is also simultaneously a reenactment of foundational violence and a promise for human institution. See, for example, Girard, *Sacrifice*, 30–61.

4. Agamben, *Homo Sacer*, 91–103.

5. For a comparable study of the Soviet Union's appropriation of Lenin's death, see Yurchak, "Re-touching the Sovereign Biochemistry of Perpetual Leninism."

6. "The state of exception [bare life] actually constituted, in its very separateness, the hidden foundation on which the entire political system rested." Agamben, *Homo Sacer*, 9.

7. Foucault, *Birth of Biopolitics*, 75–78, 187–88.

8. Jiang, "Shengsi jiemian."

9. Anonymous, "Cult of Li Wenliang."

10. Arendt, *Human Condition*, 245.

11. Gibbs et al., "#Funeral and Instagram."

12. Ye, "China Proposes Measures."

Introduction

1. Xi Jinping first proposed that all countries in the world should share the fruits of development in a speech at the Moscow State Institute of International Relations in 2013. See "Speech at the Fourth Collective Learning in the Eighteenth Central Politburo Meeting," available at http://hk.ocmfa.gov. cn/eng/jbwzlm/xwdt/zt/xzxcf/201303/t20130325_10095329.htm.

2. Arato and Cohen, "Banishing the Sovereign?" 140.

3. According to Foucault, Machiavelli's book marks the transition to a new age in which the most important political question of the time, the safety of the Prince and his territory, was gradually replaced by concerns of the modern government regarding circulation and population. Foucault, *Security, Territory, Population*, 65–66.

4. Zhang and Yang, "Lun jindai 'fatong' linian de goujian"; Zhang, "Xinhai geming bainian hua fatong."

5. Shi, "Zhonggang qiang Sun Zhongshan *fatong*."

6. The term can be found in the chapter "Qichen qizhu" 七臣七主 in *Guanzi* 管子: 惠王豐賞厚賜以竭藏, 赦姦縱過以傷法; 藏竭則主權衰, 法傷則姦門闢, available at https://ctext.org/guanzi/qi-chen-qi-zhu/zh.

7. Jin, Liu, and Chiu, "Zhongguo xiandai zhuquan guannian xingcheng," 55–56.

8. There are recent academic debates in the PRC about whether the 1911 regime change was a result of Qing's voluntary transfer of its *fatong* to the Republican government. Those who argue for this view emphasize that the Qing court gave up its power voluntarily, meaning that the legitimate *fatong* was not broken by the Republican government and was instead carried forward. Yang, *Gegu dingxin*, 15–58.

9. Wang and Chen, "From Motherland to Daddy State."

10. Spruyt, *Sovereign State and Its Competitors*, 77–150.

11. Bodin, *On Sovereignty*, 38–39.

12. Andrew, "Jean Bodin on Sovereignty."

13. Croxton, "Peace of Westphalia."

14. Schmitt, Nomos *of the Earth*, 86–138.

15. Hobbes, *Leviathan*.

16. Rousseau, *Social Contract*, 90.

17. Hobbes, *Leviathan*, 117–29.

18. Schmitt, Nomos *of the Earth*, 143–47.

19. Schmitt, *Political Theology*, 8.

20. Kant, *Political Writings*, 108.

21. Spruyt, *The World Imagined*, 1–9.

22. Schmitt, Nomos *of the Earth*, 186–89.

23. Arendt, *Origins of Totalitarianism*, 168–77.

24. Ibid., 354.

25. Howland, *International Law*, 49–71.

26. Schmitt, Nomos *of the Earth*, 227–32.

27. Carlson, *Unifying China*, 18–20.

28. Kelly, *Sovereign Emergencies*, 134–66.

29. Benhabib, "New Sovereigntism."

30. For example, in his book *Unifying China*, Allen Carlson demonstrates how sovereignty is a tool for China both to secure its independence from the West and to integrate with the world. Maria Adele Carrai in *Sovereignty in China* offers a legal history and examines the genealogy of modern sovereignty as an international juridical concept from late Qing to contemporary China.

31. For example, in a regular press conference of the PRC's Ministry of Foreign Affairs in February of 2022, a question was raised about China's position on Russia's invasion of Ukraine. In response, the PRC spokesperson reiterated that sovereignty of all nations must be respected and protected. But he refused to comment directly on Russia's invasion of Ukraine, which is certainly a sovereign country; instead, he quickly turned to China's understanding of Russia's safety concerns. On the same day, the PRC government swiftly condemned a UK plan to expand visa eligibility for those Hong Kong young adults born after 1997. It was a solemn sovereignty issue, as the British government, it was claimed, was "grossly interfering" in China's internal affairs. Ho, "'Damp Squib.'"

32. Callahan, *Sensible Politics*, 166–73.

33. Derrida, *Rogues*, 10–11; *The Beast and the Sovereign*, 1:66–67.

34. As Michel Foucault argues, "What characterizes the end of sovereignty . . . is in sum nothing other than the submission to sovereignty. This means that the end of sovereignty is circular: this means that the end of sovereignty is the exercise of sovereignty." Foucault, "Governmentality," 95.

35. Shenila Khoja-Moolji demonstrates how both the Pakistani state and the Pakistan-based Taliban construct their sovereign legitimacy by summoning models of Islamic masculinity and kinship affections. Khoja-Moolji, *Sovereign Attachments*.

36. Povinelli, *Geontologies*, 90–91.

37. Katherine Zien explains how local artists assert the sovereign right of the people in Central America through their works. Zien, *Sovereign Acts*, 119–48.

38. Pang, *Appearing Demos*, 28–37, 44–66.

39. However, some suggest that there is indeed a liberal silent majority in today's China. See Mazzocco and Kennedy, "Public Opinion in China: A Liberal Silent Majority."

40. Gupta, *Red Tape*, 45–46.

41. See https://weibo.com/1989660417/LrL06id9y?ref=collection.

42. Alexi Yurchak describes that while it might be liberal democracy that legitimizes the sovereignty of the West, it is the Leninist Party that has occupied the center of Russian sovereignty since the 1910s. Yurchak, "Re-touching the Sovereign Biochemistry," 262.

43. Bodin, *On Sovereignty*, 58.

44. Rubinelli, "How to Think Beyond Sovereignty."

45. Simpson, "Sovereignty of Critique," 686.

46. Deleuze does not use the term "desire" to refer to the psychic structure of any individual, and it is not motivated by a lack. Instead, it is a positive force, or set of practices, circulating in the world, connecting and differentiating people as well as things.

47. Deleuze, "Desire and Pleasure," 129. Deleuze clarifies that the flight line should not be understood as created by marginal characters; rather, these are objective lines that cut across a society, where marginal figures are located. In other words, flight lines are structural.

Chapter One

1. Fifield, "Coronavirus Tests Xi's 'Heavenly Mandate.'"

2. Lowsen, "Xi Jinping's Great Leap."

3. Ho, *Challenging Beijing's Mandate of Heaven*, 17–18.

4. Anonymous, *Songs Classic*, 394–96.

5. Although the term *ming* (mandate) found in the poem is not preceded by *Tian* (Heaven), it is clearly suggested in the earlier lines that the mandate comes from Heaven.

6. Chinese originals: 天何言哉, 四時行焉, 百物生焉, in Chapter "Yanghuo" 陽貨, *The Analects* 論語: https://ctext.org/analects/yang-huo/zh; 天欲義而惡不義, in Chapter "Tianzhi" 天至, *Mozi* 墨子: https://ctext.org/mozi/will-of-heaven-i/zh; 天地不仁 以萬物為芻狗, in *Daodejing* 道德經 https://ctext.org/dao-de-jing/zh; 天公平而無私 故美惡莫不覆, in Chapter "Xingshijie" 形勢解, *Guanzi* 管子, https://ctext.org/guanzi/xing-shi-jie/zh.

7. Chen, "Yinshang de jisi zongjiao," 21–23; Mote, *Intellectual Foundations of China*, 22.

8. Eno, *Confucian Creation of Heaven*, 22–24.

9. Ibid., 84.

10. Akbarzadeh and Saeed, "Islam and Politics."

11. Bodin, *On Sovereignty*, 10.

12. Grzymała-Busse, *Nations Under God*, 7–13.

13. Schmitt, *Political Theology*, 36.

14. Poo, *In Search of Personal Welfare*, 103–4.

15. Zhao, "Mandate of Heaven and Performance," 417–18.

16. Nadeau, "Chinese Religion in the Shang and Zhou Dynasties," 30–31.

17. Yu, *Lun Tianren zhi ji*, 75–77.

18. Confucius says "he understands *Tianming* when he reaches fifty" 五十而知天命; in "Weizheng" 為政, the *Analects*; https://ctext.org/analects/wei-zheng.

19. Chinese original: 惟命不于常; in "Kanggao" 康誥, *Shangshu* 尚書; https://ctext.org/shang-shu/announcement-to-the-prince-of-kang.

20. Chinese original: 君臣無常位; in "Lord Zhao Year 32" 昭公三十二年, *Zuozhuan*; https://ctext.org/chun-qiu-zuo-zhuan/zhao-gong/zh; see also Durrant, Li, and Schaberg et al., *Zuo Tradition*, 1722–1723.

21. Chinese original: 道善則得之, 不善則失之矣; in "Daxue" 大學, *Liji* 禮記; https://ctext.org/liji/da-xue.

22. Chinese original: 天視自我民視, 天聽自我民聽; in the second essay of "Taishi" 泰誓中, *Shangshu* 尚書; https://ctext.org/shang-shu/great-declaration-ii. Xi Jinping recently quoted this line in a major political assembly to demonstrate CCP's legitimacy along the traditional political philosophy. Xi Jinping, "Speech for the Ceremony of the Sixty-Fifth Anniversary of the CPPCC."

23. Chen, "Yinshang de jisi zongjiao," 22.

24. For other passages in ancient Chinese books where the term *Tianming* appears, see Zhao, "The Mandate of Heaven and Performance," 419–20.

25. Cheng, "Nationalism, Citizenship, and the Old Text/New Text Controversy," 67.

26. Stasavage, *Decline and Rise of Democracy*, 10–16.

27. *Zuozhuan* recorded the dialogue between the statesman Cao Gui and Lord Zhuang of Lu about the chance of Lu's ability in defending the invasion of Qi. After hearing how Lord Zhuang treated the people kindly and righteously, Cao was convinced that Lu would win the war. Durrant, Li, and Schaberg et al., *Zuo Tradition*, 160–61.

28. "Delight in the Sword Fight" 說劍, *Zhuangzi* 莊子; https://ctext.org/zhuangzi/delight-in-the-sword-fight. There have been incessant debates if this essay was truly Daoist or an essay of the Zongheng School mistakenly collected into *Zhuangzi*. I will refrain from entering this debate. But in either case, the fable is clearly an advice for kingship.

29. "Identification with the Superior" 尚同, *Mozi* 墨子; https://ctext.org/mozi/identification-with-the-superior-iit.

30. Durrant, Li, and Schaberg et al., *Zuo Tradition*, 885.

31. Qin had already undergone a series of reforms to strengthen its administrative capacity during the "Warring States" period; these included the invention of new accounting methods, the learning of the actual composition of its population, and the development of a multi-level administrative system. Hui, *War and State Formation*, 79–84.

32. Pines, "Contested Sovereignty," 91–97.

33. Elman, *Cultural History*, 13–15, 248–49.

34. Lewis and Hsieh, "Tianxia and the Invention of Empire in East Asia," 38–44; Pines, "Contested Sovereignty," 218–19.

35. Lewis, *Early Chinese Empires*, 71–74.

36. Mühlhahn, *Criminal Justice in China*, 16–18.

37. Bodde and Morris, *Law in Imperial China*, 3–51.

38. Mote, *Intellectual Foundations of China*, 111–28.

39. Lo, *Law and Society in China*, 23–73.

40. Of course, we should not simply assume Magna Carta to be a reflection of a more advanced civilization. It might only show that the monarchy in Britain, and indeed throughout Western Europe, was compelled to work with representatives of the Church and towns for taxation and conscription. Stasvage, *Decline and Rise of Democracy*, 202–4.

41. Loewe, "Imperial Sovereignty."

42. Chinese original: 受命之君, 天意之所予也, 故號為天子者, 宜視天如父, 事天以孝道也; in "Shencha minghao" 深察名號, *Chunqiu fanlu* 春秋繁露; https://ctext.org/chun-qiu-fan-lu/shen-cha-ming-hao.

43. Chinese original: 故為人君者, 正心以正朝廷, 正朝廷以正百官, 正百官以正萬民, 正萬民以正四方; in "Dong Zhongshu zhuan" 董仲舒傳 (Biography of Dong Zhongshu), *Hanshu* 漢書 (Book of Han); https://ctext.org/han-shu/dong-zhong-shu-zhuan.

44. Chinese original: 古之造文者, 三畫而連其中, 謂之王。三畫者, 天、地與人也, 而連其中者, 通其道也, 取天地與人之中以為貫而參通之, 非王者孰能當是?; in "Wangdao tong san" 王道通三, *Chunqiu fanlu* 春秋繁露; https://ctext.org/chun-qiu-fan-lu/wang-dao-tong-san.

45. Chinese original: 故聖人法天而立道, 亦溥愛而亡私, 布德施仁以厚之, 設誼立禮以導之; in "Dong Zhongshu zhuan" 董仲舒傳, *Hanshu* 漢書; https://ctext.org/han-shu/dong-zhong-shu-zhuan.

46. The term first appeared in *The Book of Documents*: "Without bias and or favoritism, *wangdao* is the greatest" 無偏無黨, 王道蕩蕩; in "Hong Fan" 洪範, "Zhoushu" 周書, *Shangshu*; https://ctext.org/shang-shu/great-plan.

47. Mencius differentiated *wang* and *ba* accordingly: "He who uses force as a pretense of humaneness is a hegemon. But such a hegemon must have a large state in order to be effective. The man who uses his virtue to practice humaneness is the true king. To be a real king you don't need an especially large territory." 以力假仁者霸, 霸必有大國；以德行仁者王, 王不待大；

in "Gongsun Chou" 公孫丑 (上), *Mencius* 孟子; https://ctext.org/mengzi/gong-sun-chou-i.

48. Chinese original: 漢家自有制度, 本以霸王道雜之; in "Yuandiji" 元帝紀, *Hanshu* 漢書; https://ctext.org/han-shu/yuan-di-ji.

49. Sun Yat-sen, "Da yazhou zhuyi" (大亞洲主義 Great Asianism), speech given in Kobe, Japan, November 28, 1924. https://zh.m.wikisource.org/zh-hant/%E5%A4%A7%E4%BA%9E%E6%B4%B2%E4%B8%BB%E7%BE%A9. See also Sun, *San Min Chu I*, 4–5.

50. Chiang used primarily the *wangdao* concept developed by Ming dynasty Confucian master Wang Yangming 王陽明 (1472–1529). Huang, "Jiang Jieshi yu Yangming xue."

51. Original Chinese: 路線是王道, 紀律是霸道, 這兩者都不可少. Quoted from Mao, "Fandui zhuguan zhuyi he zongpai zhuyi."

52. Qiang, *Zhongguo Xianggang*, 92–108.

53. Huang, "Zhongguo gaibian gang xuanzhi."

54. Wang, *Zhongguo*, 17.

55. See, for example, Zhao, "All-under-Heaven and Methodological Relationism"; Bell, "Realizing Tianxia."

56. Wang, "Clash of Civilization and World Community."

57. See, for example, Callahan, *China*, 749–61; Ge, "Imagining 'All Under Heaven'"; Liang, "Imagining Tianxia."

58. Winichakul, *Siam Mapped*, 20–36.

59. Xing, *Qin Han shi lungao*, 14–15.

60. Feng, "*Fengjian*" *kaolun*, 22–35. By "feudal" I refer to the Chinese term *fengjian* 封建. The ancient Chinese *fengjian* system was replaced, more or less, by the more centralized *junxian* 郡縣 system after the Qin dynasty, in contrast to the feudal system in Europe, which lasted longer and tend to be more decentralized.

61. We also find the term *zhuxia* 諸夏 (literally many *xias*), denoting the feudal lords in the Zhou period, who were mostly the descendants of the ancient Xia Dynasty with which the Zhou dynasty identified. The intermediate Shang dynasty was largely considered by the Zhou dynasty as the improper lordship Zhou toppled. Xing, *Qin Han shi lungao*, 20–21. But *xia* was also attached with *hua* 華 to become a single term, *huaxia* 華夏, denoting a unified Chinese culture/nation composed of kingdoms or tribes of different origins. Chinese original: 華夏蠻貊, 罔不率俾 (Both the people of the Huaxia and the barbarians submitted to the rule [of the Duke of Zhou]); "Wucheng" 武成, *Shangshu* 尚書; https://ctext.org/shang-shu/successful-completion-of-the-war.

62. Hui, *War and State Formation*, 168.

63. Wang, "Diguo zhixu yu zuqun xiangxiang," 153–54.

64. Liu, "The Evolution of *Tianxia* Cosmology," 520–21.

65. Chinese original: 廿六年, 皇帝盡并兼天下諸侯, 黔首大安, 立號為皇帝; in "Shu zheng" 書證 (Documented evidence), collected in *Yanshi jiaxun* 顏氏家訓; https://ctext.org/yan-shi-jia-xun/shu-zheng.

66. Chinese original: 法度量則不壹嫌疑者, 皆明壹之; ibid. Scholars have debated the exact interpretation of certain words in this line.

67. Sanft, *Communication and Cooperation*, 57–76.

68. For example, Qin's prime minister Li Si 李斯 (246–208 BC) urged the Emperor: "With Qin's grandeur and the virtue of the Great King, it is, like cleaning the stove, easy to destroy all the princes, accomplish the imperial enterprise, and realize the unification of the world [*tianxia yitong*]" (夫以秦之彊, 大王之賢, 由灶上騷除, 足以滅諸侯, 成帝業, 為天下一統); in "Li Si lie-zhuan" 李斯列傳 (Biography of Li Si), *Shiji* 史記 (Records of the Grand Historian); https://ctext.org/shiji/li-si-lie-zhuan.

69. Chinese original: 內其國而外諸夏, 內諸夏而外夷狄; in "Wangdao" 王道, *Chunqiu fanlu* 春秋繁露; https://ctext.org/chun-qiu-fan-lu/wang-dao.

70. Chinese original: 天下之人同心歸之, 若歸父母, 故天瑞應誠而至; in "Dong Zhongshu zhuan" 董仲舒傳, *Hanshu* 漢書; https://ctext.org/han-shu/dong-zhong-shu-zhuan.

71. Jin Guantao, "Bainian shiye."

72. The so-called "nine-dash line" is the national border the PRC draws in the South China Sea to assert its sovereignty over the maritime areas. A United Nations arbitral tribunal already concluded in 2016 that this nine-dash line has no lawful effect internationally. But the PRC continues to use the "nine-dash line" as its national border, insisting that based on historical evidence, the islands within the "nine-dash line" were occupied by Chinese for centuries, if not millennia. See Akimoto, "Deciphering Island Issues from a Sinocentric Perspective"; Scott, "China's Nine-Dash Line."

73. Fei et al., *Huangquan yu shenquan*, 22–38. Mou Zongsan, another contemporary Confucian thinker, further expanded the categorization to illustrate this mechanism of compliance, and he differentiated four related concepts: sovereign power (*zhengquan* 政權), governing power (*zhiquan* 治權), ways of sovereignty (*Zhengdao* 政道), and ways of governing (*zhidao* 治道). Mou Zongsan, *Zhengdao yu zhidao*, 1–5.

74. Han Yu, "Yuandao" 原道; https://zh.m.wikisource.org/zh-hant/%E5%8E%9F%E9%81%93.

75. Yu, "Confucian Culture."

76. Combining the words *guo* (nation) and *jia* (family), the term *guojia* can be found in pre-Qin literature; it was originally used to refer to both the king and the ruling regime. Its modern connotation of the nation-state was acquired very recently. Gan, *Huangquan, liyi yu jingdian quanshi*, 152–58.

77. Gu, *Rizhi lu*, 471.

78. Chinese original: 古者以天下為主, 君為客. . . . 今也以君為主, 天下為客; in "Yuanjun" 原君 [How to be an emperor], *Mingyi daifang lu* 明夷待訪錄 [Waiting for the dawn: A plan for the prince]; https://ctext.org/wiki. pl?if=gb&chapter=267861.

79. Chinese original: 我以天下之利盡歸于己, 以天下之害盡歸于人; ibid.

80. Fei, *Xiangtu Zhongguo*, 68.

81. Yu, *Shi yu Zhongguo wenhua*, 80–82.

82. Qian, *Guo Shi Xin Lun*, 69–79.

83. Chinese original: 凡此弒而未成, 幽而復出者, 皆天命也; in Kang Youwei, "Da Nan Bei Meizhou zhuhuashang lun Zhongguo zhi kexing lixian bu kexing geming shu."

84. Ma, *Stone and the Wireless*, 156–57.

85. Chinese original: 要之, 撥亂反正, 不在「天命」之有無, 而在人力之難易。今以革命比之立憲, 革命猶易, 立憲猶難; in Zhang Taiyan, "Bo Kang Youwei lun geming shu."

Chapter Two

1. The term *dingyuyizun* 定於一尊, which can loosely be translated as "settled to one highest authority," was first found in *Records of the Grand Historian* (c. 91 BCE), in which Sima Qian recorded how Li Si, Qin's prime minister, used the term to celebrate the unification and absolute power of Qin's First Emperor. Since 2017, the CCP has used this term many times to describe the power of Xi Jinping and the Party Central in the new Chinese political system.

2. Jessen and Eggers, "Governmentality and Stratification."

3. These thinkers also utilized current geometrical knowledge—that a point, the constituting unit of the universe, is both indivisible and has area—to justify their sovereign theory. See Bartelson, "On the Indivisibility of Sovereignty."

4. Schmitt, Nomos *of the Earth*, 140–51.

5. Žižek, "Carl Schmitt in the Age of Post-Politics."

6. Schmitt, *Concept of the Political*, 19–79.

7. Yongzheng published his statement of Qing's legitimacy in *Dayi juemi lu* 大義覺迷錄 (The great reawakening) (1730), full text available: https:// ctext.org/wiki.pl?if=gb&chapter=657429. See also Wang, *Zhongguo*, 148–51.

8. If the term *Tianxia* was first popularized in the Han dynasty and then used by generations of Confucian scholars, the terms *dayitong* and *zhengtong* were used sparsely after Han, which, for example, could be found in texts of Song literati to highlight political unification as the key determinant of sovereign legitimacy. Elman, *Cultural History*, 50.

9. This Gongyang School was also known as the New Text School. See Cheng, "Nationalism, Citizenship."

10. Jiang, "Shamanism."

11. Crossley, *Translucent Mirror*, 33–34.

12. Elliott, *Manchu Way*, 63–72.

13. Sun, "Writing an Empire," 96–97.

14. Leibold, *Reconfiguring Chinese Nationalism*, 22.

15. Wang, *Xiandai Zhongguo sixiang de xingqi*, 579–99.

16. Among these military confrontations with imperialist powers, the result of the Sino-French War was most ambiguous, as neither the Qing nor the French actually won.

17. The line was found in Wei Yuan's *Illustrated Treatise on the Maritime Kingdoms* (Haiguo tuzhi 海國圖志), published in 1841.

18. Keevak, *Becoming Yellow*, 48–65.

19. Ibid., 128–29.

20. Yan, "Yuanqiang,"10.

21. Wyman, "Foreigners or Outsiders?" 31–57, 67–69.

22. Dikotter, *Discourse of Race*, 85–86.

23. Carrai, *Sovereignty in China*, 97–98.

24. Duara, *Rescuing History*, 21–23.

25. Chang, "Qingmo minchu de bianju yu shenti," 31–65.

26. Wu, *Wu Tingfang ji*, 1:116–17.

27. Mazzuca, *Latecomer State Formation*, 25–47.

28. Goodman, *Native Place, City, and Nation*, 119–46.

29. Zarrow, "Historical Trauma."

30. The original motto of the Chinese Revolutionary Alliance was highly racial: "to expel the northern barbarians and to revive Zhonghua, to establish a republic, and to distribute land equally among the people." Original Chinese: 驅除韃虜, 恢復中華, 建立民國, 平均地權. But Sun changed his political agenda a couple of years later, emphasizing his determination to establish a multiethnic Chinese sovereign nation, supported by all the Chinese citizens composed of the five major races, including the Manchus.

31. Carrico, *Great Han*, 133–58.

32. Sun, "Wuzu guomin hejinhui qi"; see also Duara, *Rescuing History from the Nation*, 32–33.

33. Arteaga and El-Hani, "Othering Processes and STS Curricula."

34. Furth, "Culture and Politics in Modern Chinese Conservatism," 23–26.

35. Zhang, "Zhonghua minguo jie." For a more elaborated description of the essay, see Schneider, *Nation and Ethnicity*, 154–67.

36. Li Hongzhang, "Chouyi zhizao lunchuan weike caiche zhe" (1872); "Chouyi haifang zhe" (1874).

37. Hill, "War, Disunity."

38. Lin, "Qingmo Minchu de sifa gaige."

39. Yang, *Gegu dingxin*, 59–92.

40. See, for example, Zhang Dongsun, "Wu ren lixiang zhi zhidu yu li-anbang"; Liang, "Jiefang yu gaizao fakan ci"; Zhang Taiyan, "Zai Hunan Changsha baojie huanyinghui shang zhi yanjiang"; Hu, "Liansheng zizhi yu junfa geju."

41. The first modern Chinese scholar to raise the idea of decentralizing power might have been Zhang Taiyan, who wrote *Fanzhen lun* 藩鎮論 (On fanzhen township) and *Fenzhen* 分鎮 (Town independence) in 1899, arguing that the ancient feudal models and the imperial *junxian* system in China already contained seeds of decentralization, which could be reinvigorated to devise a non-authoritarian modern Chinese political system. See Zhang, *Zhang Taiyan zhenglun xuanji*. Liang Qichao followed it up in 1919 and asserted that the modern nation-state must be built up from the power of the local governments, which already practice self-rule. See Liang, "Jiefang yu Gaizao fakan ci."

42. Xu, "Mapping Conservatism," 47.

43. Li, "Jizhonghua difangzhuyi yu jindai guojia jianshe."

44. Chen, *Chen Jiongming*, 126–63.

45. Xiao-Planes, "Of Constitutions and Constitutionalism," 45–47.

46. Paulès, "Warlords at Work."

47. Yang, "Difang zizhi yu tongyi guojia de jiangou," 23–24.

48. Yang, "Zouxiang geming."

49. Kobayashi, "Tibet in the Era of 1911 Revolution."

50. Wang, *East Turkestan Independence Movement, 1930s–1940s.*

51. Sun, "Zhongguo Guomindang xuanyan."

52. Carrai, *Sovereignty in China*, 109–22.

53. Wakeman, *Policing Shanghai*, 65–72.

54. Wilbur, *Nationalist Revolution in China*, 147–69.

55. Song, *Making Borders*, 171–218.

56. Duara, *Sovereignty and Authenticity*, 51–61.

57. Mitchell, "Manchukuo's Contested Sovereignty," 358–60.

58. Duara, *Culture, Power, and the State*, 86–117.

59. Strauss, "Evolution of Republican Government," 332–33.

60. Potter, *From Leninist Discipline to Socialist Legalism*, 60–62.

61. Strauss, "Morality, Coercion, and State Building," 896–906.

62. Lenin, "Right of Nations to Self-Determination."

63. Jones, *Soviet Concept*, 51–52.

64. Arato and Cohen, "Banishing the Sovereign?" 163.

65. Mao, "Lun shi da guanxi"; see also Meisner, *Mao's China and After*, 169.

66. Friedman, "Soviet Policy."

67. Qi, "Fensui xin shahuang de 'youxian zhuquan lun,'" 21; see also Carrai, *Sovereignty in China*, 161–67.

68. Mao, "Zhongjian didai you liangge," 509.

69. Mao, "Lun shi da guanxi," 244.

70. Yang, "20 shiji sanshishi niandai guogong liangdang," 93–96.

71. Carrai, *Sovereignty in China*, 157.

72. Nye, *Bound to Lead*.

73. Pang, *Creativity and Its Discontents*, 11–13; Wang, *Wenhua zhuquan lun*, 112–21.

74. In 2011, the 6th plenary session of the 17th Central Committee of the Chinese Communist Party was devoted to the development of socialist culture, and to build the country into a socialist cultural superpower. Beginning in 2013 Xi Jinping has repeatedly emphasized the promotion of China's soft power as a major task of the party and the state.

75. Kokas, *Hollywood Made in China*; Lee, "South Korean Film Industry."

76. Creemers, "China's Conception of Cyber Sovereignty," 113.

77. Ho, Chik, and Xie, "China's National Security Commission."

78. The concept was coined for the establishment of a cyberspace safety infrastructure in the PRC in 2014, in which CAC is the executive arm answering to the Central Cyberspace Affairs Commission, another central party group led by Xi himself.

79. Sun, "Fan Xi biaoyu kangyi hou."

80. King, Pan, and Roberts, "How the Chinese Government Fabricates."

81. Yang and Jiang, "Networked Practice."

82. Breslin, "Serving the Market or Serving the Party"; and Kipnis, "Neoliberalism Reified."

Chapter Three

1. Liu, "That Holy Word."

2. Perry, *Challenging the Mandate of Heaven*, ix.

3. Original Chinese: 天地革而四時成, 湯武革命, 順乎天而應乎人, 革之時大矣哉！Hexagram 49, "Ge" 革, *Yijing*; https://ctext.org/book-of-changes/ge1.

4. Chen, "Chinese 'Revolution' in the Syntax of World Revolution," 361–64.

5. Nuyen, "'Mandate of Heaven,'" 124–25.

6. "If the prince has great faults, they ought to remonstrate with him, and if he does not listen to them after they have done so again and again, they ought to dethrone him." (有大過則諫, 反覆之而不聽, 則易位). Second chapter of "Wanzhang" 萬章下, *Mencius* 孟子. https://ctext.org/engzi/wan-zhang-ii.

7. Gao, "Tongmenghui de 'ansha shidai.'"

8. Musgrove, *China's Contested Capital*, 128.

9. Tsui, *China's Conservative Revolution*, 31–32.

10. This was laid out in Sun Yat-sen's "The National Government's Leading Principles of State Building."

11. Zheng, *Minguo sixiang shilun*, 274–81.

12. Eastman, "Who Lost China?" 660.

13. Ibid., 658.

14. Becheikh, "Political Stability."

15. Grinin and Korotayev, "Institutions, Counterrevolutions, and Democracy."

16. Stasavage, *Decline and Rise of Democracy*, 256–76.

17. Slater and Wong, *From Development to Democracy*, 4.

18. Gunitsky, "From Shocks to Waves."

19. Heinzig, *Soviet Union and Communist China 1945–1950*, 51–125.

20. Chari and Verdery, "Thinking Between the Posts."

21. Lovell, *Maoism*; Cook, ed., *Mao's Little Red Book*.

22. Frazier, *East Is Black*, 37–79; Kristeva, *About Chinese Women*.

23. Rothwell, *Transpacific Revolutionaries*, 46.

24. Pang, "Mao's Dialectical Materialism."

25. Mao, "Lun shida guanxi."

26. Tian and Yan, "Self-Cultivation."

27. Marx, *Capital*, 18–19.

28. Tsui, *China's Conservative Revolution*, 32–34.

29. Li, "From Revolution to Modernization," 343–47.

30. Xi, "Speech at a Ceremony Marking the Centenary of the CPC."

31. Chiang initiated the New Life Movement in 1934, vowing to regenerate the Chinese spirit by modernizing the life of the Chinese people in terms of hygiene, physical strength, and literacy, while maintaining the traditional Confucian virtue supplemented by some Christian teaching.

32. Lin, "CCP's Exploitation of Confucianism and Legalism"; Schram, *Thought of Mao Tse-Tung*, 15–16, 125, 144–45, 181.

33. Examples include the establishment of the Confucius Institutes in 2004, the promotion of Han-style clothing, and the "national-culture fever" (*guoxue re* 國學熱) trend that began in the beginning of the twenty-first century.

34. Lin and Trevaskes, "Creating a Virtuous Leviathan."

35. Xi, "Speech at the Fourth Collective Learning in the Eighteenth Central Politburo Meeting," 57.

36. Xi, "Speech on 40th Anniversary of China's Reforms, Opening Up."

37. Veg, "Rise of China's Statist Intellectuals," 28.

38. Xie and Patapan, "Schmitt Fever."

39. Veg, "Rise of China's Statist Intellectuals," 32–33.

40. Schmitt, *Crisis of Parliamentary Democracy*, xxxii.

41. Preuß, "Carl Schmitt and the Weimar Constitution."

42. Zheng, *Politics of Rights*, 1.

43. Cohen, *Criminal Process*, 7.

44. Van der Walt, *Horizontal Effect*, 301–5.

45. Bai, *China*, 135.

46. Tsang and Cheung, "Has Xi Jinping Made China's Political System More Resilient and Enduring?"

47. Schmitt, *Political Romanticism*, 25–27.

48. Ibid., 158–61.

49. Scheuerman, "Revolutions and Constitutions," 146–47.

50. Zheng, *Carl Schmitt, Mao Zedong, and the Politics of Transition*, 113–22.

51. Liu includes Schmitt's 1962 talk "The Theory of the Partisans" in the Schmitt volume he edited, *Zhengzhi de gainian*, and Liu's comments on this essay, which date from July 26, 2007, can be found in a lecture: http://m. aisixiang.com/data/16320-3.html.

52. Xi, "Dialectical Materialism"

53. "Xi Jinping yiyi guanzhi qiangdiao"

54. Goldhammer, *Headless Republic*, 26–70.

55. Derrida, "Force of Law," 34–35.

56. Arendt, *On Revolution*, 224.

57. See, for example, Xi Jinping's speech in "'Staying True to Our Original Aspiration and Founding Mission' Major Theme Concluding Conference" ("不忘初心、牢记使命" 主题教育總結大會) in 2020.

58. Levitsky and Way, *Revolution and Dictatorship*, 85, 91–92.

Chapter Four

1. Habermas, "Popular Sovereignty as Procedure," 45.

2. Yack, "Popular Sovereignty and Nationalism," 526–28.

3. Paris, "European Populism."

4. According to its Secretary-General, the Iranian state "is the result of the popular Islamic revolution . . . a model in the Islamic world and the third world, and indeed in the world at large, for a state with full sovereignty; a state with real independence; a state with absolute freedom. . . . Real popular sovereignty exists in Iran." See "Nasrallah."

5. Yan Fu, "Xianfa dayi," 241.

6. Liang, "Jinbu dang ni Zhonghua minguo xianfa cao'an"; Liang, "Kaiming zhuanzhi lun."

7. Fitzgerald, "Nationless State," 77–78.

8. Sun, "Minquan zhuyi di yi jiang"

9. Sun, "Minquan zhuyi di wu jiang"

10. Zheng, *Politics of Rights*, 76–78, 255–58.

11. Skya, *Japan's Holy War*, 82–111.

12. Sun, *San Ming Chu I*, 23–24.

13. Sun, "Dapo jiusixiang yao yong sanmin zhuyi."

14. Osterhammel, *Transformation of the World*, 405.

15. Sun, "Zhongguo zhi tielu jihua yu minsheng zhuyi."

16. Chinese original: 共和之制, 國民為國主體共和之制, 國民為國主體, 吾黨欲使人不忘斯義也, 故顏其名曰國民黨。 Sun, "Guomindang xuanyan," 35.

17. Yuan, "Zhonghua minguo zhengshi da zongtong xuanyan." Chinese original: 共和國以人民為主體, 人民大多數之公意在安居樂業. . .. 余願極力設法使人民真享共和幸福。

18. Chen, *Chen Jiongming*, 303.

19. Yin, "Renquan yu minzhu de bianzou."

20. Paulès, "Warlords at Work," 46–47.

21. Lam, *Passion for Facts*, 41.

22. Li, "Zhongguo shehui diaocha yundong."

23. Chen, *Chinese Sociology*, 17–22.

24. Foreman, "Racial Modernity in Republican China."

25. Sakamoto, "The Cult of 'Love and Eugenics' in May Fourth Movement Discourse."

26. Culp, *Articulating Citizenship*, 163–208.

27. Henrietta, *The Making of the Republican Citizen*, 60–64.

28. Johnson, *Childbirth in Republican China*, 35–72.

29. Stanton, "Popular Sovereignty," 320–24.

30. Jenco, "'Rule by Man' and 'Rule by Law' in Early Republican China."

31. See, for example, Hu Shi, "Zhongguo wu ducai de biyao yu keneng."

32. Van de Ven, *From Friend to Comrade*, 17–18.

33. Clinton, *Revolutionary Nativism*, 161–90.

34. Ni, *Minzu xiangxiang*, 19–75.

35. Hon, "From Babbitt to 'Bai Bide'."

36. Yeh, *Chinese Political Novel*, 163–230.

37. Zeng Pu, *Niehai hua*.

38. Liang, "Xin Zhongguo weilai ji."

39. Liang, "Lun xiaoshuo yu qunzhi zhi guanxi."

40. Lew, "China's Renaissance—the Christian Opportunity," 301.

41. Pan Guangdan, for example, believed that many deep-rooted bad characteristics of the Chinese people were the product of China's frequent natural disasters. The people became selfish and incapable of sympathy because they had to focus on their own survival. Therefore, he believed that to improve the character of the Chinese race, the people had to learn to prevent drought and flood, and to commit to reforestation. Pan, "Minzu texing yu minzu weisheng."

42. Hu, "Buxiu: wo de zongjiao"

43. Lee, *Romantic Generation*, 266.

44. Lu Xun, "Huran xiangdao," 16.

45. Lu, "Medicine," in *Diary of a Madman and Other Stories*, 49–58.

46. Lu, "Hometown," in ibid., 89–100.

47. Murthy, "Resistance to Modernity," 528–32.

48. Tang, *Global Space*, 22.

49. Yu, "Chenlun," 53.

50. Tsu, *Failure, Nationalism, and Literature*, 177.

51. Ibid., 184–88.

52. Pang, *Building a New China in Cinema*.

Chapter Five

1. Translation retrieved from Marxists Internet Archive. https://www.marxists.org/reference/archive/mao/selected-works/poems/poems18.htm.

2. The term *jiangshan* has been used for more than two millennia; it can be found, among other early sources, in the "Mountain and Wood" 山木 chapter of *Zhuangzi* 莊子, referring literally to river and mountain: 彼其道遠而險, 又有江山。我無舟車, 奈何？("The road is long and dangerous, blocked with rivers and mountains. I have neither cars nor boats. What can I do?"). The meaning of the term gradually expanded to refer also to sovereign territory. For example, in "Book of Wu" 吳書 of *Records of the Three Kingdoms* 三國志, we find the line: 割據江山, 拓土萬里 (Occupying parts of the *jiangshan*, and expanding ten thousand li of the territory).

3. Chinese original: 人民就是江山, 共產黨打江山、守江山, 守的是人民的心, 為的是讓人民過上好日子。http://politics.people.com.cn/n1/2021/0628/c1001-32141933.html.

4. Chan, "In Search of the Southeast."

5. Sun, "Mogao yishi."

6. Brady, *Marketing Dictatorship*, 35–37.

7. The most important advocate in this regard was senior party member Jiang Feng 江豐 (1910–1982), who was in charge of the art policy in the first half of the 1950s. He made it clear that a large part of traditional Chinese aesthetics must go. See Jiang, "Guohua gaizao de diyibu."

8. Wang Zhaowen 王朝聞 (1909–2004), responsible for art and cultural policies in the Central Propaganda Department, emphasized the effectiveness of the use of lines in Chinese paintings—in contrast to the emphasis on light in European arts—in extracting the core tensions and displaying the major relations of a scene. He also argued that traditional Chinese paintings could become Marxist so long as they were capable of reflecting reality, expressing emotions, and teaching the masses. See Wang, "Jingque miaoxie bu dengyu xianshi zhuyi."

9. The idea of New National Painting first appeared in the early Republican period, when a new generation of artists and painters advanced to reform traditional Chinese paintings with Western techniques. The most representative advocates were the members of the Lingnan School.

10. Cai, "Guanyu guohua gaige wenti."

11. The first "New National Painting Exhibition" took place in Beijing in April 1949.

12. These artists' works were first presented in Beijing's Beihai Garden, at an exhibition that was widely documented and discussed around the country. See Qiu, "Guanyu guohua chuangzuo jieshou yichan de yijian."

13. Many art critics discussed the piantings; see the essays published in the most prestigious art magazine *Art* (*Meishu*) in 1955.

14. Gu, *Chinese Ways of Seeing*, 193–207.

15. Wan, "Fu Baoshi 'Mao Zedong shiyi hua' chuangzuo zhi yanjiu."

16. For example, in 1959, the Zhejiang Academy of Arts put forward two major campaigns titled "For Truly Great Men, Look to This Age Alone" (數風流人物還看今朝) and "This Land So Rich with Beauty" (江山如此多嬌), which are both lines from Mao's poem "Snow, Adopted after the Tune of Chin Yuan Chun." The two campaigns were meant to encourage the painters to depict the new people and the new faces of nature respectively, showing that figure and landscape were both treasured. Editorial, "Li dazhi, gu ganjin, shenru shenghuo, fanrong chuangzuo."

17. Wu, *Yongwu tantu*, 117.

18. Croizier, "Hu Xian Peasant Painting," 137.

19. Cerella, "Space and Sovereignty."

20. Cams, "At the Borders of Qing Imperial Cartography."

21. Wang, *Zhongguo*, 156–69.

22. Huang, *Bimo jiangshan*, 111.

23. This is summarized in the theory of Tang dynasty artist Zhang Zao 張璪, who famously argued that the essence of art involves both naturalism and expressionism, so that artists should "study the external form and acquire the internal mind" (外師造化, 中得心源).

24. The Guangdong-based Lingnan School was among the first to emphasize the importance of life drawing in traditional Chinese painting.

25. Gu, *Chinese Ways of Seeing and Open-Air Painting*, 17–20, 88–89.

26. Li, *Utopian Ruins*, 100–149.

27. Shuai, "Zhongguo huajia zai daqihuang Zhong."

28. In addition to the trip he took with Zhang Ding and Luo Ming as well as two other domestic trips, Li was also invited to East Germany in 1957 for four months.

29. Chen, "Landscape Painting of Li Keren," 129.

30. Li and Wang, "Li Keran 'hongse shanshui' yishu fengge fenxi."

31. Dialectic thinking was extremely important to the socialist aesthetics at that time. For more information, see Pang, "Can Dialectic Materialism Produce Beauty?"

32. Faure, "Lineages as a Cultural Invention."

33. Tilly, *Coercion, Capital, and European States*, 97–99.

34. Stilz, *Territorial Sovereignty*, 33–34, 157–58.

35. Mao, *On Khrushchov's Phoney Communism*.

36. Foucault, *Security, Territory, Population*, 20–23.

37. Strauss, "Campaigns of Redistribution Land Reform and State Building."

38. Pang, "Mao's Dialectical Materialism," 113–14.

39. The PRC has never released the figures for the death toll caused by the Great Famine. The most official data can be found in Zhonggong Zhongyang danshi yanjiushi, *Zhongguo Gongchandang lishi dierjuan*, which quoted from State Statistics that China's national population in the year of 1960 witnessed a drop of 10 million (563). But most scholars offer much higher estimates. Yang Jisheng estimates the death toll to be 16 million, while Frank Dikötter believes 45 million people died from starvation. See Yang, *Tombstone*, 409; Dikötter, *Mao's Great Famine*, 333.

40. Li and Yang, "Great Leap Forward."

41. Shapiro, *Mao's War Against Nature*.

42. The other one is *A Glimpse of the Coal Capital* (Meidu yipie 煤都一瞥), which is reprinted in Chung, *Chinese Art in an Age of Revolution*, 171.

43. Fu, *Fu Baoshi yishu suibi*, 231–32. A part of Fu's reflection is translated into English in Chung, *Chinese Art*, 170.

44. Fu, *Fu Baoshi yishu suibi*, 231–32.

45. Dong, "Coal, Which Built a Chinese City."

46. Fushun City CPPCC History Committee, *Fushun meikuang bainian*, 140.

47. Stilz, *Territorial Sovereignty*, 170–71.

48. Ruggie, "Territoriality and Beyond"; Mitchell, *Colonising Egypt*, viii.

49. Cosgrove, *Social Formation*, 16–17.

50. Shapiro, *Methods and Nations*, 105–40.

51. Foong, *Efficacious Landscape*, 64–73.

52. Bush, *Chinese Literati on Painting*.

53. Hay, *Shitao*, 30.

54. For the difficult adaptation of republican intellectuals and cultural workers to the new political environment, see Pickowicz, "Acting Like Revolutionaries."

Chapter Six

1. Pye, "On Chinese Pragmatism in the 1980s."

2. Weber, *How China Escaped Shock Therapy*.

3. Chang, *Capitalist Development in Korea*.

4. Chen, ed. *China's Integration*.

5. Hartcher, "Money or Our Sovereignty"; For more on Australia's recent panic over China's intrusion of Australian sovereignty, see Brophy, *China Panic*, 19–21.

6. Polanyi, *Great Transformation*, 117–21.

7. See Foucault's trilogy of biopower: *"Society Must Be Defended"*; *Security, Territory, Population*; and *The Birth of Biopolitics*.

8. Bargu, *Starve and Immolate*, 43–54.

9. Marx and Engels, *German Ideology*, 79–81.

10. But the meanings of state security are state-specific. For example, Akhil Gupta criticizes that to Agamben, exclusion is the basis for violence in states of exception, shown most obviously in the killing of Jews, homosexuals, and gypsies in Nazi Germany. But in India, the poor are killed despite their inclusion in projects of national sovereignty and despite their centrality to democratic politics and state legitimacy. The main force in this structure of violence is not the state's survival drive, but the bureaucracy's indifference to the arbitrary outcomes it produced. Gupta, *Red Tape*, 6.

11. Xi, "Xi Jinping zai qiyejia zuotanhui shang de jianghua."

12. Economy, *Third Revolution*, 124.

13. Chen, *Manipulating Globalization*, 13–14.

14. Geertz, *Agricultural Involution*.

15. Huang, *Peasant Family*.

16. See https://new.qq.com/rain/a/20201203A0EGL700.

17. Grey, "Chinese Youth More Confident."

18. Yang, *Wuhan Lockdown*.

19. Wu et al., "Chinese Citizen Satisfaction."

20. The crisis was a result of the over-lending of some of these platforms. Many people were lured by the high returns these lending companies promised and poured in their savings as lenders. But when a good number of borrowers were not able to pay back their borrowings, it created much fear among the debtors, and the industry collapsed.

21. Li, *Jiucai de ziwo xiuyang*.

22. See, for example, a collection of these amateur dance video along the "Song of Garlic Chives," www.youtube.com/watch?v=AjC-P47bLk4.

23. Ye, "'Ge jiucai' fa peiyang houbei rencai."

24. Zhang, "How Much Do State-owned Enterprises Contribute to China's GDP?" 5.

25. Xi, "Xi Jinping zai qiyejia zuotanhui shang jianghua."

26. Bilibili was set up in 2012 in China, modeled after the Japanese video platform Niconico. It was vastly popular among young people: as of 2020, there are 17.2 million active users, 75 percent of whom are under the age of 24.

27. According to official Chinese sources, by the end of 2019 there were more than 180,000 Chinese citizens working in Africa, a number that declined by 10 percent compared with 2018. See China Africa Research Initiative, http://www.sais-cari.org/data-chinese-workers-in-africa. But the

actual number is believed to be much higher. There are all kinds of Chinese workers involved, from managers and foremen to laborers, and most have not been given what they were promised. See Halegua, "Where is the Belt and Road Initiative Taking International Labour Rights?"

28. "Zhi qianlang" 致前浪 (To the preceding waves), https://www.youtube.com/watch?v=QsD9uFKtoRY; "Qianlang: yinghe buluo xiangei qianlang de yanjiang" 前浪 硬核部落獻給前浪的演講 "The preceding waves: The speech given by the hardcore tribe to the preceding waves," www.youtube.com/watch?v=5WRR-nFbq-k.

29. "Zheyang ge jiucai, keyi duoshou haojige cha, chide shijian chang," 這樣割韭菜, 可以多收好幾個茬, 吃得時間長 (With this method of cutting garlic chives, we can harvest a few more times, and eat longer), https://www.bilibili.com/video/BV1rV411z7S2?from=search&seid=10375705564126712183&spm_id_from=333.337.0.0.

30. Roberts, *Censored*, 2.

31. Hu et al., "Aphrodisiac Properties."

32. My thanks to Guo Yijiao for reminding me of this folk saying.

33. Li, "Report on the Work of the Government."

34. Schucher, "Fear of Failure," 80.

35. This infrastructure, provided mostly by a handful of state-approved conglomerates such as Tencent and Alibaba, is made up of a mass entrepreneurship online sales platform (Taobao), social media (QQ and Wechat), online banks (WeBank and MyBank), digital payments (WeChat Pay and Alipay), and commodity shipment (SF Express and STO Express).

36. World Bank, "Financial Inclusion."

37. Sarma and Pais, "Financial Inclusion and Development."

38. Loubere, "China's Internet Finance Boom and Tyrannies of Inclusion," 12.

39. "Chinese Dream" refers to the collective efforts of the Chinese people to participate in the great rejuvenation of the Chinese nation. It is a state slogan first proposed in 2012 by Xi, who had just become the CCP leader and formulated his statecraft emphasizing the cultivation of national pride among the citizens.

40. Magnus, *Red Flags*.

41. Arrighi, *Adam Smith in Beijing*, 351–89.

42. Burak Gürel and Eylem Taylan consulted many critical responses to Arrighi's book, summarizing that its analysis of contemporary China economy is considered the most serious shortcoming of this influential book. Gürel and Taylan, "Critique of the Critics of Giovanni Arrighi's Adam Smith in Beijing."

43. Andreas, "Changing Colors in China."

44. See, for example, Yao, "Yadang simi zai Beijing"; Yang and Gan, "Shehui zhuyi hexin jiazhi.".

45. Locke, *Promise and Limits of Private Power*.

46. "The farmers set out at daybreak and come back at dusk, diligently sowing seeds and planting trees to produce much soy beans and millet, and dare not be negligent. Why do they do this? They think diligence will result in wealth, and negligence in poverty; diligence will produce plenty, and negligence famine. Therefore they dare not be negligent. The women get up at dawn and retire in the night, diligently weaving and spinning to produce much silk, flax linen, and cloth, and dare not be negligent. Why do they do this? They think diligence will produce wealth and negligence poverty; diligence will produce warmth and negligence cold. Therefore they dare not be negligent." *Anti-Fatalism*, vol. 3 非命下, Mozi 墨子. For full text see https://ctext.org/mozi/anti-fatalism-iii/zh?en=on.

47. Wang, "Statement at the United Nations General Assembly"; Xi, "Speech on 40th Anniversary of China's Reforms."

48. Anonymous, "Zhongxuanbu, Quanguo zonggonghui xiang quan shehui gongkai fabu."

49. Responding to recent heated discussions on the internet about the relevance of Lu Xun's short story "Kun Yiji" to today's social downward mobility among college graduates, the state mouthpiece CCTV.com urges young people not to complain but to work harder. See https://news.sina.com.cn/s/2023-03-16/doc-imykznfz7788561.shtml.

50. Changxi, "Renkuang."

51. Chrostowska, *Utopia in the Age of Survival*, 89.

Conclusion

1. This book was initiated by my reflections on the discussion of sovereignty in my previous book, where I advanced the concept of multiple sovereignties to come to terms with the "One-country-two-system" framework that is given to Hong Kong. It is clear that I did not give enough attention to the centrality of indivisibility in state sovereignty, as well as the fact that there is a unique history to each sovereignty. This book is an attempt to further an immature idea of mine. See Pang, *Appearing Demos*, 6–11.

2. Derrida, *Beast and the Sovereign*, 1:76.

3. Fraser, *Scales of Justice*, 155–57.

Bibliography

Agamben, Giorgio. *Homo Sacer: Sovereign Power and Bare Life*. Trans. Daniel Heller-Roazen. Stanford, CA: Stanford University Press, 1998 [1995].

Akbarzadeh, Shahram, and Abudullah Saeed. "Islam and Politics." In *Islam and Political Legitimacy*, ed. Shahram Akbarzadeh and Abudullah Saeed, 1–13. London: RoutledgeCurzon, 2003.

Akimoto, Kazumine. "Deciphering Island Issues from a Sinocentric Perspective." *Review of Island Studies*, March 24, 2014, islandstudies//readings/b00006. Translated from "Chuka shiso kara yomitoku tosho mondai," *Tosho Kenkyu Journal* 2, no. 2 (April 2013): 128–34.

Anderson, Benedict. *Imagined Communities*. London: Verso, 1983.

Andreas, Joel. "Changing Colors in China." *New Left Review* 54 (2008): 123–42.

Andrew, Edward. "Jean Bodin on Sovereignty." *Republics of Letters: A Journal for the Study of Knowledge, Politics, and the Arts* 2, no. 2 (2011): 75–84.

Anonymous. "The Cult of Li Wenliang, the Doctor Who Spotted COVID-19." *The Economist*. January 12, 2023. https://www.economist.com/china/2023/01/12/the-cult-of-li-wenliang-the-doctor-who-spotted-covid-19.

Anonymous. "Daxue" 大學 [*Great learning*]. *Xinyi liji duben xia* 新譯禮記讀本 (下) [New Translation of Great Learning], vol. 2. Taipei: Sanmin Shuju, 2012 [c. 475–221 BCE].

Anonymous. *Mencius* 孟子. Beijing: Zhonghua Shuju, 1998 [c. 340–250 BC].

Anonymous. *Mozi* 墨子. Beijing: Zhonghua Shuju, 1985 [c. 490–221 BC].

Anonymous. "Nasrallah: Let Whoever Claims to Want a State of Sovereignty, Liberty and Independence, Confront the Destructive American Influence." National News Agency, February 10, 2022. https://www.nna-leb.gov.lb/en/%D8%B3%D9%8A%D8%A7%D8%B3%D8%A9/521164/nasrallah-let-whoever-claims-to-want-a-state-of-so.

Anonymous. "Qichen qizhu" 七臣七主 [Seven types of courtier and seven types of lord]. *Guanzi* 管子, vol. 17. Beijing: Zhonghua Shuju, 1965 [c. 475–220 BCE].

Anonymous. *Shangshu* 尚書 [Book of documents]. Beijing: Zhonghua Shuju, 2009 [c. 772–476 BCE].

Anonymous. *Songs Classic: China's Earliest Poetry Anthology*. Trans. William Dolby. Edinburgh: Carreg, 2005 [c. 1046–771 BCE].

Anonymous. "Xi Jinping yiyi guanzhi qiangdiao 'ba dang de weida ziwo geming jinxing daodi'" 習近平一以貫之強調"把黨的偉大自我革命進行到底" [Xi Jinping repeatedly emphasizes "to follow through the implementation the party's great self-revolution to the end"]. CPC News. January 11, 2023. http://cpc.people.com.cn/BIG5/n1/2023/0111/c164113-32604542.html

Anonymous. *Xinyi Zhuangzi duben* 新譯莊子讀本 [A reader of new interpretations of Zhuangzi]. Taipei: Sanmin Shuju, 1974 [c. 350–250 BCE].

Anonymous. "Zhongxuanbu, Quanguo zonggonghui xiang quan shehui gongkai fabu 'Zhongguo meng, laodong mei' zuimei zhigong" 中宣部、全國總工會向全社會公開發佈 '中國夢. 勞動美' 最美職工 [Propaganda Department and National Federation of Trade Unions announce to society the most beautiful worker of "Chinese Dream, Beauty of Labor"]. *Guangming Daily* 光明日報, April 25, 2015, http://epaper.gmw.cn/gmrb/html/2015-04/25/nw.D110000gmrb_20150425_9-07.htm.

Arato, Andrew, and Jean L. Cohen. "Banishing the Sovereign? Internal and External Sovereignty in Arendt." In *Politics in Dark Times Encounters with Hannah Arendt*, ed. Seyla Benhabib, 137–71. Cambridge: Cambridge University Press, 2010.

Arendt, Hannah. *The Origins of Totalitarianism*. New York: Schocken Books, 2004 [1951].

Arendt, Hannah. *The Human Condition*. Chicago: University of Chicago Press, 1998 [1958].

Arendt, Hannah. *On Revolution*. New York: Penguin, 2006 [1963].

Arrighi, Giovanni. *Adam Smith in Beijing: Lineages of the Twenty-First Century*. London: Verso, 2017.

Arteaga, Juan Manual Sánchez, and Charbel N. El-Hani, "Othering Processes and STS Curricula: From Nineteenth Century Scientific Discourse on Interracial Competition and Racial Extinction to Othering in Biomedical Technosciences." *Science and Education* 21 (2012): 607–29.

Bai Tongdong. *China: The Political Philosophy of the Middle Kingdom.* London: Zed Books, 2012.

Ban Gu 班固. "Dong Zhongshu Zhuan" 董仲舒傳 [Biography of Dong Zhongshu]. *Hanshu* 漢書, vol. 56. Beijing: Zhonghua Shuju, 1962 [c. 36–111].

Bargu, Banu. *Starve and Immolate: The Politics of Human Weapons.* New York: Columbia University Press, 2014.

Bartelson, Jens. "On the Indivisibility of Sovereignty." *Republics of Letters: A Journal for the Study of Knowledge, Politics, and the Arts* 2, no. 2 (2011): 85–94.

Becheikh, Nizar. "Political Stability and Economic Growth in Developing Economies: Lessons from Morocco, Tunisia and Egypt Ten Years after the Arab Spring." *Insights into Regional Development* 3, no. 2 (2021): 229–51.

Bell, Daniel A. "Realizing Tianxia: Traditional Values and China's Foreign Policy." In *Chinese Visions of World Order: Tianxia, Culture, and World Politics*, ed. Ban Wang, 129–46. Durham, NC: Duke University Press, 2017.

Benhabib, Seyla. "*The New Sovereigntism and Transnational Law: Legal Utopianism, Democratic Scepticism and Statist Realism,*" *Global Constitutionalism* 5, no. 1 (2016): 109–44.

Bodde, Derk and Clarence Morris. *Law in Imperial China.* Cambridge, MA: Harvard University Press, 1967.

Bodin, Jeans. *On Sovereignty: Four Chapters from the Six Books of the Commonwealth.* Trans. and ed. Julian H. Franklin. Cambridge: Cambridge University Press 1992 [1576].

Brady, Anne-Marie. *Marketing Dictatorship: Propaganda and Thought Work in Contemporary China.* Boulder, CO: Rowman and Littlefield, 2008.

Breslin, Shaun. "Serving the Market or Serving the Party in China: Neoliberalism in China." In *The Neo-Liberal Revolution: Forging the Market State*, ed. R. Robison, 114–31. London: Palgrave Macmillan, 2006.

Brophy, David. *China Panic: Australia's Alternative to Paranoia and Pandering.* Melbourne: La Trobe University Press, 2021.

Bush, Susan. *The Chinese Literati on Painting: Su Shih (1037–1101) to Tung Ch'i-ch'ang (1555–1636).* Hong Kong: Hong Kong University Press, 2012 [1971].

Cai Ruohong 蔡若虹. "Guanyu guohua gaige wenti: kanle xin guohua yuzhan zhihou," 關於國畫改革問題--看了新國畫預展之後 [About the reform of Chinese paintings—after watching preview of new Chinese arts]. *People's Daily* (Beiping), May 22, 1949.

Callahan, William A. *China: The Pessoptimist Nation.* Oxford: Oxford University Press, 2010.

Callahan, William A. *Sensible Politics: Visualizing International Relations.* New York: Oxford University Press, 2020.

Cams, Mario. "At the Borders of Qing Imperial Cartography." Newsletter, International Institute for Asian Studies, no. 84 (Autumn 2019). https://www.iias.asia/the-newsletter/article/borders-qing-imperial-cartography.

Carlson, Allen. *Unifying China, Integrating with the World: Securing Chinese Sovereignty in the Reform Era.* Stanford, CA: Stanford University Press, 2005.

Carrai, Maria Adele. *Sovereignty in China: A Genealogy of a Concept Since 1840.* Cambridge, MA: Cambridge University Press, 2019.

Carrico, Kevin. *The Great Han: Race, Nationalism, and Tradition in China Today.* Oakland, CA: University of California Press, 2017.

Cerella, Antonio. "Space and Sovereignty: A Reverse Perspective." In *Art and Sovereignty in Global Politics*, ed. Douglas Howland, Elizabeth Lillehoj, and Maximilian Mayer, 31–57. New York: Palgrave Macmillan, 2017.

Chan, Pedith. "In Search of the Southeast: Tourism, Nationalism, and Scenic Landscape in Republican China." *Twentieth-Century China*, 43, no. 3 (October 2018): 207–31.

Chang Dae Oup. *Capitalist Development in Korea: Labour, Capital, and the Myth of the Development State.* London: Routledge, 2009.

Chang, Shih-ying 張世瑛. "Qingmo minchu de bianju yu shengti" 清末民初的變局與身體 [The changing world and bodies during late Qing and early republican period]. PhD dissertation, Department of History, National Chengchi University, 2006.

Changxi 昌西. "Renkuang: Zhege bei Zhongguo hulianwang shencha de wanguo xinci, weishenmo rang tongzhizhe gandao jingti?" 人礦：這個被中國互聯網審查的網絡新詞，為什麼讓統治者感到警惕？ [Human mines: Why are the rulers on guard against this new term censored in China's cyber world?]. *The Initium*, February 2, 2023. https://theinitium.com/article/20230202-opinion-china-human-mines/

Chari, Sharad, and Katherine Verdery. "Thinking Between the Posts: Postcolonialism, Postsocialism, and Ethnography After the Cold War." *Comparative Studies in Society and History* 51, no. 1 (2009): 6–34.

Chen, Chunlai ed. *China's Integration with the Global Economy: WTO Accession, Foreign Direct Investment, and International Trade.* Cheltenham, UK: Edward Elgar, 2009.

Chen, Hon Fai. *Chinese Sociology: State Building and the Institutionalization of Globally Circulated Knowledge.* London: Palgrave Macmillan, 2018.

Chen Jianhua 陳建華. "Chinese 'Revolution' in the Syntax of World Revolution." In *Tokens of Exchange: The Problem of Translation in Global Circulations*, ed. Lydia H. Liu, 355–74. Durham, NC: Duke University Press, 1999.

Chen Lai 陳來. "Yinshang de jisi zongjiao yu Xi Zhou de tianming xinyang" 殷商的祭祀宗教與西周的天命信仰 [The worship and religious practices in the Yinshang period and the belief in Heaven's Mandate in Western Zhou dynasty] 中原文化研究 [The Central Plains culture research), no. 2 (2014): 18–24.

Chen, Leslie H. Dingyan. *Chen Jiongming and the Federalist Movement: Regional Leadership and Nation Building in Early Republican China*. Ann Arbor: University of Michigan Press, 1999.

Chen, Ling. *Manipulating Globalization: The Influence of Bureaucrats on Business in China*. Stanford, CA: Stanford University Press, 2018.

Chen Shou 陳壽. "Wu Shu" 吳書 [Book of Wu]. *Sanguozhi* 三國志, vol. 65. Shanghai: Zhonghua Shuju, 1960 [c. 265–300].

Chen Weihe. "The Landscape Painting of Li Keren and Its Special Qualities." PhD Dissertation, University of Durham, 1997.

Cheng, Anne. "Nationalism, Citizenship, and the Old Text/New Text Controversy in Late Nineteenth Century China." In *Imagining the People: Chinese Intellectuals and the Concept of Citizenship, 1890–1920*, ed. Joshua A Fogel and Peter G. Zarrow, 61–81. Armonk, NY: M.E. Sharpe, 1997.

Chrostowska, S. D. *Utopia in the Age of Survival: Between Myth and Politics*. Stanford: Stanford University Press, 2021.

Chung, Anita ed. *Chinese Art in an Age of Revolution: Fu Baoshi (1904–1965)*. New Haven, CT: Yale University Press, 2012.

Clinton, Maggie. *Revolutionary Nativism: Fascism and Culture in China, 1925–1937*. Durham, NC: Duke University Press, 2017.

Cohen, Jerome Alan. *The Criminal Process in the People's Republic of China, 1949–1963: An Introduction*. Cambridge, MA: Harvard University Press, 2013 [1968].

Cook, Alexander C. ed. *Mao's Little Red Book: A Global History*. Cambridge: Cambridge University Press, 2014.

Cosgrove, Denis E. *Social Formation and Symbolic Landscape*. Clifton, NJ: Barnes & Noble, 1984.

Creemers, Rogier. "China's Conception of Cyber Sovereignty: Rhetoric and Realization." In *Governing Cyberspace: Behavior, Power, and Diplomacy*, ed. Dennis Broeders and Bibi van den Berg, 107–42. Lanham: Rowman and Littlefield, 2020.

Croizier, Ralph. "Hu Xian Peasant Painting: From Revolutionary Icon to Market Commodity." In *Art in Turmoil: The Chinese Cultural Revolution, 1966–76*, ed. Richard King, 136–65. Vancouver: UBC Press, 2010.

Crossley, Pamala Kye. *A Translucent Mirror: History and Identity in Qing Imperial Ideology*. Berkeley: University of California Press, 1999.

Croxton, Derek. "The Peace of Westphalia of 1648 and the Origins of Sovereignty." *International History Review* 21, no. 3 (2005): 569–91.

Culp, Robert Joseph. *Articulating Citizenship: Civic Education and Student Politics in Southeastern China, 1912–1940*. Cambridge, MA: Harvard University Asia Centre, 2007.

Deleuze, Gilles. "Desire and Pleasure." In *Two Regimes of Madness: Texts and Interviews 1975–1995*, ed. David Lapoujade, trans. Ames Hodges and Mike Taormina, 122–34. New York: Semiotext(e), 2006.

Derrida, Jacques. "Force of Law: The 'Mystical Foundations of Authority." In *Deconstruction and the Possibility of Justice*, ed. Drucilla Cornell, Michael Rosenfeld, and David Carlson, 3–67. London: Routledge, 1992.

Derrida, Jacques. *Rogues: Two Essays on Reason.* Stanford, CA: Stanford University Press, 2005.

Derrida, Jacques. *The Beast and the Sovereign.* Vol. 1. Trans. Geoffrey Bennington. Chicago: Chicago University Press, 2009.

Dikötter, Frank. *The Discourse of Race in Modern China.* Hong Kong: Hong Kong University Press, 1992.

Dikötter, Frank. *Mao's Great Famine: The History of China's Most Devastating Catastrophe, 1958–62.* London: Bloomsbury, 2010.

Dong, Yifu. "Coal, Which Built a Chinese City, Now Threatens to Bury It." *The New York Times.* October 6, 2015. https://www.nytimes.com/2015/10/07/world/asia/china-coal-mines-fushun.html.

Dong Zhongshu 董仲舒. "Shencha minghao" 深察名號; "Wangdao tong san" 王道通三; "Wangdao" 王道, *Chunqiu fanlu* 春秋繁露. Beijing: Zhonghua Shuju, 2011[c. 206–9 BCE].

Duara, Prasenjit. *Culture, Power, and the State: Rural North China, 1900–1942.* Stanford, CA: Stanford University Press, 1988.

Duara, Prasenjit. *Rescuing History from the Nation: Questioning Narratives of Modern China.* Chicago: Chicago University Press, 1995.

Duara, Prasenjit. *Sovereignty and Authenticity: Manchukuo and the East Asia Modern.* Lanham, MD: Rowman and Littlefield, 2003.

Durrant, Stephen Wai-yee Li and David Schaberg, trans. and eds. *Zuo Tradition/Zuozhuan: Commentary on the "Spring and Autumn Annals."* Seattle: University of Washington Press, 2016.

Eastman, Lloyd E. "Who Lost China? Chiang Kai-shek Testifies." *China Quarterly*, no. 88 (1981): 658–68.

Economy, Elizabeth. *The Third Revolution: Xi Jinping and the New Chinese State.* Oxford: Oxford University Press, 2018.

Editorial. "Li dazhi, gu ganjin, shenru shenghuo, fanrong chuangzuo" 立大志鼓干勁 深入生活 繁榮創作 [Being ambitious, courageous, entering deep in life, making prosperous creations]. *Meishu* 美術 [Art], no. 1 (1960): 46.

Ekbladh, David. "From Consensus to Crisis: The Postwar Career of Nation-building in U.S. Foreign Relation." In *Nation Building: Beyond Afghanistan and Iraq*, ed. Francis Fukuyama, 19–41. Baltimore, MD: Johns Hopkins University Press, 2006.

Elliott, Mark C. *The Manchu Way: The Eight Banners and Ethnic Identity in Late Imperial China.* Stanford, CA: Stanford University Press, 2001.

Elman, Benjamin A. *A Cultural History of Civil Examinations in Late Imperial China.* Berkeley: University of California Press, 2000.

Faure, David. "The Lineages as a Cultural Invention: The Case of the Pearl River Delta." *Modern China* 15, no. 1 (1989): 4–36.

Fei Xiaotong 費孝通. *Xiangtu Zhongguo* 鄉土中國 [Rural China]. Shanghai: Guanchashe, 1948.

Fei Xiaotong 費孝通. et al. *Huangquan yu shenquan* 皇權與紳權 [The rights of sovereign and the rights of gentry]. Shanghai: Guanchashe, 1948.

Feng Tianyu 馮天瑜. *"Fengjian" kaolun* 「封建」考論 [An investigation of "feudalism"]. 2nd ed. Wuhan: Wuhan daxue chubanshe, 2007.

Fifield, Anna. "Coronavirus Tests Xi's 'Heavenly Mandate,' but Proves a Godsend for His Surveillance State." *The Washington Post*, March 3, 2020. https://www.washingtonpost.com/world/asia_pacific/coronavirus-tests-xis-heavenly-mandate-but-proves-a-godsend-for-his-surveillance-state/2020/03/03/454f6880-59fb-11ea-8efd-0f904bdd8057_story.html.

Fitzgerald, John. "The Nationless State: The Search for a Nation in Modern Chinese Nationalism." *Australian Journal of Chinese Affairs* 33 (1995): 75–104.

Foong Ping. *The Efficacious Landscape: On the Authorities of Painting at the Northern Song Court.* Cambridge, MA: Harvard University Asia Center, 2015.

Foreman, Matthew Wong. "Racial Modernity in Republican China, 1927–1937." *Asian Ethnicity* 23, no. 2 (2022): 377–97.

Foucault, Michel. *The Birth of Biopolitics: Lectures at the Collège de France, 1978–1979.* Trans. Graham Burchell. New York: Picador, 2008 [2004].

Foucault, Michel. "Governmentality." In *Foucault Effect: Studies in Governmentality*, ed. Graham Burchell, Colin Cordon, and Peter Miller, 87–104. Chicago: University of Chicago Press, 1991.

Foucault, Michel. *Security, Territory, Population: Lectures at the Collège de France, 1977–78.* Trans. Graham Burchell. New York: Palgrave Macmillan, 2007 [2004].

Foucault, Michel. *"Society Must Be Defended": Lectures at the Collège de France, 1975–1976.* Trans. David Macey. New York: Picador, 2003 [1997].

Fraser, Nancy. *Scales of Justice: Reimagining Political Space in a Globalizing World.* New York: Columbia University Press, 2009.

Frazier, Robeson Taj. *The East Is Black: Cold War China in the Black Radical Imagination.* Durham, NC: Duke University Press, 2014.

Friedman, Jeremy. "Soviet Policy in the Developing World and the Chinese Challenge in the 1960s." *Cold War History* 10, no. 2 (2010): 247–72.

Fu Baoshi 傅抱石. *Fu Baoshi yishu suibi*, 傅抱石藝術隨筆 [Art essays of Fu Baoshi]. Cheng Mingshi 承名世, ed. Shanghai: Shanghai wenyi chubanshe, 2001.

Furth, Charlotte. "Culture and Politics in Modern Chinese Conservatism." In *The Limits of Change: Essays on Conservative Alternatives in Republican China*, ed. Charlotte Furth, 22–53. Cambridge, MA: Harvard University Press, 1976.

Fushun City CPPCC History Committee 撫順市政協文史資料委員會, ed. *Fushun meikuang bainian 1901–2001* 撫順煤礦百年 1901–2001 [One hundred years of Fushun coal mine, 1901–2001]. Shenyang: Liaoning renmin chubanshe, 2004.

Gan Huaizhen 甘懷真. *Huangquan, liyi yu jingdian quanshi: Zhongguo gudai zhengzhi shi yanjiu* 皇權,禮儀與經典詮釋:中國古代政治史研究 [Imperial sovereignty, rites, and hermeneutics of classics: A study of the history of politics in ancient China]. Shanghai: Huadong shifan daxue, 2008.

Gao Hua 高華. "Tongmenghui de 'ansha shidai'" 同盟會的"暗殺時代" [The "assassinations period" of the Chinese Revolutionary Alliance]. "*Minjian lishi*" 民間歷史 [Folk history], Universities Service Center, Chinese University of Hong Kong, 1989.

Ge Zhaoguang. "Imagining 'All Under Heaven': The Political, Intellectual, and Academic Background of a New Utopia." Trans. Michael S. Duke and Josephine Chiu-Duke. In *Utopia and Utopianism in the Contemporary Chinese Context: Texts, Ideas, Spaces*, ed. David Der-wei Wang, Angela Ki Che Leung, and Zhang Yide, 15–35. Hong Kong: Hong Kong University Press, 2020.

Geertz, Clifford. *Agricultural Involution: The Processes of Ecological Change in Indonesia*. Berkeley: University of California Press, 1963.

Gibbs, Martin, et al. "#Funeral and Instagram: Death, Social Media, and Platform Vernacular," *Information, Communication, and Society* 18, no. 3 (2015): 255–68.

Girard, René. *Sacrifice*. Trans. Matthew Pattillo and David Dawson. East Lansing, MI: Michigan State University Press, 2011.

Goldhammer, Jesse. *The Headless Republic: Sacrificial Violence in Modern French Thought*. Ithaca, NY: Cornell University Press, 2005.

Goodman, Bryna. *Native Place, City, and Nation: Regional Networks and Identities in Shanghai, 1853–1937*. Berkeley: University of California Press, 1995.

Gradin, Carlos, Murry Leibbrandt, and Finn Tarp. "Global Inequality May Be Falling, but the Gap Between Haves and Have-nots is Growing." *The Conversation*, September 2, 2021. https://theconversation.com/global -inequality-may-be-falling-but-the-gap-between-haves-and-have -nots-is-growing-159825.

Grey, Jerry. "Chinese Youths More Confident in China's Future, Don't Admire the West." *Global Times*, May 8, 2022. https://www.globaltimes.cn/ page/202205/1265055.shtml.

Grinin, Leonid, and Andrey Korotayev. "Institutions, Counterrevolutions, and Democracy." In *Handbook of Revolutions in the 21st Century*, ed. Jack A. Goldstone, Leonid Grinin, and Andrey Korotayev, 105–36. Cham, Switzerland: Springer International Publishing, 2022.

Grzymała-Busse, Anna Maria. *Nations under God: How Churches Use Moral Authority to Influence Policy*. Princeton, NJ: Princeton University Press, 2015.

Gu Yanwu 顧炎武. *Rizhi lu* 日知錄 [Records of daily progressive knowledge]. Changsha: Yuelu Book Press, 1994 [c. 1695].

Gu Yi. *Chinese Ways of Seeing and Open-Air Painting*. Cambridge, MA: Harvard University Asia Center, 2020.

Gunitsky, Seva. "From Shocks to Waves: Hegemonic Transitions and Democratization in the Twentieth Century." *International Organization* 68 (Summer 2014): 561–97.

Gupta, Akhil. *Red Tape: Bureaucracy, Structural Violence, and Poverty in India*. Durham, NC: Duke University Press, 2012.

Gürel, Burak, and Taylan, Eylem. "Critique of the Critics of Giovanni Arrighi's *Adam Smith in Beijing*." *Alternatif Politika* 11, no. 2 (2019): 430–47.

Habermas, Jürgen. "Popular Sovereignty as Procedure." In *Deliberative Democracy: Essays on Reason and Politics*, ed. James Bohman and William Rehg, 35–65. Cambridge: MA: MIT Press, 1997.

Halegua, Aaron. "Where is the Belt and Road Initiative Taking International Labour Rights? An Examination of Worker Abuse by Chinese Firms in Saipan." In *The Belt and Road Initiative and Global Governance*, ed. A. Maria Carrai, Jan-Christophe Defraigne, and Jan Wouters, 225–57. Cheltenham, UK: Edward Elgar, 2020.

Hardt, Michael, and A. Negri. *Commonwealth*. Cambridge, MA: Harvard University Press, 2009.

Harrison, Henrietta. *The Making of the Republican Citizen: Political Ceremonies and Symbols in China, 1911–1929*. Hong Kong: Oxford University Press, 2000.

Hartcher, Peter. "The Money or Our Sovereignty: China Leaves Us No Choice." *Sydney Morning Herald*, May 1, 2020, www.smh.com.au/pol itics/federal/the-money-or-our-sovereignty-china-leaves-us-no -choice-20200501-p54p57.html.

Hastings, Adrian. *The Construction of Nationhood: Ethnicity, Religion, and Nationalism*. Cambridge: Cambridge University Press, 1997.

Hay, Jonathan. *Shitao: Painting and Modernity in Early Qing China*. New York: Cambridge University Press, 2001.

Heinzig, Dieter. *The Soviet Union and Communist China, 1945–1950: The Arduous Road to the Alliance*. Armonk, NY: M.E. Sharpe, 2004.

Hill, Emily M. "War, Disunity, and State Building in China, 1912–1949." *Twentieth-Century China* 47, no. 1 (2022): 20–29.

Ho, Kelly. "'Damp Squib': Beijing Condemns UK's Plan to Expand Visa Eligibility for Younger Hongkongers." *Hong Kong Free Press*, February 25, 2022, https://hongkongfp.com/2022/02/25/damp-squib-beijing-condemns -uks-plan-to-expand-visa-eligibility-for-younger-hongkongers.

Ho, Matt, Holly Chik, and Echo Xie. "China's National Security Commission Met in Secret Amid Coronavirus Pandemic." *South China Morning Post*, June 29, 2020.

Ho Ming-sho. *Challenging Beijing's Mandate of Heaven: Taiwan's Sunflower Movement and Hong Kong's Umbrella Movement*. Philadelphia: Temple University Press, 2019.

Hobbes, Thomas. *Leviathan*. Cambridge: Cambridge University Press, 1991.

Hobsbawm, Eric J. *Nations and Nationalism Since 1780*. Cambridge: Cambridge University Press, 1990.

Hon Tze-ki. "From Babbitt to 'Bai Bide': Interpretations of New Humanism in Xueheng." In *Beyond the May Fourth Paradigm: In Search of Chinese Modernity*, ed. Kai-wing Chow et al., 253–67. Lanham, MD: Lexington Books, 2008.

Howland, Douglas. *International Law and Japanese Sovereignty: The Emerging Global Order in the 19th Century*. New York: Palgrave Macmillan, 2016.

Hu Gaohus, et al. "Aphrodisiac Properties of Allium Tuberosum Seeds Extract." *Journal of Ethnopharmacology* 122, no. 3 (2009): 579–82.

Hu Shi 胡適. "Buxiu: wo de zongjiao" 不朽——我的宗教 [Immortality: My religion]. *Hu Shi xuanji* 胡適選集 [Selected collection of Hu Shi], 68–77. Tianjin: Tianjin renmin chubanshe, 1991 [1919].

Hu Shi 胡適. "Liansheng zizhi yu junfa geju (da Chen Duxiu) 聯省自治與軍閥割據 (答陳獨秀). [Self-ruled provinces alliance and separatism of warlords (Reply to Chen Duxiu)]. *Nuli zhoubao* 努力週報, September 10, 1922. In *Hu Shi wenji* 胡適文集 [Collected works of Hu Shi] 12 vols., ed. Ouyang Zhesheng 歐陽哲生. Beijing: Peking University Press, 2013 3:331–35.

Hu Shi 胡適. "Zhongguo wu ducai de biyao yu keneng." 中國無獨裁的必要與可能 [There is no need and no possibilities for China to practice dictatorship]. *Independent Criticism* 獨立評論, December 9, 1934. In *Hu Shi Wenji*, 11:501–6.

Huang Ko-wu 黃克武. *Jiang Jieshi yu Yangming xue: yi Qingmo tiaoshi chuantong wei beijing zhi fenxi* 蔣介石與陽明學：以清末調適傳統為背景之分析 [Jiang Jieshi and The Yangming School: Analysis with the background of late Qing's tradition adaptation]. In *Jiang Zhongzheng yu jindai Zhong-Ri guanxi* 蔣中正與近代中日關係, ed. Huang Tzu-chin 黃自進, 1–26, Taipei: Daoxiang, 2006.

Huang Mingqian 黃名芊. *Bimo jiangshan: Fu Baoshi shuai tuan xiesheng shilu*. 筆墨江山：傅抱石率團寫生實錄 [*Jiangshan in brush and ink: Records of Fu Baoshi leading a life-drawing team*]. Beijing: Renmin meishu chubanshe, 2005.

Huang, Philip C. C. *The Peasant Family and Rural Development in the Yangzi Delta, 1350–1988*. Stanford, CA: Stanford University Press, 1990.

Huang Yu-jen 黃育仁. "Zhongguo gaibian gang xuanzhi, Minjindang qianze: jiquan badao chengnuo shiru wuwu [Democratic Progressive Party condemns China changing Hong Kong's election structure: Dictatorial *baodao* ignoring prior promises] 中國改變港選制 民進黨譴責：極權霸道承諾視如無物, March 12, 2021, https://news.cts.com.tw/cts/politics/202103/202103122034459.html.

Huang Zong Xi 黃宗羲. "Yuanjun" 原君 [*How to be an emperor*], *Mingyi daifang lu* 明夷待訪錄. Beijing: Zhonghua Shuju, 1985 [c. 1662].

Hui, Victoria Tin-bor. *War and State Formation in Ancient China and Early Modern Europe*. Cambridge: Cambridge University Press, 2005.

Jenco, Leigh K. "'Rule by Man' and 'Rule by Law' in Early Republican China: Contributions to a Theoretical Debate." *Journal of Asian Studies* 69, no. 1 (2010): 181–203.

Jessen, Mathias Hein, and Nicolai Won Eggers. "Governmentality and Stratification: Towards a Foucauldian Theory of the State." *Theory, Culture, and Society* 37, no. 1 (2020): 53–72.

Jiang Feng 江豐. "Guohua gaizao de diyibu" 國畫改造的第一步 [The first step in *guohua* reform]. *People's Daily* 人民日報, May 25, 1949.

Jiang Hong 姜紅, Hu Anqi 胡安琪, and Fang Xiaxuan 方俠旋. "Shengsi jiemian: yu shizhe de shuzi 'jiaowang'" 生死界面：與逝者的數字「交往」 [The Interface between life and death: digital communication with the deceased]. *Communication and Society* 傳播與社會學刊 62 (2022): 69–103.

Jiang, Xiaoli. "Shamanism and the Manchu Bannermen of the Qing Dynasty." *Religions* 13, no 10 (2022). https://doi.org/10.3390/rel13100884.

Jin Guantao 金觀濤, "Bainian shiye: tianxia guan he dongya shehui de guoji guanxi" 百年視野：天下觀和東亞社會的國際關係 [A hundred year's vision: *tianxian guan* and the international relations of East Asian society]. *ICCS Journal of Modern Chinese Studies* 4, no. 2 (2012): 3–8.

Jin Guantao 金觀濤, Liu Qingfeng 劉青峰, and Chiu Weiyun 邱偉雲. "Zhongguo xiandai zhuquan guannian xingcheng de shuwei renwen yanjiu" 中國現代主權觀念形成的數位人文研究 [Digital Humanities Research of the formation of the concept of modern sovereignty in China]. *Ershiyi shiji* 二十一世紀, no. 172 (April 2019): 49–67.

Johnson, Tina Phillips. *Childbirth in Republican China: Delivering Modernity*. Lanham, MD: Rowman and Littlefield, 2011.

Jones, Robert A. *The Soviet Concept of "Limited Sovereignty" from Lenin to Gorbachev: The Brezhnev Doctrine.* New York: Palgrave Macmillan, 1990.

Kang Youwei 康有為. "Da Nan Bei Meizhou zhuhuashang lun Zhongguo zhi kexing lixian bu kexing geming shu" 答南北美洲諸華商論中國只可行立憲不可行革命書 [Answering the various Chinese merchants in South and North America that we should practice constitutionalism, not revolution]. In *Kang Youwei quanji,* 康有為全集 [Complete works of Kang Youwei], 20 vols, ed. Jiang Yihua 姜義華 and Zhang Ronghua 張榮華. Beijing: Beijing renmin daxue chubanshe, 7:312–33, 2007 [1902].

Keevak, Michael. *Becoming Yellow: A Short History of Racial Thinking.* Princeton, NJ: Princeton University Press, 2011.

Khoja-Moolji, Shenila. *Sovereign Attachments: Masculinity, Muslimness, and Affective Politics in Pakistan.* Berkeley: University of California Press, 2021.

King, Gary, Jennifer Pan, and Margaret E. Roberts. "How the Chinese Government Fabricates Social Media Posts for Strategic Distraction, Not Public Engagement." *American Political Science Review* 111, no. 3 (2017): 484–501.

Kipnis, Andrew. "Neoliberalism Reified: Suzhi Discourse and Tropes of Neoliberalism in the People's Republic of China." *Journal of the Royal Anthropological Institute* 13, no. 2 (2007): 383–400.

Kokas, Aynne. *Hollywood Made in China.* Berkeley: University of California Press, 2017.

Krasner, Stephen. *Sovereignty: Organized Hypocrisy.* Princeton, NJ: Princeton University Press, 1999.

Kristeva, Julia. *About Chinese Women.* Trans. Anita Barrows. New York: Marion Boyars, 1986.

Lam Tong. *A Passion for Facts: Social Surveys and the Construction of the Chinese Nation-state, 1900–1949.* Berkeley: University of California Press, 2011.

Lee Leo Ou-fan. *The Romantic Generation of Modern Chinese Writers.* Cambridge, MA: Harvard University Press, 1973.

Lee Sangjoon. "The South Korean Film Industry and the Chinese Film Market." *Screen* 60, no. 2 (2019): 332–41.

Leibold, James. *Reconfiguring Chinese Nationalism: How the Qing Frontier and Its Indigenes Became Chinese.* New York: Palgrave Macmillan, 2007.

Lenin, V.I. "The Right of Nations to Self-Determination." In V.I. *Lenin Collected Works,* vol. 20, trans. Bernard Isaacs and Joe Fineberg, 393–454. Moscow: Progress, 1972.

Levitsky, Steven, and Lucan Way. *Revolution and Dictatorship: The Violent Origins of Durable Authoritarianism.* Princeton, NJ: Princeton University Press, 2022.

Lew, Timothy Tingfang. "China's Renaissance—the Christian Opportunity." *The Chinese Recorder and Missionary Journal*, May 1921, 301–23.

Lewis, Mark Edward. *The Early Chinese Empires: Qin and Han*. Cambridge, MA: Harvard University Press, 2022 [2007].

Lewis, Mark Edward. *Sanctioned Violence in Early China*. Albany: State University of New York Press, 1990.

Lewis, Mark Edward, and Mei-yu Hsieh. "Tianxia and the Invention of Empire in East Asia." In *Chinese Visions of World Order: Tianxia, Culture, and World Politics*, 25–48. Durham, NC: Duke University Press, 2017.

Li Chao 李超 and Wang Peidong 王培棟. "Li Keran 'hongse shanshui' yishu fengge fenxi: yi *Wanshan hongbian* wei li." 李可染"紅色山水"藝術風格分析——以《萬山紅遍》為例 [Analysis of the artistic style of Li Keran's "Red landscape": *Redness all over Ten Thousand Mountain* as an example"]. *Dongfang shoucang* 東方收藏 [Oriental collection], no. 1 (2021): 67–72.

Li Hongzhang 李鴻章. "Chouyi zhizao lunchuan weike caiche zhe" 籌議製造輪船未可裁撤摺 [Memorial to the Emperor about the negative consequences of shipbuilding budget cut] (1872). In *Li Hongzhang quanji* 李鴻章全集 [Complete volume of Li Hongzhang], 9 vols. (Shanghai: Shanghai renmin chubanshe, 1986), 2:676–78.

Li Hongzhang "Chouyi haifang zhe" 籌議海防摺 [Memorial to the Emperor about coastal defense] (1874). In *Li Hongzhang quanji*. 李鴻章全集 [Complete volume of Li Hongzhang)], 9 vols. Shanghai: Shanghai renmin chubanshe, 1986, 2:825–32.

Li Huaiyin. "From Revolution to Modernization: The Paradigmatic Transition in Chinese Historiography in the Reform Era." *History and Theory* 49 (2010): 336–60.

Li Huaiyin 李懷印. "Jizhonghua difangzhuyi yu jindai guojia jianshe: Minguo Beijing zhengfu shiqi junfa zhengzhi de zai renshi" 集中化地方主義與近代國家建設——民國北京政府時期軍閥政治的再認識 [Centralized localism and modern nation building: Re-understanding the warlord politics of the Beijing government in the Republican period]. *Jindaishi yanjiu* 近代史研究, no. 5 (2018): 67–84.

Li Jie. *Utopian Ruins: A Memorial Museum of the Mao Era*. Durham, NC: Duke University Press, 2020.

Li Jinghan 李景漢. "Zhongguo shehui diaocha yundong." 中國社會調查運動 [Chinese Social Survey Movement], *Shehui xuejie* 社會學界, no. 1 (June 1927).

Li Keqiang. "Report on the Work of the Government." Delivered at the Third Session of the 12th National People's Congress on 5 March, 2015." http://english.www.gov.cn/archive/publications/2015/03/05/content_281475066179954.htm.

Li Shi, Terry Sicular, and Finn Tarp. "China: Structural Chang, Transition, Rent-Seeking and Corruption, and Government Policy." In *Inequality in the Developing World*, ed. Carlos Gradin, Murry Leibbrandt, and Finn Tarp, 133–56. Oxford: Oxford University Press, 2021.

Li Wen and Dennis Tao Yang. "The Great Leap Forward: Anatomy of a Central Planning Disaster." *Journal of Political Economy* 113, no. 4 (2005): 840–77.

Li Xiaolai 李笑來. *Jiucai de ziwo xiuyang* 韭菜的自我修養 [Self-cultivation of the garlic chives]. Jiangsu: Fenghuang wenyi chubanshe, 2018.

Liang Qichao 梁啟超. "Jiefang yu gaizao fakan ci" 解放與改造發刊詞 [Foreword to the inaugural issue of *Liberation and Reform*]. *Yinbingshi wenji* 飲冰室文集 [Essays collection of Yinbingshi], 45 vols. (Taipei: Zhonghua shuju, 1960) 35:19–22 [1920].

Liang Qichao 梁啟超. "Jinbu dang ni Zhonghua minguo xianfa cao'an" 進步黨擬中華民國憲法草案 [Draft of Republic of China Constitution by Progressive Party], *Liang Qichao quanji* 梁啟超全集 [The complete volume of Liang Qichao], 20 vols. (Beijing: Beijing chubanshe, 1999), 9:2615–2626 [1913].

Liang Qichao 梁啟超. "Kaiming zhuanzhi lun" 開明專制論 [On Liberal autocracy] *Yinbingshi wenji*. 飲冰室文集 [Essays collection of Yinbingshi], 45 vols. (Taipei: Zhonghua shuju, 1960) 35:13–83 [1906].

Liang Qichao 梁啟超. "Lun xiaoshuo yu qunzhi zhi guanxi" 論小說與群治之關係 [About the relation between novels and politics]. *Liang Qichao quanji* 梁啟超全集 [The complete volume of Liang Qichao], 20 vols. (Beijing: Beijing chubanshe, 1999), 20:884 [1902].

Liang Qichao 梁啟超. "Xin Zhongguo weilai ji" 新中國未來記 [The future of new China]. Originally published in *Xin xiaoshuo* 新小說 [New fictions] nos. 1, 2, 3, 7 (1902); *Liang Qichao quanji* 梁啟超全集 [The complete volume of Liang Qichao] 20 vols. (Beijing: Beijing chubanshe, 1999), 19:5609–5637.

Liang Zhiping. "Imagining 'Tianxia'" Building Ideology in Contemporary China." Original Chinese: 梁治平, "想像'天下': 當代中國的意識形態建構," *Reflexion* 思想 36 (December 2018): 71–177. Trans. David Ownby, https://www.readingthechinadream.com/liang-zhiping-tianxia-and-ideology.html.

Lin, Delia. "The CCP's Exploitation of Confucianism and Legalism." In *Routledge Handbook of the Chinese Communist Party*, ed. Willy Wo-Lap Lam, 47–58. London: Routledge, 2017.

Lin, Delia, and Susan Trevaskes. "Creating a Virtuous Leviathan: The Party, Law, and Socialist Core Value." *Asian Journal of Law and Society* 6, no. 1 (2019): 41–66.

Lin Mingde 林明德. "Qingmo Minchu de sifa gaige" 清末民初的司法改革 [Juridical reform during late Qing and early Republican period]. *Lishi xuebao* 歷史學報 [Academic Journal of History] 26 (1998): 135–65.

Liu, Junping. "The Evolution of *Tianxia* cosmology and Its Philosophical Implications." *Frontiers of Philosophy in China* 1, no. 4 (2006): 517–38.

Liu Xiaobo. "That Holy Word, 'Revolution.'" In *Popular Protest and Political Culture in Modern China*, ed. Jeffrey Wasserstrom and Elizabeth Perry, 309–24. Boulder, CO: Westview Press, 1994.

Liu Xiaofeng 劉小楓 ed. (Originally written by Carl Schmitt.) *Zhengzhi de gainian* 政治的概念 [Political concepts]. Shanghai: Shanghai renmin chubanshe, 2015.

Lo, Vai L. *Law and Society in China.* Cheltenham: Edward Elgar, 2020.

Locke, Richard M. *The Promise and Limits of Private Power: Promoting Labour Standards in a Global Economy.* Cambridge: Cambridge University Press, 2013.

Loewe, Michael. "Imperial Sovereignty: Dong Zhongshu's Contribution and His Predecessors." In *Foundation and Limits of State Power in China*, ed. Stuart R. Schram, 11–32. Hong Kong: Chinese University Press, 1987.

Loubere, Nicholas. "China's Internet Finance Boom and Tyrannies of Inclusion." *China Perspectives* 4 (2017): 9–18.

Lovell, Julia. *Maoism: A Global History.* London: The Bodley Head, 2019.

Lowsen, Ben. "Xi Jinping's Great Leap." *The Diplomat*, January 5, 2023. https://thediplomat.com/2023/01/xi-jinpings-great-leap/

Lu Fakui 陸發聵. "Observing the Public Opinions: The Night on the Internet When Li Wenliang Died" 輿情觀察：李文亮去世後互聯網上的一夜. Initium Media 端傳媒, February 7, https://theinitium.com/article/20200207-liwenliang-public-opinion/.

Lu Xun 魯迅. "Huran xiangdao" 忽然想到 [I suddenly realize]. *Lu Xun quanji* 魯迅全集 [Complete works of Lu Xun], 18 vols. Beijing: Renmin wenxue chubanshe, 2005, 3:14–21.

Lu Xun. *Diary of a Madman and Other Stories.* Trans. William A. Lyell. Honolulu: University of Hawaii Press, 1990.

Ma, Shaoling. *The Stone and the Wireless: Mediating China, 1861-1906.* Durham, NC: Duke University Press, 2021.

Magnus, George. *Red Flags: Why Xi's China Is in Jeopardy.* New Haven, CT: Yale University Press, 2018.

Mao Zedong 毛澤東. "Fandui zhuguan zhuyi he zongpai zhuyi" 反對主觀主義和宗派主義 [Opposing subjectivism and sectarianism]. September 10, 1941; *Mao Zedong wenji* 毛澤東文集 [Writings of Mao Zedong], 86 vols. (Beijing: Renmin chubanshe, 1993), 2:372–73.

Mao Zedong 毛澤東. "Lun shi da guanxi" 論十大關係 [On ten major relationships], April 25, 1956; *Mao Zedong wenji* 毛澤東文集 [Writings of Mao Zedong] 8 vols (Beijing: Renmin chubanshe, 1999), 7:23–49.

Mao Zedong 毛澤東. *On Khrushchov's Phoney Communism and Its Historical Lessons for the World — Comment on the Open Letter of the Central*

Committee of the CPSU (IX). July 14, 1964. Peking: Foreign Language Press, 1964.

Mao Zedong 毛澤東. "Zhongjian didai you liangge" 中間地帶有兩個 [There are two middle areas] (1963/1964); *Mao Zedong waijiao wen xuan* 毛澤東外交文選,ed. PRC Ministry of Foreign Affairs and Party Literature Research Center, CPC Central Committee. Beijing: Zhongyang wenxian chuban-she, 1994, 506–9.

Marx, Karl. *Capital: A Critique of Political Economy.* London: ElecBook, 1998.

Marx, Karl, and Frederick Engels. *The German Ideology.* New York: International Publishers, 1970.

Mazzocco, Ilaria, and Scott Kennedy. "Public Opinion in China: A Liberal Silent Majority." Center for Strategic and International Studies, February 9, 2022, https://www.csis.org/features/public-opinion-china-liberal-silent-majority.

Mazzuca, Sebastián. *Latecomer State Formation: Political Geography and Capacity Failure in Latin America.* New Haven, CT: Yale University Press, 2021.

Meisner, Maurice. *Mao's China and After: A History of the People's Republic.* 3rd ed. New York: The Free Press, 1999.

Mitchell, Ryan. "Manchukuo's Contested Sovereignty: Legal Activism, Rights Consciousness, and Civil Resistance in a 'Puppet State.'" *Asian Journal of Law and Society* 3, no. 2 (2016): 351–76.

Mitchell, Timothy. *Colonising Egypt.* Berkeley: University of California Press, 1988.

Mote, Frederick W. *Intellectual Foundations of China.* New York: Alfred A. Knopf, 1971.

Mou Zongsan 牟宗三. *Zhengdao yu zhidao* 政道與治道 [Sovereignty and governance]. Taiwan: Xuesheng shuju, 1987.

Mühlhahn, Klaus. *Criminal Justice in China: A History.* Cambridge, MA: Harvard University Press, 2009.

Murthy, Viren. "Resistance to Modernity and the Logic of Self-Negation as Politics: Takeuchi Yoshimi and Wang Hui on Lu Xun." *positions: asia critique* 24, no. 2 (2016): 513–54.

Musgrove, Charles D. *China's Contested Capital: Architecture, Ritual, and Response in Nanjing.* Honolulu: University of Hawaii Press, 2013.

Nadeau, Randall. "Chinese Religion in the Shang and Zhou Dynasties." In *The Wiley-Blackwell Companion to Chinese Religions,* ed. Randall Nadeau, 25–49. Malden, MA: Blackwell, 2012.

Ni Wei 倪偉. *Minzu xiangxiang yu guojia tongzhi: 1928–1949 nian Guomin-dang de wenyi zhengce ji wenxue yundong* 民族想像與國家統制：1928–1949年國民黨的文藝政策及文學運動 [Imagination of nation and the governance of state: The literary policy and movement of the Chinese Nationalist Party between 1928 and 1949]. Taipei: Renjian chubanshe, 2011.

Nuyen, A. T. "The 'Mandate of Heaven': Mencius and the Divine Command Theory of Political Legitimacy." *Philosophy East and West*, 63, no. 2 (2013): 113–26.

Nye, Joseph. *Bound to Lead: The Changing Nature of American Power*. New York: Basic Books, 1990.

Osterhammel, Jürgen. *The Transformation of the World: A Global History of the Nineteenth Century*. Trans. Patrick Camilla. Princeton, NJ: Princeton University Press, 2014 [2009].

Pan Guangdan 潘光旦. "Minzu texing yu minzu weisheng" 民族特性與民族衛生 [National character and national hygiene]. In *Pan Guangdan wenji* 潘光旦文集 [Writings of Pan Guangdan], 14 vols. Beijing: Peking University Press, 2000, 3:27–35 [1937].

Pang, Laikwan. *The Appearing Demos: Hong Kong During and After the Umbrella Movement*. Ann Arbor: University of Michigan Press, 2020.

Pang, Laikwan. "Can Dialectic Materialism Produce Beauty? The "Great Aesthetic Debates" (1956–1962) in the People's Republic of China." *International Journal of Asian Studies*, June 29, 2022, 1–14. doi:10.1017/S1479591422000171.

Pang, Laikwan. *Creativity and Its Discontents: China's Creative Industries and Intellectual Property Rights Offences*. Durham: Duke University Press, 2012.

Pang, Laikwan. "Making Sense of Labor: Works of Art and Arts of Work in China's Great Leap Forward." In *Sensing China: Modern Transformation of Sensory Culture*, ed. Xuelei Huang and Shengqing Wu, 151–73. London: Routledge, 2022.

Pang, Laikwan. "Mao's Dialectical Materialism: Possibilities for the Future." *Rethinking Marxism* 28, no. 1 (2016): 108–23.

Paris, Roland. "European Populism and the Return of 'Illiberal Sovereignty': A Case-study of Hungary." *International Affairs* 98, no. 2 (2022): 529–47.

Paulès, Xavier. "Warlords at Work: Four Crucial Realms and Four Dynamics of State Building in Republican China, 1916–1937." *Twentieth-Century China* 47, no. 1 (2022): 40–49.

Perry, Elizabeth J. *Challenging the Mandate of Heaven: Social Protest and State Power in China*. Oxford: Taylor & Francis, 2002.

Pickowicz, Paul. "Acting Like Revolutionaries: Shi Hui, the Wenhua Studio, and Private-Sector Filmmaking, 1949-52." In *Dilemmas of Victory: The Early Years of the People's Republic of China*, ed. Jeremy Brown and Paul Pickowicz, 256–87. Cambridge, MA: Harvard University Press, 2007.

Pines, Yuri. "Contested Sovereignty: Heaven, the Monarch, the People, and the Intellectuals in Traditional China." In *The Scaffolding of Sovereignty:*

Global and Aesthetic Perspectives on the History of a Concept, ed. Zvi Ben-dor Benite, Stefanos Geroulanos, and Nicole Jerr, 80–101. New York: Columbia University Press, 2017.

Polanyi, Karl. *The Great Transformation: The Political and Economic Origins of Our Time*. Boston: Beacon Press, 2001 [1944].

Poo Mu-chou. *In Search of Personal Welfare: A View of Ancient Chinese Religion*. Albany: State University of New York Press, 1998.

Potter, Pitman. *From Leninist Discipline to Socialist Legalism: Peng Zhen on Law and Political Authority in the PRC*. Stanford, CA: Stanford University Press, 2003.

Povinelli, Elizabeth A. *Geontologies: A Requiem to Late Liberalism*. Durham, NC: Duke University Press, 2016.

Preuß, Ulrich K. "Carl Schmitt and the Weimar Constitution." In *The Oxford Handbook of Carl Schmitt*, ed. Jens Meierhenrich and Oliver Simons, 474–89. Oxford: Oxford University Press, 2017.

Pye, Lucian W. "On Chinese Pragmatism in the 1980s." *China Quarterly* no. 106 (1986): 207–34.

Qi Xiangyang 齊向陽. "Fensui xin shahuang de 'youxian zhuquan lun'" 粉碎新沙皇的"有限主權論" [Smash the new tsar's theory of 'limited sovereignty"]. *Hong qi* 紅旗 [Red flag], no. 5; English translation in *Peking Review*, May 23, 1969, 21.

Qian Mu 錢穆. *Guoshi xinlun* 國史新論 [New Discussions of national history]. Taipei: Dongda tushu, 2004.

Qiang Shigong 強世功. *Zhongguo Xianggang: wenhua yu zhengzhi de shiye* 中國香港：文化與政治的視野 [Chinese Hong Kong: Perspectives of culture and politics]. Hong Kong: Oxford University Press, 2008.

Qiu Shiming 邱石冥. "Guanyu guohua chuangzuo jieshou yichan de yijian" 關於國畫創作接受遺產的意見 [My opinions about heritage in *guohua* production]. *Meishu* 美術 [Art], no. 1 of 1955: 37–41.

Roberts, Margaret E. *Censored: Distraction and Diversion Inside China's Great Firewall*. Princeton, NJ: Princeton University Press, 2019.

Rothwell, Matthew. *Transpacific Revolutionaries: The Chinese Revolution in Latin America*. London: Routledge, 2013.

Rousseau, Jean-Jacques. *The Social Contract and Other Later Political Writings*, ed. and trans. Victor Gourevitch. Cambridge: Cambridge University Press, 1997.

Rubinelli, Lucia. "How to Think beyond Sovereignty: On Sieyes and Constituent Power." *European Journal of Political Theory* 18, no.1 (2019): 47–67.

Ruggie, John. "Territoriality and Beyond: Problematizing Modernity in International Relations." *International Organization* 47, no. 1 (1993): 139–74.

Sakamoto, Hiroko. "The Cult of 'Love and Eugenics' in May Fourth Movement Discourse." *positions: east asia cultures critique* 12, no. 2 (2004): 329–76.

Sanft, Charles. *Communication and Cooperation in Early Imperial China: Publicizing the Qin Dynasty.* Albany: State University of New York Press, 2014.

Sarma, Mandira, and Pais, Jesim. "Financial Inclusion and Development." *Journal of International Development* 23 (2011): 613–28.

Scheuerman, William E. "Revolutions and Constitutions: Hannah Arendt's Challenge to Carl Schmitt." *Canadian Journal of Law and Jurisprudence* 10, no. 1 (1997): 141–61.

Schmitt, Carl. *The Concept of the Political.* Trans. George Schwab. Chicago: University of Chicago Press, 2007 [1932].

Schmitt, Carl. *The Crisis of Parliamentary Democracy.* Trans. Ellen Kennedy. Cambridge, MA: MIT Press, 1985 [1923].

Schmitt, Carl. *The Nomos of the Earth in the International Law of the Jus Publicum Europaeum.* New York: Telos Press, 2003 [1950].

Schmitt, Carl. *Political Romanticism.* Trans. Guy Oakes. Cambridge, MA: MIT Press, 1986 [1919].

Schmitt, Carl. *Political Theology: Four Chapters on the Concept of Sovereignty.* Trans. George Schwab. Cambridge, MA: MIT Press, 1985 [1922].

Schneider, Julia C. *Nation and Ethnicity: Chinese Discourses on History, Historiography, and Nationalism (1900s–1920s).* Leiden: Brill, 2017.

Schram, Stuart. *The Thought of Mao Tse-Tung.* Cambridge: Cambridge University Press, 1989.

Schucher, Günter. "The Fear of Failure: Youth Employment Problems in China." *International Labour Review* 156, no. 1 (2017): 73–98.

Scott, Shirley. "China's Nine-Dash Line, International Law, and the Monroe Doctrine Analogy." *China Information* 30, no. 3 (2016): 296–311.

Shanmu 山木. *Xinyi Zhuangzi duben* 新譯莊子讀本 [A reader of new interpretations of Zhuangzi]. Taipei: Sanmin Shuju, 1974 [c. 350–250 BCE].

Shapiro, Judith. *Mao's War Against Nature: Politics and the Environment in Revolutionary China.* Cambridge: Cambridge University Press, 2001.

Shapiro, Michael. *Methods and Nations: Cultural Governance and the Indigenous Subject.* New York: Routledge, 2014.

Shi Hsiao-kuang, "Zhonggong qiang Sun Zhongshan *fatong*, Hong jing yao dang zixing." 中共搶孫中山法統, 洪竟要黨自省 [CCP robs Sun Zhongshan's *fatong*, Hong asks the Party for self-reflection]. Liberty Times Net, November 13, 2016. https://news.ltn.com.tw/news/politics/paper/1051578

Shuai Hao 帥好. "Zhongguo huajia zai daqihuang zhong" 中國畫家在大饑荒中 [Chinese artists during the Great Famine]. Reprinted in *Open Magazine* 開放雜誌 [Kaifang zazhi], June 14, 2011. http://www.open.com.hk/about_us.php/content.php?id=299#.W4ovIM4zaUk

Sima Qian 司馬遷. "Li Si liezhuan" 李斯列傳 [Biography of Li Si]. *Shiji* 史記, vol. 87. Beijing: Zhonghua shuju, 1982 [c. 109–91 BCE].

Sima Qian and K. E. Brashier, *The First Emperor: Selections from the Historical Records*. Oxford: Oxford University Press, 2007.

Simpson, Audra. "The Sovereignty of Critique." *South Atlantic Quarterly* 119, no. 4 (2020): 685–99.

Skya, Walter. *Japan's Holy War: The Ideology of Radical Shinto Ultranationalism*. Durham, NC: Duke University Press, 2009.

Slater, Dan, and Joseph Wong. *From Development to Democracy: The Transformations of Modern Asia*. Princeton, NJ: Princeton University Press, 2022.

Song, Nianshen. *Making Borders in Modern East Asia: The Tumen River Demarcation, 1881–1919*. Cambridge: Cambridge University Press, 2018.

Spruyt, Hendrik. *The Sovereign State and Its Competitors: An Analysis of Systems Change*. Princeton, NJ: Princeton University Press, 1994.

Spruyt, Hendrik. *The World Imagined: Collective Beliefs and Political Order in the Sinocentric, Islamic and Southeast Asian International Societies*. Cambridge: Cambridge University Press, 2020.

Stanton, Timothy. "Popular Sovereignty in an Age of Mass Democracy: Politics, Parliament and Parties in Web, Kelsen, Schmitt and Beyond." In *Popular Sovereignty in Historical Perspective*, ed. Richard Bourke, 320–58. Cambridge: Cambridge University Press, 2016.

Stasavage, David. *The Decline and Rise of Democracy: A Global History from Antiquity to Today*. Princeton, NJ: Princeton University Press, 2020.

Stilz, Anna. *Territorial Sovereignty: A Philosophical Exploration*. Oxford: Oxford University Press, 2019.

Strauss, Julia. "Morality, Coercion, and State Building by Campaign in the Early PRC: Regime Consolidation and After, 1949–1956." *China Quarterly* 188 (December 2006): 891–912.

Strauss, Julia. "The Evolution of Republican Government." *China Quarterly* 150 (June 1997): 329–51.

Strauss, Julia. "Campaigns of Redistribution Land Reform and State Building." In *States in the Developing World*, ed. Miguel A. Centeno and Deborah J. Yashur, 339–62. Cambridge: Cambridge University Press, 2017.

Sun Cheng 孫誠. "Fan Xi biaoyu kangyi hou 'Beijing' yu 'yonggan' cheng Zhongguo hulianwang minganci" 反習標語抗議後"北京"與"勇敢"成中國互聯網敏感詞 [After the anti-Xi slogan protest 'Beijing' and 'bravery' have become sensitive words in China's internet]. RFA, October 13, 2022; https://www.rfa.org/mandarin/yataibaodao/meiti/sc-10132022141124.html.

Sun Lin. "Writing an Empire: An Analysis of the Manchu Origin Myth and the Dynamics of Manchu Identity." *Journal of Chinese History* 1 (2017): 93–109.

Sun Ruxian 孫儒僩. "Mogao yishi: wo de Dunhuang shengya (3)" 莫高軼事：我的敦煌生涯(3) [Mogao anecdote: My life in Dunhuang]. *Dunhuang Research* 敦煌研究, no. 3 (2013): 15–21.

Sun Yat-sen [Sun Zhongshan 孫中山]. "Dapo jiusixiang yao yong sanmin zhuyi" 打破舊思想要用三民主義 [Using Three Principles of the people to dismantle old thinking]. In *Guofu quanji* 國父全集 [Complete volume of the Father of the Nation], 12 vols. Taipei: Party History Committee of KMT Central Committee, 1973, 2:570–71 [1923].

Sun Yat-sen [Sun Zhongshan 孫中山]. "Da yazhou zhuyi" [大亞洲主義 Great Asianism]. Speech given in Kobe, Japan, November 24, 1924. In *Sunwen xuanji*, vol. 2 孫文選集（下冊）(Sun Wen Collection, vol. 2), 619–29. Guangzhou: Guangdong renmin chubanshe, 2006.

Sun Yat-sen [Sun Zhongshan 孫中山]. "Guomin zhengfu jianguo dagang" 國民政府建國大綱 [The National Government's leading principles of state building] (1924). In *Guofu quanji*, 國父全集 [Complete volume of the Father of the Nation] 12 vols. (Taipei: Party History Committee of KMT Central Committee, 1989), 1:623–25.

Sun Yat-sen [Sun Zhongshan 孫中山]. "*Guomindang xuanyan*" 國民黨宣言 [Manifesto of KMT] (1912). In *Guofu quanji* 2:33–35.

Sun Yat-sen [Sun Zhongshan 孫中山]. "Minquan zhuyi di wu jiang" 民權主義第一講 [The first lecture of popular sovereignty] (1924). In *Guofu quanji*, 1:55–67.

Sun Yat-sen [Sun Zhongshan 孫中山]. "Minquan zhuyi di wu jiang" 民權主義第五講 [The fifth lecture of popular sovereignty] (1924). In *Guofu quanji*, 1:99–113.

Sun Yat-sen [Sun Zhongshan 孫中山]. *San Min Chu I: The Three Principles of the People*. Vancouver: Soul Care, 2011 [1927].

Sun Yat-sen [Sun Zhongshan 孫中山]. "Wuzu guomin hejinhui qi" 五族國民合進會啟 [For the five-race citizenry cooperation association]. Collected in *Sun Zhongshan cangdang xuanbian (Xinhai geming qianhou)* 孫中山藏檔選編（辛亥革命前後）[Selected essays of the Sun Zhongshan collection (Before and after Xinhai Revolution)], 398–401. Beijing: Zhonghua shuju, 1986 [1912].

Sun Yat-sen [Sun Zhongshan 孫中山]. "Zhongguo guomindang xuanyan" 中國國民黨宣言 [Manifesto of China's KMT] (1923). In *Guofu quanji*, 2:110–13.

Sun Yat-sen [Sun Zhongshan 孫中山]. "Zhongguo zhi tielu jihua yu minsheng zhuyi" 中國之鐵路計劃與民生主義 [China's railway plan and people's livelihood] (1921). In *Zongli guanyu guoqing jinian de yijiao* 總理關於國慶紀念的遺教 [The posthumous teachings of the President about the national day celebration], 1–11. Nanjing: KMT Central Party Propaganda Department, 1929.

Tang, Xiaobing. *Global Space and the Nationalist Discourse of Modernity: The Historical Thinking of Liang Qichao*. Stanford, CA: Stanford University Press, 1996.

Tian, Li, and Yunxiang Yan. "Self-Cultivation of the Socialist New Person in Maoist China: Evidence from a Family's Private Letters, 1961–1986." *China Journal* 82 (2019): 88–110.

Tilly, Charles. *Coercion, Capital, and European States, AD 990–1992*. Cambridge, MA: Blackwell, 1992.

Tsang, Steve, and Olivia Cheung. "Has Xi Jinping Made China's Political System More Resilient and Enduring?" *Third World Quarterly* 43, no. 1 (2022): 225–43.

Tsu, Jing. *Failure, Nationalism, and Literature: The Making of Modern Chinese Identity, 1895–1937*. Stanford, CA: Stanford University Press, 2005.

Tsui, Brian. *China's Conservative Revolution: The Quest of a New Order, 1927–1949*. Cambridge: Cambridge University Press, 2018.

Van de Ven, Hans J. *From Friend to Comrade: The Founding of the Chinese Communist Party, 1920–1927*. Berkeley: University of California Press, 1991.

Van der Walt, Johan. *The Horizontal Effect Revolution and the Question of Sovereignty*. Berlin: De Gruyter, 2014.

Veg, Sebastian. "The Rise of China's Statist Intellectuals: Law, Sovereignty, and 'Repoliticization.'" *China Journal*, no. 82 (2019): 23–45.

Wakeman, Frederic E. *Policing Shanghai, 1927–1937*. Berkeley: University of California Press, 1995.

Wan Xin-Hua 萬新華. "Fu Baoshi 'Mao Zedong shiyi hua' chuangzuo zhi yanjiu" 傅抱石'毛澤東詩意畫'創作之研究 [A study of Fu Baoshi's 'Paintings based on Mao Zedong's poems']. *Journal of National Taichung University* 台中教育大學學報 22, no. 2 (2008): 71–114.

Wang, Ban. "The Clash of Civilization and World Community: The West and China." *Telos* 199 (2022): 48–56.

Wang Chaowen 王朝聞. "Jingque miaoxie bu dengyu xianshi zhuyi" 精確描寫不等於現實主義 [Precise depiction is not realism]. *Meishu* 美術, no. 3 (1950): 15–17.

Wang, Clyde Yicheng, and Zifeng Chen. "From 'Motherland' to 'Daddy State': A Genealogical Analysis of the Gender Undertone in China's Nationalist Discourses." *Nations and Nationalism* 29, no. 2 (2023): 751–767. Wang Hui 汪暉. *Xiandai Zhongguo sixiang de xingqi* 現代中國思想的興起 [The rise of modern Chinese thoughts]. 4 vols. Beijing: Sanlian shudian, 2004.

Wang Jianwen 王健文. "Diguo zhixu yu zuqun xiangxiang: dizhi Zhongguo chuqi de huaxia yishi" 帝國秩序與族群想象：帝制中國初期的華夏意識 [The order of empire and the imagination of ethnic groups: The *huaxia* consciousness of early imperial China]. In *Dongya lishi shang de tianxia yu*

Zhongguo gainian 東亞歷史上的天下與中國概念 [The concept of *tianxia* and China in East Asian history], ed. Gan Huaizhen, 149–80. Taipei: National Taiwan University Press, 2007.

Wang Jingsheng 王京生. *Wenhua zhuquan lun* 文化主權論 [Theory of cultural sovereignty]. Beijing: Hongqi chubanshe, 2013.

Wang Ke. *The East Turkestan Independence Movement, 1930s–1940s.* Hong Kong: Chinese University Press, 2018.

Wang Ke. 王珂. *Zhongguo: Cong 'Tianxia" dao minzu guojia.* 中國：從「天下」到民族國家 [China: From "Tianxia" to nation-state]. Taipei: National Chengchi University Press, 2017.

Wang, Linzhu. *Self-determination and Minority Rights in China.* Leiden: Brill, 2019.

Wang Yi. "Statement at the United Nations General Assembly." September 28, 2019. English translation available at http://newyork.china-consulate.org/eng/xw/t1703216.htm

Wasserstorm, Jeffrey N. "Questioning the Modernity of the Model Settlement: Citizenship and Exclusion in Old Shanghai." In *Changing Meanings of Citizenship in Modern China,* ed. Merle Goldman and Elizabeth J. Perry, 110–32. Cambridge, MA: Harvard University Press, 2002.

Weber, Isabella. *How China Escaped Shock Therapy: The Market Reform Debate.* London: Routledge, 2021.

Wilbur, Martin C. *The Nationalist Revolution in China.* Cambridge: Cambridge University Press, 1983.

Winichakul, Thongchai. *Siam Mapped: A History of the Geo-Body of a Nation.* Honolulu: University of Hawaii Press, 1994.

World Bank. "Financial Inclusion." 2018. https://www.worldbank.org/en/topic/financialinclusion/overview.

Wu, Cary, et al. "Chinese Citizen Satisfaction with Government Performance during COVID-19." *Journal of Contemporary China* 30, no. 132 (2021): 930–44.

Wu Guanzhong 吳冠中. *Yongwu tantu* 永無坦途 [Never a smooth path]. Hong Kong: Open Page, 2016.

Wu Tingfang 伍廷芳. *Wu Tingfang ji,* 伍廷芳集 [Collection of Wu Tingfang]. 2 vols. Beijing: Zhonghua shuju, 1993.

Wyman, Judith. "Foreigners or Outsiders? Westerners and Chinese Christians in Chongqing, 1870s-1900." In *New Frontiers: Imperialism's New Communities in East Asia, 1842-1953,* ed. Robert Bickers and Christian Henriot, 75–87. Manchester: Manchester University Press, 2000.

Xi Jinping 習近平. "Dialectical Materialism is the Worldview and Methodology of Chinese Communists." *Qiushi Journal* (English edition) 11, no. 1 (January–March 2019), https://www.ccdpch.com/dialectical-materialism-is-the-worldview-and-methodology-of-chinese-communists/.

Xi Jinping 習近平. "Jiangshan jiushi renmin, renmin jiushi jiangshan: Xi Jinping zongshuji guanyu yi renmin wei zhongxin zhongyao lunshu zongshu" 江山就是人民, 人民就是江山—習近平總書記關於以人民為中心重要論述綜述 [*Jiangshan* is the people, the people are *Jiangshan*: An overview of the important discussions by General Secretary Xi Jinping about people as center]. *People's Net*, June 28, 2021. http://politics.people.com.cn/n1/2021/0628/c1001-32141933.html

Xi Jinping 習近平. "Speech at a Ceremony Marking the Centenary of the CPC." *Xinhua Net*, July 1, 2021. http://www.xinhuanet.com/english/special/2021-07/01/c_1310038244.htm.

Xi Jinping 習近平. "Speech at the Fourth Collective Learning in the Eighteenth Central Politburo Meeting." February 23, 2013. Excerpt collected in *Xi Jinping guanyu quanmian yifa zhiguo lunshu zhaibian* 習近平關於全面依法治國論述摘編 [A collection of Xi Jinping's discussions about ruling the country through law], 57. Beijing: Zhongyang wenxian chubanshe, 2015.

Xi Jinping 習近平. "Speech on 40th Anniversary of China's Reforms, Opening Up." December 18, 2018. English translation available at: www.transcend.org/tms/2018/12/xi-jinpings-speech-on-40th-anniversary-of-chinas-reforms-opening-up-full-text.

Xi Jinping 習近平. "Xi Jinping zai qiyejia zuotanhui shang de jianghua" 習近平在企業家座談會上的講話 [Xi Jinping's speech in a symposium with entrepreneurs]. *People's Net*, July 22, 2020. Available at http://cpc.people.com.cn/BIG5/n1/2020/0722/c64094-31792488.html.

Xiao, Muyi, Isabelle Qian, Tracy Wen Liu, and Chris Buckley. "How a Chinese Doctor Who Warned of COVID-19 Spent His Final Days." *The New York Times*, October 6, 2022. Available at https://www.nytimes.com/2022/10/06/world/asia/covid-china-doctor-li-wenliang.html.

Xiao-Planes, Xiaohong. "Of Constitutions and Constitutionalism: Trying to Build a New Political Order in China, 1908–1949." In *Building Constitutionalism in China*, ed. Stéphanie Balme and Michael W. Dowdle, 37–58. New York: Palgrave Macmillan, 2009.

Xie Libin and Haig Patapan. "Schmitt Fever: The Use and Abuse of Carl Schmitt in Contemporary China." *International Journal of Constitutional Law* 18, no. 1 (2020): 130–46.

Xing Yitian 邢義田. *Qin Han shi lungao* 秦漢史論稿 [Manuscript of Qin and Han history]. Taipei: Dongda tushu, 1987.

Xu, Aymeric. "Mapping Conservatism of the Republican Era; Genesis and Typologies." *Journal of Chinese History* 4 (2020): 135–59.

Yack, Bernard. "Popular Sovereignty and Nationalism." *Political Theory* 29, no. 4 (2001): 517–36.

Yan Fu 嚴復. "Xianfa dayi" 憲法大義 [Great meanings of the Constitution]. In *Yan Fu Ji* 嚴復集, 2:238–45. Beijing: Zhonghua shuju, 1986.

Yan Fu 嚴復. "Yuanqiang" 原強 [The originally strong]. In *Yan Fu Ji*, vol. 1, 5–31.

Yan Zhi Tui顏之推. "Shuzheng" 書證 [*Documented evidence*]. *Yanshijiaxun* 顏氏家訓,vol. 6. Beijing: Zhonghua Shuju, 1985 [c. 420–581].

Yang, Guobin. *The Wuhan Lockdown*. New York: Columbia University Press, 2022.

Yang, Guobin, and Min Jiang. "The Networked Practice of Online Political Satire in China: Between Ritual and Resistance." *International Communication Gazette* 77, no. 3 (2015): 215–31.

Yang Jisheng. *Tombstone: The Great Chinese Famine, 1958–1962*. Trans. Stacy Mosher and Guo Jian. New York: Farrar Straus and Giroux, 2012.

Yang Siji 楊思機. "20 shiji sanshishi niandai guogong liangdang guanyu guonei minzu zhengce wenti de lunzheng," 20世紀三四十年代國共兩黨關於國內民族政策問題的論爭 [The KMT and CCP debates around China's nationalities policies in the 1930s and 1940s]. In *Yincang de renqun: jindai zhongguo zuqun yu bianjiang* 隱藏的人群：近代中國族群與邊疆 [Modern China: Minority nationalities], ed. Huang Ko-wu 黃克武, 90–132. Taipei: Show We, 2012.

Yang Tianhong 楊天宏. *Gegu dingxin: Minguo qianqi de falü yu zhengzhi* 革故鼎新：民國前期的法律與政治 [Discarding the past and supporting the new: Law and politics in early Republican China]. Beijing: Sanlian, 2018.

Yang Tianhong 楊天宏. "Difang zizhi yu tongyi guojia de jiangou: Beiyang shiji 'liansheng zizhi' yundong zai yanjiu" 地方自治與統一國家的建構：北洋時期"聯省自治"運動再研究 [The construction of local self-rule and national unification: Reinvestigating the "Self-ruled Provinces Alliance" movement during the Beiyang period]. *Journal of Sichuan University (Social Science Edition)* 四川大學學報 （哲學社會科學版) 182, no. 5, 2012: 20–29.

Yang Yifan 楊一帆. "Zouxiang geming: Zhonggong dangren yu liansheng zizhi de fenhe." 走向革命：中共黨人與聯省自治的分合 [Toward revolution: The separation and cooperation of the CCP members and the movement of self-ruled provinces alliance]. *Dangshi yanjiu yu jiaoxue* 黨史研究與教學 [Party history research and teaching] 286, no. 2 (2022): 50–59.

Yao Yang 姚洋. *Yadang Simi zai Beijing chongxin renshi Zhongxiaoxuenong jingji* 《亞當·斯密在北京》重新認識中小學農經濟 [*Adam Smith in Beijing* re-examines Chinese petty farmer economy]. *Xiangyin* 鄉音 11 (2009): 38–39.

Ye Jianbo 葉劍波. "'Ge jiucai' fa peiyang houbei rencai" '割韭菜' 法培養後備人才 ['Garlic chives harvesting' method to cultivate reserved talents]. *Chinese Power Enterprise Management* 中國電力企業管理, 13 (2011): 92–93.

Ye, Josh. "China Proposes Measures to Manage Generative AI Services." Reuters, April 11, 2023. Available at https://www.reuters.com/technology/china-releases-draft-measures-managing-generative-artificial-intelligence-2023-04-11.

Yeh, Catherine Vance. *The Chinese Political Novel: Migration of a World Genre*. Cambridge, MA: Harvard University Press, 2015.

Yin Shuxuan 尹淑鉉. "Renquan yu minzhu de bianzou: Wusi yundong qianhou minquan gainian de yanbian" 人權與民主的變奏——五四運動前後民權概念的演變 [The variation of human rights and democracy: The transformation of the concept of popular sovereignty before and after the May Fourth movement]. *Twentieth First Century* 二十一世紀, 180 (2020): 33–51.

Yu Dafu 郁達夫. "Chenlun" 沉淪 [Sinking]. In *Yu Dafu wenji*郁達夫文集 [Collected works of Yu Dafu], 1:16–53. Hong Kong: Joint Publishing, 1982 [1921].

Yu Ying-shih 余英時. "Confucian Culture vs Dynastic power in Chinese History." *Asia Major* 34, no. 1 (2021): 1–10.

Yu Ying-shih 余英時. *Lun Tianren zhi ji:Zhongguo gudai sixiang qiyuan shitan* 論天人之際：中國古代思想起源試探 [About the relation between heaven and human: Attempts to explore the origins of Chinese ancient thoughts]. Taipei: Linking, 2021.

Yu Ying-shih 余英時. *Shi yu Zhongguo wenhua* 士與中國文化 [Literati and Chinese culture]. Shanghai: Shanghai renmin chubanshe, 2003.

Yuan Jiuhong 袁久紅 and Gan Wenhua 甘文華. "Shehui zhuyi hexin jiazhi yu Zhongguo jingshen de xinsheng" 社會主義核心價值與 '中國精神' 的新生 [Socialist core values and the revival of the spirit of China]. *Journal of Southeast University (Philosophy and Social Sciences* 東南大學學報 (哲學社會科學版) 15, no. 5 (2013): 5–16.

Yuan Shikai 袁世凱. "Dazongtong liren xuanyan bugao" 大總統蒞任宣言佈告 [Declaration of the President of the Republic of China]. *Yuan Shikai quanji* 袁世凱全集 [Complete works of Yuan Shikai], 36 vols. Zhengzhou: Henan University Press, 2013, 24:41–43 [1913].

Yurchak, Alexi. "Re-touching the Sovereign: Biochemistry of Perpetual Leninism." In *The Scaffolding of Sovereignty: Global and Aesthetic Perspectives on the History of a Concept*, ed. Zvi Ben-dor Benite, Stefanos Geroulanos, and Nicole Jerr, 246–74. New York: Columbia University Press, 2017.

Zarrow, Peter. "Historical Trauma: Anti-Manchuism and Memories of Atrocity in Late Qing China." *History and Memory*, 16, no. 2 (2004): 67–107.

Zeng Pu 曾樸, with Jin Songcen金松岑. *Niehai hua* 孽海花 [Flower in the sea of retribution]. Hong Kong: Tsunami, 1998 [1905].

Zhang Chunlin. "How Much Do State-owned Enterprises Contribute to China's GDP and Employment?" World Bank, Geneva, 2019.

Zhang Dongsun 張東蓀 (Dongsun 東蓀). "Wu ren lixiang zhi zhidu yu lian-bang" 吾人理想之制度與聯邦 [Our ideal institution and federation]. *Jiayin* 甲寅 1, no. 10 (October 10, 1915): 1–16.

Zhang Jinfan 張晉藩. "Xinhai geming bainian hua fatong." 辛亥革命百年話法統 [Understanding *fatong* in a century after Xinhai Revolution]. *Faxue zazhi* 法學雜誌 11 (2011): 1–5.

Zhang, Qi. *Carl Schmitt, Mao Zedong, and the Politics of Transition.* London: Palgrave Macmillan, 2016.

Zhang Renshan 張仁善 and Yang Yujian 楊宇劍. "Lun jindai 'fatong' linian de goujian yu yuanshikai dui minchu 'fatong' de gaizao" 論近代「法統」理念的構建與袁世凱對民初「法統」的改造 [On the construction of *fatong* in modern times and the transformation introduced by Yuan Shikai during early Republican period]. *Fazhi yanjiu* 法治研究 3 (2015): 150–59.

Zhang Taiyan 章太炎. "Bo Kang Youwei lun geming shu" 駁康有為論革命書 [Extending Kang Youwei's writings about revolution]. *Zhang Taiyan quanji* 章太炎全集 [Complete works of Zhang Taiyan], 8 vols. Shanghai: Shanghai Renmin chubanshe, 1985, 4:173–84 [1903].

Zhang Taiyan 章太炎. "Fenzhen" 分鎮 [Town independence]. *Zhang Taiyan zhenglun xuanji* 章太炎政論選集上 [Selected political commentaries by Zhang Taiyan], 2 vols. Beijing: Zhonghua shuju, 1977, 1:104–7 [1899].

Zhang Taiyan 章太炎. "Guojia lun" 國家論 [About nation]. *Zhang Taiyan quanji* 章太炎全集 [Complete works of Zhang Taiyan], 8 vols. Shanghai: Shanghai Renmin chubanshe, 1985, 4:457–65 [1907].

Zhang Taiyan 章太炎. "Zai Hunan Changsha baojie huanyinghui shang zhi yanjiang" 在湖南長沙報界歡迎會上之演講 [Speech given at the welcoming ceremony by the press of Changsha, Hunan]. *Zhang Taiyan yanjiangji* 章太炎演講集 [Speeches of Zhang Taiyan], November 1, 1920, 213. Shanghai: Shanghai Renmin chubanshe, 2011.

Zhang Taiyan 章太炎. "Zhonghua minguo jie" 中華民國解 [Explaining the Republic of China]. *Zhang Taiyan quanji* 章太炎全集 [Complete works of Zhang Taiyan], 8 vols. Shanghai: Shanghai Renmin chubanshe, 1985, 4:252–62 [1907].

Zhao Dingxin. "The Mandate of Heaven and Performance Legitimation in Historical and Contemporary China." *American Behavioral Scientist* 53, no. 3 (2009): 416–33.

Zhao Tingyang. "All-under-Heaven and Methodological Relationism: An Old Story and New World Peace." In *Contemporary Chinese Political Thought: Debates and Perspectives*, ed. Fred Dallmayr and Zhao Tingyang, 46–66. Lexington: University Press of Kentucky, 2012.

Zhao, Yongle. "History, Culture, Revolution, and Chinese Constitutionalsm." In *The Constitution of Ancient China*, ed. Zhang Yongle and Daniel Bell, 198–208. Princeton, NJ: Princeton University Press, 2018.

Zheng Dahua 鄭大華. *Minguo sixiang shilun* 民國思想史論 [History of thoughts in Republic of China]. Beijing: Shehuikexue wenxian chuban-she, 2006.

Zheng Xiaowei. *The Politics of Rights and the 1911 Revolution in China*. Stanford, CA: Stanford University Press, 2018.

Zhonggong Zhongyang dangshi yanjiushi 中共中央黨史研究室 (Party History Research Center of the CPC Central Committee), *Zhongguo Gongchandang lishi dierjuan xiace* 中國共產黨歷史第二卷下冊 (Party History of the CPC, second volume, no. 2). Beijing: Zhonggang dangshi chubanshe, 2011.

Zien, Katherine. *Sovereign Acts: Performing Race, Space, and Belonging in Panama and the Canal Zone*. New Brunswick, NJ: Rutgers University Press, 2017.

Žižek, Slavoj. "Carl Schmitt in the Age of Post-Politics." In *The Challenges of Carl Schmitt*, ed. Chantal Mouffe, 18–37. London: Verso, 1999.

Index

Page locators in *italics* indicate figures.

Printed and bound by CPI Group (UK) Ltd, Croydon, CR0 4YY

05/03/2024

14465713-0003